# Directing the Baccalaureate Social Work Education Program

*Second Edition*

**Harry J. Macy**

**Rebecca Turner**

**Scott Wilson**

*eddie bowers publishing co., inc.*

Exclusive marketing and distributor rights for U.K., Eire,
and Continental Europe held by:

Gazelle Book Services Limited
Falcon House
Queen Square
Lancaster
LA1 1RN
U.K.

---

*eddie bowers publishing co., inc.*
14744 Highway 20 West
Dubuque, Iowa 52003 USA


ISBN 1-57879-019-0

Printed in the United States of America.

9  8  7  6  5  4  3  2  1

## CONTRIBUTORS

**Harry J. Macy**, MSW, MAPA, Ed.D., is Professor and Chair of the Department of Social Work, Ball State University. He has over thirty years of social work education and administrative experience in graduate and baccalaureate degree programs. His practice experience includes family and child welfare services, program administration, and community development. As a Peace Corps volunteer, he taught upper primary school children in Tabora, Tanzania. He has authored numerous publications on social work education administration and practice, and serves on editorial boards of a number of social work education and practice journals. He has completed several terms on the Council on Social Work Education Board of Directors, and has served as a member of the Conferences and Faculty Development, Standards and Accreditation, and Educational Policy Commissions of the Council. Macy is an experienced program consultant, a CSWE Site Team Member/Chair, and has served as an officer of numerous social work education and professional organizations including the Association of Baccalaureate Program Directors.

**Rebecca Turner** practiced social work in the public child welfare system for eight years before joining a developing BSW at a regional state university as one of two faculty in 1981. She was named the program's first director in 1987, head of its host department in 1991, and in 1998 assumed the position of Associate Vice President for Academic and Student Affairs. Active in the AL/MS Social Work Education Conference since 1980, and BPD since 1988, she served on the Board of Directors of BPD and chaired the Membership Committee. Turner is a Child Welfare Research Fellow whose research project focused on therapeutic foster care in Alabama. She has been a member of the Commission on Educational Policy of CSWE and a CSWE Site Team Chairperson. She holds three social work degrees at baccalaureate, master's, and doctoral levels, is a member of the Academy of Certified Social Workers, and is a Licensed Certified Social Worker in the State of Alabama.

**Scott Wilson** is a Senior Educational Specialist with the Council on Social Work Education, Division of Standards and Accreditation, where he has served since 1991. He completed seventeen years teaching macro practice, applied research, social policy, and organizational and power theory at Temple University and Bryn Mawr College before joining the CSWE staff. His social work practice experience in two states included state-level social welfare planning and organizational consultation. As a Peace Corps volunteer, he performed national child welfare planning in Lima, Peru. He holds an MSSW and Ph.D. from Bryn Mawr College's Graduate School of Social Work and Social Research. Wilson is the author of several published articles in social work journals, and co-author of a book on community organizing; and he has made numerous presentations at conferences and meetings on topics including program evaluation, curriculum development, and accreditation issues.

# CONTENTS IN BRIEF

# Contents

## CHAPTER 2: Academic Affairs 23

**CHAPTER 4:    Academic Program Governance    69**

## CHAPTER 6:    Faculty and Staff Resources    137

**CHAPTER 7: Accreditation and the Direction of Baccalaureate Social Work Education Programs    177**

# Acknowledgements

The authors wish to acknowledge the continuing efforts of the Association of Baccalaureate Social Work Program Directors to promote social work education excellence. Gratitude is acknowledged for the gracious support of Mildred Joyner and Jack Sellers, the current and immediate past Presidents of the Association, along with the assistance of Douglas Burnham, former Chairperson of the Publications Committee, who has been especially helpful to the authors. To Alison Gillespie, special thanks are extended for processing the many drafts of the manuscript and for her editorial work throughout this project.

A special note of appreciation is expressed to all current and future program directors whose notable administrative services are an invaluable contribution to social work education advancement.

# Foreword

As we move into the twenty-first century, the second edition of *Directing the Baccalaureate Social Work Program* has been published to assist current and future directors in all of the areas of academic program administration. As former BPD President Lorrie Greenhouse Gardella noted in the Forward of the first 1995 edition of this volume, new program directors generally learn to do their job through a combination of trial and error experiences, informal networking, participation in professional associations and attending specialized workshops. Few directors have formal educational preparation prior to assuming their directorship positions. Therefore, one of the main questions that BPD presidents continue to be asked is how to direct a baccalaureate program. Issues such as program governance, resource procurement, working with central administrative officials, promoting program quality and managing personnel matters continue to be problematic for new and experienced directors.

The second goal of the BPD 1999-2000 strategic plan is to provide social work opportunities for the development and support of baccalaureate social work program administrators and faculty. Both the initial 1995 volume and this revised edition fall under the BPD Strategic Plan and have evolved with BPD support and the continuing sponsorship of annual workshops for new program directors. These administrative workshops help new directors gain a theoretical orientation to their administrative position, think analytically about their position responsibilities within their colleges and universities, analyze innovative approaches to complete program leadership tasks, and establish collaborative and information networks to provide ongoing support.

This edition updates contemporary academic program administrative practices and strengthens the application of an ecological orientation to completing position responsibilities common to various institutional settings. For a new program director, the content provides a guide for examining position responsibilities, identifies administrative tasks within basic program operations and examines administrative leadership within the institutional and professional structures and contexts of the academic enterprise. For the experienced director, the volume presents a "fresh look" at an academic administrative paradigm that can mobilize the collective efforts of program stakeholders, expand the perspective needed to address persistent academic and administrative issues, and promote an outcome-oriented social work educational process.

The first two authors, Harry Macy and Rebecca Turner, are very experienced Program Directors who, between them, have served on the Council on Social Work Education's Commission on Accreditation, Commission on Conferences and Faculty Development, and Commission on Educational Policy. They have served as site visit chairs and site team members for CSWE accreditation site visits. Together with the third author, Scott Wilson, a long-serving Senior Educational Specialist with CSWE, they have worked with hundreds of undergraduate social work programs to develop programs in concert with accreditation standards. Each of the authors have staffed the annual BPD Conference "New Program Directors" workshops where much of the content presented in this book was honed. The authors have astutely written on the subjects of how programs generically carry out the administrative assignments and other program issues in baccalaureate social work education.

Throughout this volume, the authors identify fundamental administrative practices and guidelines that can be applied as templates to foster program advancement. This book can be a reference to directors when working with administration, faculty members, students, staff, advisory boards, and other program stakeholders as they embark on developing a program. Seasoned directors of programs will use this book as a resource when monitoring and developing new aspects of their programs.

*Directing the Baccalaureate Social Work Program*, 2nd edition is published by Eddie Bowers Publishing Company, with the authors contributing a percentage of the purchase price of each book to BPD in order to help fund member services. BPD sponsors an annual conference and publishes the UPDATE and the Journal of Baccalaureate Social Work twice yearly.

On behalf of BPD members, we would like to thank the authors, the BPD Board of Directors, the Publications Committee, and Eddie Bowers for this contribution to undergraduate social work education. We are certain that this resource will guide you and your program into the future.

Mildred C. Joyner, MSW, LSW
President
Association of Baccalaureate Social Work Program Directors

Jack Sellers, Ph.D.
Past President
Association of Baccalaureate Social Work Program Directors

# Preface

The choice of this book may mean that after a period of successful work within the academic realms of the social work program, you have accepted appointment as a program director or are thinking about becoming a director and thereby adding program administration to your faculty teaching, research, service, and student advising responsibilities. For the readers who are currently serving in the role of a program director, this book may provide a resource to increase one's understanding of the administrative position or to serve as a reference source when confronted with administrative challenges. Directors of baccalaureate social work programs are typically experienced social work practitioners and often expert in the content areas in which they teach. Many may have had administrative experience in social work agencies. However, few possess that combination of educational preparation and academic administrative experience that would best prepare them to carry out the roles and responsibilities of a program director. Aware of this fact, the Association of Baccalaureate Social Work Program Directors (BPD) has for some time sponsored training sessions for program directors. The authors of this book have been engaged in new director training for the past four years. Much of the book's content has evolved from or through these training sessions, but here we provide a more fully developed format.

The first edition, published in 1995, was found to be very useful by both new and experienced program directors. This new, completely re-written edition was spurred by continuing demand for such a source of accumulated wisdom, and the perception that an updated and expanded version of the first edition would best address the tasks that today's program directors face. While BPD has been fully supportive of this project, the approach and content are the authors'.

The content shared in this book is intended to help program directors conceptualize academic administration and understand the position-based tasks associated with the operational domains of a baccalaureate social work academic program. Directors who understand how their role and its inherent position responsibilities fit into a larger organizational and professional whole will be able to administer with increased efficiency, work more purposefully toward program goals, and respond more successfully to unanticipated challenges in the interest of program development. Some of the content you will read in this volume is familiar and may bring comfort from knowing that you have a solid grounding in academic program administration. Some content may be thought provoking as you consider new approaches to your administrative responsibilities.

The authors hope that the book will be supportive of your efforts to develop more effective administrative practices.

In this volume, we view directing an undergraduate social work education program through several thematic lenses. We want these themes to pervade the content of each chapter, so that the themes unify and give focus to the work program directors are called on to accomplish. These themes fall into three categories:

## 1. Themes Reflecting the Program Itself

- **Program purpose, scope, role and significance as a higher education operational unit.**

    A baccalaureate social work education program is a fundamental academic, instructional, research, service, governance, and administrative unit of a higher education institution. It is where the mission, goals, and policies of the college or university are operationalized and the major stakeholders that participate in the educational enterprise are served. Readers will be invited repeatedly to "think programmatically" where this level of unit is critical (e.g. rather than a focus on larger or smaller units). While this perhaps unique focus on the social work program itself cannot be understated, directors will encounter the continuing dynamic that they must also "think contextually" about their programs, placing the program within an ecological framework set by the institution, the social work profession, social work personnel needs of evolving health and human service delivery systems, and accreditation standards.

- **Program Quality**

    The assumed underlying purpose of social work program directing is to promote quality in all aspects of the program's teaching curriculum, professional services, scholarship, student performance and administration. This commitment to educational excellence is anchored in the ability of program graduates to use the knowledge, skills, and values gained - as systematically documented by program outcome evaluations. The reality that social work service clientele rely on the quality of practice provided by program graduates adds to the importance of this purpose. Social work education and practitioners have, over the decades, refined operational definitions of the term program quality, and produced expectation for education (the CSWE accreditation standards) and practice (the NASW Code of Ethics) that capture current definitions. New accreditation standards are being written, reviewed and revised for use beginning in 2001 or 2002. The contents of this book have been crafted to be applicable to either set of accreditation standards. Likewise, changes in a future Code of Ethics should not make the focus of this book less timely or applicable.

- **Professional Education Is Different**

  Directors of social work programs carry a responsibility quite beyond that of non-professional educational disciplines: the requirements of practice and the needs and rights of consumers reach well into the basic operational domains of an educational enterprise. These fundamental or basic domains include student and academic affairs, decision-making or governance, funding and personnel. Thus, the contingencies for even seemingly minor program decisions within these domains are often "stretched" beyond the parent institution into the community at large and the professional community. This adds to program complexity and possible conflict among competing actors or interests.

2. **Themes Reflected in the Work of the Program Director**[1]

- **Centrality of Director Position**

  The position of academic program director is a functional axis or center within the educational enterprise and serves the differing and competing needs and interests of program stakeholders. Information flow, including communication within the institutional hierarchy, is an inherent part of program directing since the position is the conduit for downward, upward, and horizontal or lateral information flow within the administrative hierarchy of the institution. Administrative tasks or events inevitably involve people (staff, students, etc.) who make requests and communication is an essential ingredient of motivation, coordination, evaluation, collaboration, and so forth, which are essential strategic aspects of program leadership.

- **Leadership**

  The program director role, while collegial in some ways, also requires a great deal of personal, academic, and professional leadership. The director initiates, creates structure, acts as a role model, networks, communicates and energizes and engages others.

The term applies also to the social work program: we see the program providing leadership within the educational institution (program assessment, anti-discrimination) and within the social work practice and wider communities (research, training, experimental programs, legislation, social action).

- **Scope, Number and Diversity of Administrative Tasks/Functions**

    The administrative tasks and decisions related to academic resources, student services, and personnel matters when combined with the teaching, research and service responsibilities inherent in a faculty position, represent a challenging set of role responsibilities. The total number of administrative responsibilities also represents more tasks than one individual can personally complete. Therefore, a director must develop academic program administrative approaches that include a combination of direct involvement in selected high priority management functions found within each of the domains, and delegation of some of the administrative functions to faculty and staff program-based committees, while retaining overall administrative oversight and evaluation responsibilities.

3. **Themes Reflecting Contexts in Which the Program Functions**

- **Administrative Contextual Perspective of a Program Director**

    The five major program domains of a baccalaureate social work program require a director to acquire a broad institution-wide administrative perspective affording the ability to identify the resources, supports and constraints in order to strategically administer the baccalaureate program. The application of a strengths, weaknesses, opportunities, and threats (SWOT), mixed scanning planning approach is an important component of this administrative perspective.

- **Academic Program - Institutional Goal-Related Tensions**

    The overall academic program goal of selecting and preparing students for entry level professional generalist social work practice has inherent tensions with the mission and goals of the institution. These tension points, which include such program operations as selective admission and retention of students, field practicum requirements, integration of academic and professional advising of students, outcome oriented curriculum and structured instructional approaches, and a faculty reward system which prizes professional service, represent administrative challenges related to promoting the fit of the goals and operations of the social work program with those of its institution.

- **Blended Administrative Paradigms**

  Higher education administrative and governance structures, policies and procedures require the program director to utilize a blended mixture of bureaucratic, collegial, and political administrative processes to differentially administer academic, personnel, fiscal and student centered program operations. The unique governance and decision procedures in higher education require the adaptive use of a hybrid model of academic program administration.

- **Contingency Thinking**

  There are a very large number of factors inside and outside a social work education program that impinge on the director and on the responsibilities of this position. Effective action requires that these factors be analyzed by situation, opportunity, and challenge. Also referred to as "environmental scanning" in the ensuing chapters, this complex and careful analysis leads to well-informed decisions and courses of action, not quick and ill-informed reactions.

## 4. Combined Programs

Just under a quarter of all baccalaureate social work education programs exist in a "combined program" context. That is, they are organizationally combined with a master's of social work educational program in a school, college, or departmental format within the institution. This structure presents some opportunities and challenges distinct from the majority of baccalaureate programs not joined with a social work master's program, but we view most of the book's content as very much applicable in combined program contexts.

Differences are apparent with reference to the thematic lenses previously discussed in this Preface. Some themes may present fewer problems for combined programs. Because there are now two professional social work programs (MSW and BSW) and their combined visibility may be high, the need may be less to stress differences between professional and other academic disciplines. Relating to the institutional context is likely to change, with the baccalaureate program director relating mostly only to university undergraduate elements while a combined program administrator carries primary relational responsibilities to graduate studies and central administration.

Many of the themes are the same or very similar as for non-combined programs. The baccalaureate program is no longer the only social work education unit in the institution, and may be viewed as the more minor unit compared to the master's program. However, those associated with the baccalaureate program in a combined context will find it very necessary to "think programmatically" about this unit to ensure its integrity is maintained within the combined program and relative to other undergraduate programs on campus. Program quality is of equal concern. The director's leadership is still central to the program's welfare. Contingency thinking and the use of a blended administrative paradigm remain necessary.

In some cases the combined context may suggest more emphasis on some themes. The scope, number and diversity of administrative tasks and functions of the baccalaureate program director may increase, as duties in the combined program get added (although some roles may move from this position to an administrator of the combined program). Where we believe larger differences will occur for baccalaureate program director in combined contexts we will address these special circumstances at those points in the on-going discussion.

## 5. Social Work Contributions to Enhancing Baccalaureate Education

Related particularly to the institutional context of the social work program is the theme that social work education has some important ideas and experiences to share - some "better ideas". This theme involves thinking of the social work education program as a center of excellence in terms of innovation. Social work education should not always be viewed only as the consumer of others' ideas and resources, but also as the holder and source of ideas with important implications for other disciplines or units in the institution.

Several examples can be cited, and others may well occur to the reader. Service learning has gained great currency with the opening of the 21$^{st}$ century. Social work has a long and detailed history of use of an educational model in which field-based learning is structured as an integral part of an overall learning plan for students; as other disciplines become aware of an attracted to service-learning components for their students it is the social work program that has the expertise to model, consult with, and advise these new efforts. Institution-wide implications include development of a learning model that incorporates service and community engagement as intrinsic aspects.

Social work's field practicum is a strong model of learning, far more organized and rigorous than that of most observational, interning, or apprenticeship models. As engagement with the community and its institutions and organizations is considered within the institution, social work educators have the ability to assist other units to evolve learning models and relationships that fit the educational ends in question, yet also have real meaning and impact for those in the community who become involved.

Social work education has evolved close working relationships with social welfare agencies and other community actors through advisory boards to the social work education program. While some of the focus is on the field practica of students, other focuses include feedback to the program on how its curriculum "fits" the world of the community, and service and other projects (research, advocacy) in the community.

Social work education has developed a model of holistic advising that goes far beyond the advising approaches of most disciplines, and is in a position to help other disciplines consider the utility of more intensive means for working with students. Social work advising engages not just academic advising issues, but also career preparation and personal development aspects; and these are treated as parts of a whole, and not as a possible series of questions strung out haphazardly over the student's time in the university. A closely related aspect of this approach is student - centeredness - an empowering approach geared to providing the student necessary information to deal effectively with the student and learning environments; and formal access to decision-making procedures that make students into "players" in the program in which they are enrolled. Student evaluations in social work education often go far beyond the minimal assessment of a course and instructor, to full consumer feedback on the program in general, and on their field practicum in specific. Course syllabi in social work are typically far more developed and detailed than their counterparts in other disciplines - a straight-forward result of the desire to fully inform students about intentions for instruction and learning so they can engage in and critique those intentions and their realization.

Social work education has embraced outcomes-oriented education in an overt manner since 1994, when accreditation standards were revised to upgrade the nature of the focus on assessment of pre-stated program objectives - for student learning and other program effects. The intervening years have given social work educators time to become experienced with stating objectives, fashioning means to evaluate the attainment of those objectives, and then the accomplishment of program revisions responsive to the outcomes findings. These are the skills that institutions nationwide need to do discipline-specific and institution-wide assessments.

Thus, the theme of social work educators having the capacity to act as leaders in educational innovations will recur as the pages of this book unfold.

We hope that the content shared in this book, intended to help program directors to become more effective administrators, is a useful reference to that end.

Harry J. Macy

Rebecca Turner

Scott Wilson

[1] College and universities use different terms for the faculty member who is the chief administrative officer in an academic program. These differences reflect unique institutional characteristics such as the academic organizational structure of a program, governance procedures, efforts to achieve gender-neutral administrative titles, and variations in institutional decision structures. Terms for this position found in the literature include "department chief officer," "chair," and "chairperson", "head", and "program director". The authors use the term "program director" because the focus of this publication is on the academic program irrespective of organization structure (e.g., combined BSW and MSW degree, or an academic department that offers a number of allied disciplines including social work, etc.). In addition, a consistent theme of this publication is that quality social work education requires the completing of a set of fundamental position responsibilities either by the program director or by another administrative official, which results in the director needing to provide administrative oversight.

# Chapter 1

# Role Responsibilities of A Baccalaureate Social Work Program Director

This chapter introduces position and administrative leadership responsibilities of a program director. Program administration responsibilities will be examined within the context of five operational components or domains that comprise an academic program. These domains include: (1) academic affairs; (2) financial/physical resources; (3) governance; (4) student affairs; and (5) faculty/staff resources. These domains, when combined, represent an organizing framework for examining administrative practices within the institutional, professional, organizational and program accreditation parameters of a social work program. The program advancement or development and the information management practices are inherent throughout the position responsibilities. They are described as intrinsic program administrative leadership processes that flow across each of the five interrelated operational domains.

Chapter 8, a companion chapter, describes the ecologically oriented administrative model that provides the basis for an assertive leadership model in promoting excellence within each of the five program domains. Key institutional, professional and environmental factors that form the administrative context for the position are examined. A focus on the use of strategic administrative leadership is designed to advance program effectiveness by mobilizing the resource, governance and management systems found within colleges and universities. Readers are connected to recommended sources in the literature for further examination of academic program administration, which is a dynamic, complex theoretical research and practice field of inquiry that extends far beyond the scope of any one publication.

A "what-how-why" framework is used to examine the program director's administrative responsibilities. The "what" portion of the framework is represented by specific administrative tasks related to each of the domains. Illustrations and examples of administrative practices and guidelines for completing the position-based responsibilities of the five domains represent the "how" portion of the framework. Promoting overall program quality, which is anchored in the Council on Social Work Education (CSWE) accrediting standards and the practice guidelines defined by the National Association of Social Workers (NASW), represents the "why" portion of the framework. The focus of the next five sequential chapters of this book is on each of these five domains.

## Position Responsibilities

As one completes this review, it is important to keep in mind the ecological nature of academic program administration. The overlapping position responsibilities are embedded in the institution's mission, administrative structure and governance policies. Administrative support and oversight related to each of the five program domains are provided by an array of specialized support and oversight officers located throughout the institutional hierarchy. Resources and the authority to offer an academic program are delegated by the institution to the program. Therefore, the administrative orientation of the director must become an integrated one that incorporates both program and institutional perspectives when completing position tasks.

An examination of the job or position description of a director is a helpful orientation step for becoming a program director. Even though specific administrative responsibilities are shaped by such institutional factors as the program size or the organizational structure of the academic unit where the program may be located (e.g., combined BSW-MSW degree program located in a school of social work structure), it is also important that the generic position responsibilities listed in Figure 1.1 be viewed as essential program-based administrative tasks to be systematically completed at some administrative level within the academic enterprise. Each of the fifteen overlapping administrative tasks may be: (1) directly completed by a program director, (2) delegated by a director to an administrative assistant, (3) completed by centralized institutional officials within the administrative hierarchy of the institution, or (4) done by another faculty member who has overall administrative responsibility for an academic unit in which the baccalaureate program is located.

In settings where each of the fifteen administrative tasks is not a formal position responsibility of the program director and thereby not done directly by that faculty member, there remains, however, the need for program-level administrative oversight or monitoring by the director to be certain that these responsibilities are routinely completed in a competent manner to help assure that a high-quality program is being provided.

The generic position responsibilities listed in Figure 1.1 have been, for identification purposes, placed within the five operational domains of an academic program (1) academic affairs; (2) financial/physical resources; (3) governance; (4) student affairs; and (5) faculty/staff resources. As one reads the definition of and program operations found within each of the five domains presented in this chapter, the overlapping nature of the position responsibilities becomes apparent. Comparing scholarship, service, teaching and administrative responsibilities contained in the sixteen position responsibilities in Figure 1.1 to those identified in one's own official job description can help define the types and scope of a director's position responsibilities in a particular college or university. If there is no formal position description, the listing of generic responsibilities can be used as a reference to draft a director's position description. The comparative review is an important position orientation and a beginning point for examining the locus of direct administrative control within a program, for defining position priorities and boundaries, and for identifying the administrative superiors and collaterals who have some level of indirect involvement in or administrative responsibilities for directing a baccalaureate social work program.

## FIGURE 1.1

## Academic Program Domains -Corresponding Administrative Position Responsibilities

1.  Academic Affairs

    Generic Position Responsibilities:

    - Promotes the quality of curriculum content and instructional effectiveness within the contexts of the mission, program goals, objectives, and evaluative outcomes.
    - Teaches as required by program needs.
    - Engages in scholarly or creative endeavors and professional and university service provision.

    ---

2.  Financial and Physical Resources

    Generic Position Responsibilities:

    - Acts as the financial agent for the program to acquire, allocate, and utilize funds and resources to advance the academic enterprise in compliance with institutional policies and procedures.

    ---

*(continued)*

**FIGURE 1.1** *(concluded)*

## Academic Program Domains -Corresponding Administrative Position Responsibilities

3. Academic Program Governance

Generic Position Responsibilities:

- Provides leadership in the strategic program planning, advancement, operation and evaluation of the academic enterprise.
- Serves as the primary spokesperson for and representative of the program within the institution, with all program stakeholders, and with external academic, administrative, regulatory, professional and legal entities.
- Provides day-to-day administrative oversight and supervision of the program, including but not limited to such tasks as establishing appropriate office and student advising times for faculty, chairing program meetings, creating committee structures, overseeing work assignments, and hearing formal appeals.
- Promotes the effectiveness of formal program-based decision-making within the official faculty, staff and student governance structures, procedures, and policies of the college or university.
- Resolves personnel conflicts, complaints, grievances and appeals in a timely and effective manner.
- Promotes the program's quality, reputation, and visibility within the educational, institutional, and professional contexts of the academic enterprise.
- Provides leadership to the program stakeholders in obtaining and/or maintaining Council on Social Work Education accreditation.
- Oversees and evaluates printed and electronic program-based records, documents, reports and promotional information to ensure content accuracy, design quality and distribution effectiveness.

---

4. Student Affairs

Generic Position Responsibilities:

- Administers program-based student recruitment, matriculation, admission, advising, dismissal and degree-verification processes that comply with the academic governance and administrative policies, procedures and standards of the institution.
- Provides opportunities and resources for students to organize. Informs them of their rights and responsibilities and promotes their formal participation in program governance in accordance with institutional policies and procedures.

---

5. Faculty and Staff Resources

Generic Position Responsibilities:

- Administers all program personnel appointments, promotions and advancement decisions within the institutional guidelines, policies, and procedures.
- Recruits, hires, supervises, and promotes the job performance of faculty, staff, technical and student employees of the program; conducts systematic performance evaluations of all personnel, and addresses unsatisfactory performance within the personnel policies and procedures of the institution.
- Advocates for program personnel in such matters as promotion, advancement, salary, and development opportunities.

# Dynamics of Position Responsibilities

The number, scope, and diversity of administrative responsibilities that converge at the baccalaureate program decision and operational levels soon become a position reality for a new program director. This reality is amplified by the daily mix of the routine, predictable, formally-assigned role tasks intermixed with a diversity of unanticipated tasks and decisions that flow to the director position. This position is viewed by the program stakeholders as the locus of decision authority - the program official whose job it is to see that things get done. The posture of a program director can be exemplified by that of Janus, the ancient Roman god of gates and doors who is characteristically represented with two opposite faces; one, in this case, pointed toward the program and its stakeholders and the other toward the institution and the external environments that influence the academic enterprise.

Routine or anticipated program maintenance responsibilities such as the scheduling of courses, providing oversight of student advising and supervising secretarial services represent a first level of anticipated responsibilities that must be systematically completed. These routine or formally assigned administrative responsibilities are supplemented by daily unanticipated tasks that represent a second level of responsibilities that also require a director's attention. Examples of daily, unanticipated tasks include "last minute," program-based information requests from administrative superiors, being informed that the copy machine has stopped working, having a faculty member report that because of illness she is unable to teach her classes that day, and being confronted by a student who wants to complain about the quality of teaching in a required course.

A third level of administrative responsibility relates to program advancement or development-related position responsibilities that are both planned and spontaneous; tend to combine both program and institutional interests and needs; and are instigated by institutional officials who request program participation. Examples of this third level of tasks would include such requests as program participation in institutional fundraising efforts to increase student financial assistance levels; enrolling all program personnel in the completion of a series of workshops to learn a new campus-wide information technology system; assisting the student recruitment efforts of the institution by conducting a series of program-based presentations to potential students; and having a social work faculty member direct a major institutional search, governance, or advancement committee.

These three levels of administrative responsibilities and commensurate tasks are further complicated by the institutional trends of asking academic program directors to participate in institutional-wide initiatives such as hosting dignitaries serving in major campus leadership and governance capacities and participating in public relations type events. Institutional requests for the director to participate in institutional sponsored initiatives contribute to the range and complexity of position responsibilities as higher education institutions adapt to more rigorous external controls, expectations, and political contingencies (Blostein, 1999). Such development participation requests represent potential opportunities for the program director to provide leadership within the institution, which, in turn, can improve the visibility, appreciation, and credibility of the social work educational enterprise. Consequently, a social work program director might be left with a mixture of feeling being overwhelmed yet excited about the potential for change and opportunities to advance the program within the institution. In fact, the opportunity to make a difference is a primary motivator for faculty who accept a program leadership position (Macy, 1990; Swaine and Flax, 1992).

A program director becomes a very busy faculty member whose typical day can be filled by committee meetings, stacks of paperwork, encounters with colleagues, students, staff and central administrators, drop-in visitors, and telephone calls; all of which combine to create a reactive oriented administrative approach. The director easily can be left with time only to react to a continuous stream of administrative demands, tasks, and information that naturally flow to the program director position. This can cause the office holder to lose the ability to strategically focus administrative attention on the most significant needs and priorities of the program in a proactive manner. The subsequent chapters provide information that a program director can apply in order to maintain personal and professional vitality as a faculty member while serving in a demanding leadership position. We examine such administrative strategies as identifying and prioritizing position responsibilities, applying administrative leadership approaches, and developing functional relationships with officials support systems needed to promote program advancement, increase administrative efficiency, and mobilize collective efforts that program stakeholders require to complete essential academic program responsibilities.

The program director position represents a "middle management" administrative role which requires the faculty member to assume the inherent responsibilities of linking or coordinating within the institutional administrative structure, to mediate among the various institutional stakeholders served by the program, and to serve as an official communication channel between faculty, students, alumni, institutional administrators, and external professional entities who have differing and competing interests, needs, and expectations. An examination of the administrative implications of the "middle management" role phenomena is extended in Chapter 8.

The academy historically has been built on a foundation of participation and involvement of faculty in basic academic program operations such as curriculum, governance, and budgeting. Academic program administration therefore built toward a shared process that consists of involving faculty and staff members in completing delegated responsibilities as individuals, ad hoc task groups and as member of formal or standing committees. Even though faculty members have the freedom to pursue individual career interests and professional goals, these pursuits can be linked in a meaningful way to the program mission and to the broad mission of the institution (Creswell, Wheeler, Seagren, Egly, Beyer 1990). Benefits of clarity about such institutional matters as historical precedents, current program initiatives, priorities of key administrators are factors that help a program set realistic goals and expectations. An essential function of administrative leadership, therefore, is facilitating the efforts of the individual faculty members toward common program-based goals. This is done by creating cooperative relationships with institutional and professional resource, support and collaborative systems needed to promote overall effectiveness of the education enterprise.

The program director position therefore is located on an "organizational boundary" between the program and (1) the institutional operations and official offices related to each of the five program domains, (2) the external regulatory and professional standards entities that shape education and (3) the stakeholder groups that comprise the educational enterprise. Given the diversity of competing interests and needs of the program, administrative leadership remains focused on creating a work environment and collective vision that benefits the long-range needs of the program.

The increasing number, diversity, and range of position-related responsibilities that a director manages represents a formidable administrative challenge. This challenge is exacerbated by the need to successfully manage the adaptations inherent in the process as a faculty member transitions to the program director position and becomes both an administrator of and a colleague in the academic enterprise.

Administrative leadership is another role performance dimension that a director brings to the position to strategically guide program stakeholders toward collective efforts to develop the academic enterprise. The nature of academic program leadership, which is a theme throughout the subsequent chapters, includes the blended application of such administrative actions as institutional networking, organizational visioning, strategic planning, culture building, and human resource development, all of which are firmly anchored in a careful assessment and understanding of the institutional auspices and contexts of the program.

# Program Operational Domains - Definitions

The major operational domains or components that comprise an academic program define the parameters for position responsibilities of a program director. They are used in this publication as a means to examine the administrative framework or context of a program directorship. Five operational domains - (1) academic affairs, (2) financial affairs, (3) governance, (4) human resources, and (5) student affairs - are viewed, as the essential functional areas where program administration must be focused. The generic position responsibilities identified in Figure 1.1 that are related to academic program administration responsibilities are viewed as the duties of a program director that flow across each of these five interrelated domains. A definition and descriptive "snapshot" of each domain is provided below. An in-depth examination of program operations and detailed administrative responsibilities inherent in each of the five domains is provided in the five subsequent chapters. It is within each of these program domains that the work of a program director is done and, as consistently noted in research findings, where the overall quality of the program depends on the relative effectiveness of the director in completing administrative tasks associated with each of these domains (Woodburne, 1958; Fisher, 1977; Roach, 1976; & Tucker, 1984).

## (1)    Academic Affairs

The area of academic affairs represents the heart of the academic enterprise and comprises the curriculum, instruction, and research operations of the academic program. As previously noted, social work education, as an applied academic discipline, views the educational process as an integration of academic and professional development. The requirement of students to apply theoretical knowledge, professional ethics and discipline-based skills to demonstrate competent service provision is an educational paradigm that is being increasingly adopted at many colleges and universities. In social work, the field practicum for example, is a significant component of the academic affairs domain where students, under supervision, learn to apply responsive practice interventions to accommodate contemporary practice realities, systematically evaluate the efficacy of their professional competencies and demonstrate the attributes of life-long learners.

The growing application by higher education of a "teacher-scholar" model of faculty performance, means that faculty members complete four inseparable responsibilities of "...the scholarship of discovery, of integration, of application and of teaching..." in order to complete scholarly works (Boyer, 1990).

Professional service provision by the program is an important dimension of a baccalaureate social work program and is consistent with the "Boyer" model. Quality academic programs in social work remain closely linked to the social work practice and professional communities to reinforce evolving program and curriculum relevance. CSWE accrediting standards reinforce this quality program feature. One method, for example, of addressing this program quality need is to develop program-agency partnerships, systematically providing release time assignments so that social work faculty can provide various types of professional services to community-based social service systems in the role of technical and evaluation consultants. Agency-based social workers, in turn, provide practitioner-based perspectives to the educational program (Ruffolo & Miller, 1994). Even though the nature of professional service activities selected often are left to individual faculty members, the director needs to monitor service activities to ascertain that such activities are consistent. For example, activities should be consistent with program goals, promote a positive public image of the program, create program advancement opportunities, and should be appropriately documented in faculty workload accountability reports. Linking faculty professional service initiatives and the service-learning or field-practicum requirements faced by students is also desirable so that field agencies are more fully in partnership with the educational program.

Systematic grant submissions by a director to fund institutional developments such as piloting computer-assisted instructional innovations, creating service-learning projects to strengthen experiential learning, and providing in-service teaching methods workshops are examples of resource development initiatives. Administrative tasks range from such routine responsibilities as scheduling required classes that provide the greatest access by students to acquiring library holdings, measuring outcomes using a range of academic program and institutional assessments, and mobilizing resources to promote curriculum and institutional effectiveness. Providing administrative oversight of systematic procedures to collect, analyze and apply program-based outcome data to promote incremental improvement in the curriculum, instructional, and student performance quality is a fundamental responsibility.

The operational domain of academic affairs is the focus of Chapter 2.

## (2)    Financial and Physical Resource Affairs

The financial affairs area consists of preparing, administrating, and evaluating the annual program budget, allocating funds, and completing internal and external financial reports. Program-based resource management including space, staff, equipment, supplies are also implicit within other position responsibilities including program leadership, advancement, governance and personnel. Within the financial affairs domain, administrative oversight includes the utilization of allocated resources by the college or university to meet the inherent expenses of the program's daily operations.

A broad range of administrative responsibilities such as approving monthly expenditures for telephone service, signing time-sheets reports for personnel to be paid, authorizing equipment repairs, ordering office supplies and addressing problematic clerical procedures are examples of daily program operations that require administrative oversight. The associated physical resources responsibilities, related to this domain, consists of obtaining, using, storing, maintaining, securing, and disposing of all of the tangible materials used by an academic program to achieve program goals. Such resources range from paper supplies, to classroom space, to equipment maintenance contracting, and to software acquisitions. A program director monitors program revenues to be certain, for example, that all expenditures are consistent with the program's annual and long-term priorities and are made in strict adherence to the financial policies and procedures of the college or university.

Numerous offices at the institutional level manage budgeting, purchasing, inventory control, contracts and grants administration, institutional development or advancement, alumnae/alumni affairs, student financial aid, and payroll and employee benefits. Each of these academic support offices, located throughout the college or university, provides specialized and technical services that can assist the program director with financial and physical resource administrative responsibilities.

Although a program director might not have the final word in financial affairs, administrative oversight responsibilities of financial expenditures, documenting resource needs, as well as setting funding priorities such as faculty travel funds are inherent responsibilities of this position. The director is, in general, the custodian of program space, equipment, and financial resource allocations.

Data management is a physical resource of the program that the director administers. As noted in the "reporting" function of Figure 1.1, the responsibility for the program's record or data keeping systems includes the collection, storage, and distribution of information related to each of the five program domains is a director's responsibility. The effective use of finite resources is a major role performance consideration by the institution in determining the overall quality of the program and its administrator. The operational domain of financial and program resources is the focus of Chapter 3.

## (3)    Program Governance

Governance in higher education administration lacks a common, uniform definition. The term governance describes an array of relationships among decision-making units and decision-oriented processes in higher education institutions. The term is also used to describe the units and structures comprising the administrative hierarchy, the legal relationships among institutional entities, the formal authority supplemented by the informal influencing patterns among institutional participants, the rights and responsibilities of internal and external institutional constituencies, and the formal institutional decision-making processes related to resource allocation. The CSWE Evaluative Standards related to program structure, organization, governance, and resources are guidelines related to program governance considerations and the reader should refer to those evaluative standards. For the purpose of this book, however, governance is defined as the structures, processes, and personnel involved in formal decision making at the academic program level.

Administrative tasks that support academic program governance range from building consensus among stakeholders regarding program mission to the development of long-range policies, procedures, standards, and services that enhance program effectiveness. Program directors, in collaboration with faculty members, are responsible for all program-based policies; procedures and administrative practices related to formal decision processes of the stakeholders. Found within the program-based governance domain is the largest number of core administrative responsibilities as illustrated in Figure 1.1.

Governance responsibilities require program directors to have a thorough understanding of the institution's policies, procedures, and decision making structure, be superb facilitators and team builders of program personnel, function as effective communicators and conflict managers, and provide competent leadership to mobilize and coordinate the individual efforts of all program personnel and stakeholders. The operational domain of governance is the focus of Chapter 4.

## (4)    Human Resource Affairs

The area of human resource affairs consists of administrative activities designed to obtain, support, develop, and evaluate the academic, staff, and technical personnel needed to achieve the purposes of the academic program. Academic work is labor-intensive; consequently, the annual expenditure for personnel is by far the largest portion of the annual budget and can be considered a foundation for the other four operational domains of the academic program.

In a social work program, human resource management includes the recruitment, orientation, supervision, development, and evaluation of faculty and staff. In order to adhere to all legal, personnel, union, professional, and institutional policies that govern human resources, the director works in collaboration with a number of institutional offices. Furthermore, the director is accountable for work assignments that build on individualized strengths in order to maximize the collective success of the human resources.

Evaluating the collective performance effectiveness of all program-based personnel including faculty members, who as academicians prefer to work independently, is a fundamental administrative responsibility. These "staffing responsibilities," as identified in Figure 1.1, may be directly assigned to a program director or depending on the nature of the governance structure, may be a shared responsibility with another administrator. Effective performance in human resource affairs determines the overall success of an academic program; thus, it is not surprising to find that this area is near the top of all administrative challenges, frustrations and management efforts reported by program directors (Carroll, 1974; Swaine and Flax, 1992; Tucker, 1984; and Waltzer, 1975). The operational domain of human resources is the focus of Chapter 5.

## (5)   Student Affairs

Students are the major stakeholders in the program and matters related to them fall within the administrative responsibilities of a program director. The overall purpose of student affairs is to ensure that the program meets the academic and professional development needs of students, and includes the administration of institutional policies and procedures that are designed to recruit, admit, retain, and evaluate the professional competence of social work students. Such policies and procedures in a professional degree program, as previously noted, require the provision of academic and professional development services that focus on the whole person. An academic program provides learning at the cognitive, affective and experiential levels, along with instructional methods that involve students in ongoing self-assessment to complement systematically completed faculty evaluations. Personal attributes such as values, attitudes, and professional beliefs, for example, are defined by the Code of Ethics of the National Association of Social Workers (NASW).

A key focus in student affairs is the program's determination of the ability of every social work student to demonstrate defined professional competencies embodied in defined program outcomes. A program helps students integrate personal and professional attributes. This fundamental demonstration of program resources and opportunities designed to foster outcomes is a formidable instructional challenge. It considers the personal, academic, and professional maturation of students, coupled with the requirement that they demonstrate mastery of basic knowledge values and skills under actual professional practice conditions in a supervised field practicum setting. Consequently, a particularly challenging position responsibility for a program director is related to providing administrative oversight of the program-based student admissions, retention, dismissal, and instructional policies and procedures.

A current major focus of higher education is student retention strategies designed to not only enroll capable students, but also to retain a critical mass of qualified matriculates so as to maintain institutional budgets, images and rankings (Reisbert, 1999). Efforts to reduce the exodus of students to other institutions, employment opportunities, or to simply drop out may include such ideas as the creation of "campus or learning communities" in which students are provided opportunities to (1) enroll in clustered courses to learn with a common cohort of classmates, (2) select resident halls to reside close to friends, (3) have informal contacts with faculty in their academic programs of interests, (4) receive institutionally sponsored out-reaching efforts to students who fit a profile of becoming a "drop-out," and (5) engage students in collegially-oriented community service and volunteer projects with faculty. These types of institutional-based student retention initiatives directly impact every academic program and represent a particularly complex issue for a director of an accredited baccalaureate social work education program that is mandated to screen and reject students who are not qualified for program-based admission.

The social work program not only delivers a high quality academic curriculum, but also provides faculty-based academic and professional advising on an individual basis to students. At the point of formal program admission, for example, personal behavioral patterns such as time management and personal assertiveness is formally evaluated within the context of professional standards. Deficits are addressed on an individualized basis. Academic competencies such as writing and critical thinking abilities are evaluated and if necessary, remediation completed. To supplement academic advising, faculty advisors maintain current information about the academic, personal, and professional development resources needed by advisees and the eligibility requirements to access both campus and community-based resource systems to complete successful referrals of students to these resource systems on an individualized basis. The program director responsibilities include creating and maintaining an effective operational network of institutional and community-based student services. Ideally, the network is designed to effectively address the psychological, academic, economic, social skills development, aesthetics, legal, and informational needs of students and participate as an active partner or supplement to the program-based social work faculty advising.

Another set of administrative responsibilities inherent in the student affairs domain consists of the need to provide program-based opportunities for students to plan and carry out extracurricular activities that reflect their interests and self-defined needs. These formal opportunities are designed to support the overall academic and professional development of students enrolled in the social work program. Participation in program governance is assured so those students, as a consumer group, are afforded an active voice in decisions that impact them. CSWE Evaluative Standards consistently includes a focus on the formal opportunity processes a program provides to socialize students into the profession.

Program accreditation Evaluative Standards also support the long-standing expectation of the social work profession that the educational institution serve as the gatekeeper to the profession by requiring programs to systematically evaluate students for entry into the profession and for ending their enrollment in the educational program on the basis of unsatisfactory academic performance related to professional knowledge, values, and skills standards (Moore & Urwin, 1991). This accrediting standard represents a major focus of administrative attention because admission, retention, and dismissal procedures are directly linked to such issues as enrollment numbers and trends (Berger, 1992, Singer & Strobino, 1989; Hepler & Noble, 1990; Frost, Anderson, & Sublette, 1987), recruitment and affirmative action initiatives (Raber, Tebb & Berg-Weger, 1998; Berger, 1991), legal issues, (Cole, 1991); and evaluation criteria (Gibbs, 1994; Cobb & Jordan, 1989; Moore & Urwin, 1991; Peterman & Blake, 1986).

In some institutions, selective admission and retention procedures may conflict with central administrative expectations that every academic program within the institution should continually strive to increase and retain student enrollment in order to help ensure the overall financial stability of the college or university. A policy issue conflict may result which centers on whether the specific standards of a social work program should supercede uniform institutional-based admission and academic standards. Undoubtedly, selective social work program admission and student retention standards do at some level conflict with those established by the institution. Because student recruitment, admission and dismissal standards are a feature of a quality academic program; this program-based function is a tension area for a director. Administrative efforts such as providing clear justification of the rationale for selective program-based admission, documentation of its effectiveness to help ensure program quality and systemic program-based initiatives to help admitted students achieve the standards set by the program are examples of approaches that a director promotes. In addition, it is necessary to apply systemic administrative strategies to preserve the social work program's admission, academic, and professional standards and to provide assistance in the mobilization of resources to address the continuing financial needs of the institution. Additional information about administering the recruitment, admission, retention, and dismissal process in a baccalaureate social work education program and mobilizing resources is provided in Chapters 3 and 5.

# Position-Based Information Management and Program Advancement

Program advancement is anchored in the "planning" responsibility of the director. It consists of enhancing the program's effectiveness by completing such initiatives as securing resources, identifying developmental priorities, nurturing institutional and external constituency support, and establishing relationships with institutional, community, and professional entities that can enhance academic excellence. Because the administrative tasks inherent in program advancement responsibilities cut across defined responsibilities within each of the five fundamental operational domains, program advancement is not defined as a single operational domain. In other words, program advancement occurs when a director completes administrative tasks in each of the five separate domains, provides effective overall program leadership, and successfully complies with the Council on Social Work Education program accrediting standards.

Another major program administrative task that cuts across defined position responsibilities within each of the five operational domains is communication. The informing, coordinating, mediating, persuading, negotiating, collaborating, and reporting processes inherent in the middle management position responsibilities of a program director requires effective use of written, verbal, and electronic communication. Communication can be considered the catalyst of the administrative process because it is the essential ingredient in such fundamental program administrative leadership responsibilities as:

- **Promote Image** - Promote the program's image, visibility, and creditability by serving as the program advocate and spokesperson with stakeholders, administrative, and academic support units of the institution and with external regulatory, professional, educational, legislative, business and accrediting associations, social work agencies, and interest groups.

- **Identify/Secure Resources** - Identify resource needs by talking with program faculty and staff, facilitate group discussions to achieve consensus regarding budget/resource priorities, and explicate the annual budget requests to administrative and finance officers of the institution in order to secure program resources.

- **Cultivate Stakeholder Trust** - Foster trust among program stakeholders by presenting, interpreting, and reflecting the intent of each constituency, communicating a common purpose of desired program outcomes to all parties, and facilitating productive dialog among and between stakeholders.

• **Disseminate Information** - Serve as an information conduit between and among program stakeholders and the central administrative officials of the institution by transmitting, interpreting and clarifying policies, procedures, directives and information that flow within the institution.

• **Foster Administrative Support** - Create an effective cooperative working relationship with the program director's administrative superior (e.g. dean, division head, provost vice president, etc.) position by developing mutual trust, respect, and creditability by informing that official about the social work discipline, program achievements, documented resource needs, pending issues, or problems confronting the program.

• **Collaborative Problem-Solving** - Promote the use of a program-based, collaborative problem solving orientation to prevent, reduce, and effectively resolve student, staff, and faculty grievances, appeals, and conflicts using communication that relies on trust, respect and honesty in work relationships.

• **Delegating Responsibilities/Decision Making** - Facilitate the planning and governance process within the program by delegating position responsibilities to individuals and committees, engage stakeholders in decision-making opportunities, and encourage ideas for improving the quality of the educational enterprise.

• **Inform Students** - Recruit, advise, and counsel students by the effective use of both formal and informal methods of providing timely, accurate verbal, written, and electronic-based information.

Added to the traditional communication processes is the expectation that a director apply information technology as an essential communication competency. The "future compatible or connected campus" is defined as one

.... that will allow higher education to develop a technology-enabled environment that consists of three components; connected learning, connected service to the community, and connected management. Enabled by the network infrastructure, higher education will be able to use technology to redesign the academic and administrative aspects of colleges and universities to further enhance the quality of the learning experience. This new approach will be based on networks, communication and computer technology using learning-on-demand, learner-centered instruction, student-centered services and digital libraries. (Obligner and Rush, 1998, p. xvi)

It is difficult to overestimate the profound changes that information technology will have on the future of higher education and academic program administration. As noted in the publication, The Learning Revolution by Oblinger & Rush, 1998, Farrington wrote:

> Several changes seem inevitable. One is that learning and education will become more informal, accessible and learner-centered. Another is that the demand for education, particularly lifelong education, will grow significantly, as will competition in the education market. The new tools will open new markets for traditional educational institutions and also expose them to vigorous competition. Those universities and colleges that can change, innovate and lead are likely to thrive; those that cannot will be at risk. Surely some will disappear. (Farrington, 1997, p. 27)

Communication is a fundamental ability of an effective academic program administrator and is a central focus for preparing a faculty member for entry into an academic program directorship for the position, (Eble, 1990). The geometric rate of growth and application of information technology options such as e-mail, newsletters, networking, and teleconferencing provide an increasing number of different methods for a director to communicate. These communication options are supplemented by an increasing number and sophisticated variety of software programs to complete such administrative responsibilities as planning, budgeting, and evaluating: all supplemented by the capability to complete information searches, organization, analysis, and presentation. Consequently, an academic program director must strives to continuously improve communication and information management competencies.

The quality and manner in which the director communicates helps to shape the program's visibility, image, and reputation. The need for the director to be adept at recognizing the perspectives held by the various stakeholders and to be able to fashion communication approaches to match special interest perspectives is an important administrative skill that adds to a growing need for directors to be competent advocates, marketers, conflict managers, and planners.

## Summary

An academic program within a contemporary institution of higher education responsibilities as a significant administrative, governance, and academic programming unit that operationalizes the essential purposes of the college or university. Major internal and external institutional contexts that influence the overall operations of an accredited social work program and the administrative practices and responsibilities of a program director have been examined. The relative effectiveness of the leadership of the academic program is an important variable in shaping the overall effectiveness of the institution.

The root of the word "administer" is to serve, which defines the prime responsibility of a program director who strives to marshal the energies of others, provide vision and leadership, be resourceful in taking care of details, be responsive to opportunities and creatively overcome barriers to improved program effectiveness. The social work faculty member who serves in the role of program director completes a broad range of position-based tasks and responsibilities that require extraordinary administrative, communication, and leadership abilities within the program domains of academics, financial governance, student, and human resource affairs. Specific administrative tasks, which comprise each of these five specific program domains, are listed in an evaluation survey located at the end of this publication. The survey is designed as an assessment form to assist a new program director in setting administrative priorities within each domain and for completing periodic assessments of the need to develop management and staffing strategies for completing prioritized program-based responsibilities.

Actual work-load assignments for the program director routinely include teaching required courses, providing academic and professional student advising, delivering field instruction, communicating with alumnae/alumni and community-based social work practitioners and work with institutional-based administrators. This combination of administrative, teaching, scholarship, and professional service responsibilities inherent in the director's role requires face-to-face contact with members of the key constituencies (students, faculty, parents, alumnae/alumni, and public officials) jointly served by the institution and the social work program. The director's leadership sets an example for social work students, who view the program as their academic and professional "home." Council on Social Work Education accreditation standards explicitly define the professional credentials and duties of faculty members who serve in this formal position. The performance of program directors is a key factor in shaping the quality of the social work education that students receive, which ultimately shapes the quality of professional practice and of social welfare services.

# References

Anderson, G. L. (1962). Professional education: Present status and continuing problems. In Education for the professions, Nelson B. Henry, editor. Chicago: University of Chicago Press.

Bennett, J. B. (1983). Managing the academic department. New York: American Council on Education, Macmillan Publishing Co.

Bennett, J. B., & Figuli, D. J. (1990). Enhancing departmental leadership: The roles of the chairperson. New York, NY: Macmillan Publishing Company.

Berger, R. (1992, Winter). Student retention: A critical phase in the academic careers of minority baccalaureate social workers. Journal of Social Work Education, 28(1), 85-97.

Berger, R. (1991, Spring/Summer). Untapped sources for recruiting minority BSW students. Journal of Social Work Education, 27(2), 168-175.

Blostein, S. (1999). Social work education and university restructuring: A case study. Arete, 23(1), 23-39.

Boyer, E. L. (1990). Scholarship reconsidered: Priorities of the professorate. The Carnegie Foundation for the Advancement of Teaching. Princeton, New Jersey.

Bracy, W., & Cunningham, M. (1995). Factors contributing to the retention of minority students: Implications for incorporating diversity. The Journal of Baccalaureate Social Work, 1(1), 85-95.

Carroll, A. (1974, Spring). Role conflict in academic organizations: An exploratory examination of the department chairperson's experience. Educational Administration Quarterly, 10(3), 61.

Cobb, N. H., & Jordan, C. (1989). Students with questionable values or threatening behavior: Precedent and policy from discipline to dismissal. Journal of Social Work Education, 25(2), 87-97.

Cole, B. S. (1991). Legal issues related to social work program admissions. Journal of Social Work Education, 27(1), 18-24.

Council on Social Work Education. (1999). Guidelines for termination for academic and professional reasons. Council on Social Work Education Commission on Accreditation.

Council on Social Work Education. (1994). Handbook of accreditation standards and procedures (4th ed.). Alexandria, VA.

Creswell, J.W., Wheeler, D. W., Seagren, A. T., Egley, N. J., Beyer, K.D. (1990). The academic chairperson's handbook (pp. 22). Lincoln, NE: University of Nebraska Press.

Eble, Kenneth E. (1990). Communicating Effectively. In John B. Bennett, and David J. Figuli (Eds.), In enhancing departmental leadership: The roles of the chairperson (pp. 23-29). New York, NY: American Council on Education and Macmillan Publishing Company.

Epstein, W. M. (1995). Social work in the university. Journal of Social Work Education, 31(2), 281-291.

Farrington, G. (1997). Higher education in the information age. In D.G. Oblinger & S.C. Rush (Eds.), The learning revolution: The challenge of information technology in the academy (pp. 97-126). Bolton, MA: Anker.

Fisher, C. F. (1977, June). The evaluation and development of college and university administrators, part two: Professional development of administrators. College and University Bulletin, 5.

Flax, N, & Swaine, R. L. (1996). Influence of administrative structure on BSW program objectives. The Journal of Baccalaureate Social Work, 1(2), 41-50.

Frost, C. H., Anderson, M. F., & Sublette, S. (1987). How to increase enrollment in undergraduate and graduate schools of social work. Journal of Social Work Education, 23(2), 75-82.

Gibbs, P. (1994, Winter). Screening mechanisms in BSW programs. Journal of Social Work Education, 30(1), 63-74.

Gmelch, W. H., & Miskin, V. D. (1995). Chairing an academic department. Thousand Oaks, CA: Sage Publications.

Gulick, L., & Urwick, L. (1937). Papers on the science of administration. New York: Institute of Public Administration.

Gutierrez, L., GlenMaye, L., & DeLois, K. (1995). The organizational context of empowerment practice: Implications for social work administration. Social Work, 40(2), 249-258.

Harper, K. V. (1985). Social work education: Do female coordinators have the power to direct undergraduate programs? Unpublished paper presented at the Women's Issues Symposium, Council on Social Work Education, Washington, DC.

Harper, K. V. (1990). Power and gender issues in academic administration: A study of directors of BSW programs. Affilia, 5(1), 81-93.

Harper, K. V., Ramey, J. H., & Zook, L. J. (1991, Spring/Summer). BSW program administration: directors' perception of their power to manage. Journal of Social Work Education, 27(2), 176-186.

Hecht, I. W. D., Higgerson, M.L., Gmelch, W. H., & Tucker, A. (1999). The department chair as academic leader. Phoenix, AZ: American Council on Education and the Oryx Press, 26.

Hepler, J. B., & Noble, J. H. (1990). Improving social work education: Taking responsibility at   the door. Social Work, 35(2), 126-133.

Icard, L. D., Spearmon, M., & Curry-Jackson, A. (1996). BSW programs in black colleges: Building on the strengths of tradition. Journal of Social Work Education, 32(2), 227-235.

Johnson, H.W. (1990). Baccalaureate social work education consortia: Problems and possibilities. Journal of Social Work Education, 26(3), 254.

Johnson, H. W., & Hull, Jr., G. H. (1990). The rest of the story: Baccalaureate social work programs no longer accredited. Journal of Social Work Education, 3, 244-253.

Lennon, T. M. (1999). Statistics on social work education in the United States: 1998. Alexandria, VA: Council on Social Work Education.

Macy, H. J. (1990). Role analysis study of chairpersons in academic departments offering accredited baccalaureate social work degree programs. Unpublished doctoral dissertation, Ball State University, Muncie, Indiana.

Midgley, J., & Karger, H. J. (1993). Do schools of social work need professional deans and directors? Journal of Social Work Education, 29(2), 142-149.

Mobley, T. (1981). Selecting the department chairman. Educational Record, 52, 322.

Moore, L.S., & Urwin, C. A. (1991, Winter). Gatekeeping: A model for screening baccalaureate students for field education. Journal of Social Work Education, 27(1), 8-17.

———. (1996). Code of Ethics. Washington, DC: NASW Press.

Oblinger, D.G., & Rush, S. R. (1998). The future compatible campus: Planning, designing, and implementing information technology in the academy. Bolton, MA: Anker Publishing Company, Inc.

National Association of Social Workers. (1981). Guidelines for the selection and use of social workers. Silver Spring, MD: NASW Press.

Peterman, P. J., & Blake, R. (1986). The inappropriate BSW student. ARETE, 11(1), 27-34.

Potter-Efron, R.T. (1985). Cooperation and conflict between social workers and sociologists in combined undergraduate departments. Journal of Sociology and Social Welfare, 21(3), 27-37.

Raber, M., Tebb, S. & Berg-Weger, M. (1998). Recruitment and retention of minority students in bachelor of social work programs. The Journal of Baccalaureate Social Work, 3(2), 31-49.

Reinardy, J., & Halter, A. (1994). Social work in academia: A cast study of survival. Journal of Social Work Education, 30(3), 300.

Reisbert, L. (1999, October). Colleges struggle to keep would-be dropouts enrolled. The Chronicle of Higher Education, XLVI(7), A54-56.

Roach, J. (1976, Winter). The academic chairperson: Functions and responsibilities. Educational Record, 57, 13.

Ruffolo, M. C., & Miller, P. (1994). An advocacy/empowerment model of organizing: Developing university-agency partnerships. Journal of Social Work Education, 30(3), 310-311.

Sheafor, B. W. (1979). The social work program: Its place in higher education. In Betty Baer and Ronald Federico (Eds.), Educating the baccalaureate social worker (pp. 49-53). New York, Ballinger Press.

Singer, T. L., & Strobino, J. (1989, March). Student retention in schools of social work: The qualitative difference for the nineties. Paper presented at the Council on Social Work Education, Annual Program Meeting.

Swaine, R. L., & Flax, N. (1992). BSW program directors: Characteristics and role experiences. Arete, 17(2), 16-27.

Tucker, A. (1984). Chairing the academic department, 2nd Ed. New York: American Council on Education and Macmillan Publishing Company.

Waltzer, H. (1975). The job of academic department chairmen. Washington, DC: American Council on Education.

Weinberg, S. S. (1984). The perceived responsibilities of the departmental chairperson: A note of a preliminary study. Higher Education, 13, 301-303.

Wheeler, B. R., & Gibbons, E. (1992). Social work in academia: Learning from the past and acting on the present. Journal of Social Work Education, 28(3), 300.

Woodburne, L S. (1958). Principles of college and university administration. Stanford, CA: Stanford University Press.

# Chapter 2

# Academic Affairs

The purpose of this chapter is to provide some measure of insight into the higher education domain within which social work education programs are found: academic affairs. Representing the heart of the academic enterprise, academic affairs include curriculum, instruction, and research operations of an academic program. For social work education programs, the educational paradigm is one of professional development for career relevance in social work practice. The integration of theory, professional ethics, and practice experiences is the basis of social work education. According to Flax and Swaine (1995), the domain of academic affairs is the *raison d'être* of the academic enterprise. It is within academic affairs that the work of academic (and professional education) programs occurs and it is the domain of academic affairs that forms the structure for that work to take place. For the social work program administrator, this domain consists of all administrative tasks associated with the interrelated instructional and curricular activities of the program. In this chapter, administrative tasks in the domain of academic affairs will be considered in both the institutional and program contexts.

The program director's role in this crucial area is to provide leadership in developing, planning, implementing, and evaluating the social work curriculum, promoting faculty scholarship and instructional effectiveness, evaluating and enhancing academic programming, and facilitating faculty and/or professional development. Providing leadership does not mean that the program director works alone in accomplishing the tasks within the domain of academic affairs. On the contrary, it is the effective program director who engages faculty, staff, students, and other stakeholders in developing and maintaining a partnership for accomplishing these tasks. The administrative leader, the program director, is more effective when teamwork is a method valued and implemented routinely in the programs' academic affairs activities.

In addition to providing leadership in the academic affairs domain, the director, as a social work faculty member, is also assigned to course teaching, provide academic advising to students, serve as a curriculum development committee member, and complete other academic related assignments in the program. A list of specific administrative tasks that comprise the academic affairs domain of a social work program is found in Appendix A of this book. Along with identification of administrative tasks, there is a self report evaluation that a director may complete to identify the employee who is assigned to complete each particular task within a specific program and to help set position priorities based on an assessment of the program's needs and goals.

# Typical Services in Academic Affairs

Although universities have a variety of organizational structures and academic support services, in general one can expect to find the following services, albeit with a variety of names/titles, within the context of a university. Typical support services in the domain of academic affairs is detailed in Figure 2.1.

**FIGURE 2.1**

**Examples of Typical Support Services**

- **Library services**
- **Assessment**
- **Institutional research/analysis**
- **Distance education and instructional technologies**
- **Graduate school**
- **Honors program**
- **Continuing education and public service**
- **Off-campus programs**
- **Academic advisement (including orientation)**
- **Academic support programs such as tutoring, counseling, and instructional supports**

Student input is also necessary in order to keep the program responsive to particular needs of students. On some campuses, courses are assigned rooms by central administration, on others program directors have that responsibility, another example of the importance of understanding the structure and processes of the institution. An example of a segment from an academic affairs planning calendar is located in the Appendix G to illustrate examples of monthly activities and tasks found within the realm of academic affairs that must be completed.

## Library Services

Understanding what academic services are available in the institution and knowing how those services can support the social work education program is essential for accomplishing the director's major responsibilities in academic affairs. For example, the director knows how library materials are ordered, how programs are notified of new library holdings, and what or if any costs to the program are associated with such orders. On some campuses, a library budget is allocated within the social work program's budget, on other campuses the library budget is comprehensive and includes costs for all library expenses in the institution. It is possible, too, that a librarian is assigned to the social work program to serve as the liaison and resource person.

By all means, find out who that person is and invite them to meet with faculty at least once a semester to maintain a strong partnership between the social work program and the library.

## Institutional-Based Academic Assessment Resources

Academic assessment is another activity found in academic affairs. Knowing what assessment activities are institutionalized and which, therefore, may be accessed and integrated into systematic program reviews and planning, is another way a program director can use the unique context of the institution for program administration tasks in academic affairs. Using results of institutional alumni survey results, entering student survey information, social work licensing passages rates, and other standardized procedures to bring information about social work students and/or the program is wise for it complements the social work program's assessment plan. Finding out where assessment activities are conducted, when activities are scheduled, and how the program can obtain results of those activities is important to the social work program director's execution of academic affairs responsibilities in the area of assessment.

On many campuses, the Office of Institutional Research/Analysis typically collects data relevant to the university, including its academic programs. From this office a program director can get information on enrollments, credit hour production, graduates, and numbers of full time and part time students, for example, which can inform the director for future planning. Some institutions now make this information available on a Web Site where it can be viewed, printed out in hard copy form, or copied to a file for later use and reference. The astute program director will monitor the program's data and compare it to other programs within the institution in order to assess the program's productivity and outcomes in relation to other programs. When used strategically, this mastery of information can have a positive effect on the program's acquisition of resources needed to deliver a quality undergraduate social work program. The program director who uses solid (and official) data to demonstrate program growth over time has a stronger rationale for additional faculty resources than the program director who fails to use existing data demonstratively.

## Knowing Academic Resources

To find out what academic resources are available, the program director forms working relationships with key administrative personnel shown in the organizational chart presented previously (Swaine & Flax 1995). Furthermore, they add that developing information channels and networks which operate formally and informally helps the director gain information about the institution's curriculum, scholarship, and instructional developments and opportunities (1995). For example, in one institution faculty development travel grants are awarded twice a year. The application process takes time and the awards typically do not cover all travel expenses to a national conference, rather a portion (usually one-third) of the costs. In this case, the supportive program director will seek additional funding for faculty members from other sources. The dean, academic vice president, and program director or department chair often have funds which can be requested and used in combination to complement the faculty development travel funds, making it possible for the faculty member's travel to be fully supported with institutional funds. Further support by the program director can be demonstrated by providing samples of completed applications as references for faculty completing applications for the first time.

# Program Based Administrative Tensions

As noted in the Preface, such social work program features as selective student admissions, academic operations, and educational outcomes combine to represent some level of tension within the bureaucratically oriented institution that houses the program. Six types of tensions that a director manages are identified below.

## 1. Academic Program Tension

Because of the social work program educational goals as a professional degree program and academic goals within a university environment, academic oriented tensions are bound to exist. Tensions related to the academic affairs domain may include factors such as: educational orientation of the program, high costs associated with the program, and external involvement with the social work program. These types of tension points between the program and its institution as well as others related to the fit or complementarity of the program within its institutional environment are described in Chapter Eight. The program director assesses the institution and the program to determine where and to what extent those tensions occur, then develops strategies for managing those tensions in order to deliver a quality social work education program and reach social work program goals.

## 2. Professional Program Tension

It is commonly thought that major tensions in academic affairs typically stem from differences between the orientation of traditional academic programs and those of professional programs like social work. Sheafor (1979) identifies a number of these differences. First, higher education emphasizes intellectual development. Social work, in addition to the intellectual development of its students, focuses on their emotional and social development. This emphasis may be met with suspicion. Second, higher education tends to take a value-free, scientific approach to learning. Social work, on the other hand, focuses on the development of a strong value commitment in students to such individual development, social justice, and respect for cultural diversity (Reid and Peebles-Wilkins, 1991). The structured relationship between the value and content orientation of a social work curriculum with the liberal arts goals and requirements established by the college or university represents another type of articulation or tension issue for a program faculty. Third, higher education supports considerable autonomy in the development of program curriculum. Social work programs, however, experience considerable constraint in curriculum development because of their responsiveness to the standards of CSWE, the interests of students, and the needs of the professional practice community. These external influences, as identified in Chapter Eight, are a factor to which academia is often neither accustomed nor sympathetic.

## 3. Academic Freedom Tension

Additionally, tension exists between higher education and social work regarding individual academic freedom. Academic programs permit individual faculty to teach whatever content they choose, as long as it is relevant to the subject matter of the course. In contrast, social work programs limit individual faculty choices because of the need for delivering basic social work content, sequencing courses, and integrating content in courses across the social work curriculum. This limitation on social work faculty may be perceived as threatening to the cherished value of academic freedom.

## 4. Program Costs Tension

In a similar vein, Wheeler and Gibbons (1992) believe that many of the problems of a typical social work program arise from its dual role as an academic discipline and a professional preparation enterprise. Professional social work programs have costs that are different from those of academic programs. Costs for sufficient and competent faculty, travel costs associated with field instruction, accreditation expenses, membership fees for faculty and program in professional organizations, and travel expenses for faculty to attend national conferences on social work education are necessary for a quality social work program. These program-related costs can be a source of tension between the program and the institution. Therefore, a program director builds strong documented rationale for funding requests, and is persistent in requesting funding support for the program. Keeping good records as evidence to support a request for funding strengthens one's case.

## 5. Scholarship Tension

A major compatibility issue in the area of faculty scholarship is the tension between the scholarship expectations of many institutions and scholarship suitable for professional social work programs (Flax and Swaine, 1995). This tension exists for 2 main reasons including:

1. The trend in higher education toward increased emphasis on accountability, efficiency, and productivity.

2. A limited definition of scholarship which rewards publication to the exclusion of other activities considered scholarly by professional programs.

Institutions vary in regard to their definitions of research, so it is important that the program director be knowledgeable about his/her own institution's definition and that the definition be communicated clearly to faculty in the program. This is another example of the importance of understanding the context of the institution and using that understanding to direct the social work program.

For the well-being of the social work program, it is important that social work faculty be evaluated by criteria appropriate to professional disciplines. This may mean that the program director focuses efforts on broadening the scholarship definition used by the institution to include criteria such as professional grant service projects and reports on community-based research, presentations at professional conferences, monographs and reports, especially those emphasizing social work education. In pursuing this goal, the director may find it useful to develop coalitions with other applied disciplines, such as nursing, education, and journalism. Once again, the director looks at the institutional context when identifying potential allies for coalition building.

## 6. Practice Linkage Tension

The reciprocal and ongoing relationship of the program to its professional practice community is another unique characteristic of social work programs. This relationship is maintained through many avenues and activities. Faculty often serve as agency board members where they provide consultation, supervision, program development and evaluation services, in-service training, professional development, and continuing education. Representatives of the practice community act as field instructors, serve, on social work program committees and boards, and provide research sites and employment opportunities for program graduates. The time and costs involved in maintaining these relationships are another potential source of tension between the program and the institution. Once again, understanding the institutional context and the special needs of a professional program like social work places the program director in a stronger position when explaining the need for these activities and relationships.

# Managing Tensions

Management of tensions related to the fit of the academic discipline of social work with in its institutional/organizational environment depends on each social work program's unique situation in the context of its institution. To overcome tension, Sheafor (1979) suggests that the program director and faculty use their knowledge of the organization's structure and build relationships with key personnel. Most issues involve trade-offs that are part of every political process. The social and political skills of program personnel can affect the social work program's viability within the institution. Wheeler and Gibbons (1992) encourage social work programs to become more responsive to their professional mandate, while continuing to meet university standards for academic programs. They identify five principles for dealing with tensions between the institution and professional social work programs.

1. **Cooperation**: The program director, faculty, and staff should actively seek common ground and work towards university goals as well as its own. For example, suppose the institution wants to offer continuing education to community professionals. The social work program can respond by offering continuing education and professional development opportunities for social work professionals. An elective course on grant-writing could meet the need of a social work practice community where staff have little or no experience with proposal writing for external funding. A workshop on ethical decision making in practice could provide continuing education units for social workers while delivering solid foundation content for competent social work practice.

2. **Identity**: The program establishes an identity for itself that is compatible with academia. For example, social work faculty can collaborate in research projects with other disciplines. They can serve on institutional committees, lead focus groups studying matters of concern to the university, and participate in institutional activities. The social work program that is involved in its campus community establishes a presence and a prominent identity.

3. **Education**: The program recognizes the ongoing need to educate its institution about professional social work education. For example, the social work program stresses the contributions of professional programs to the university mission. Reporting program activities for Board of Trustees meetings, institutional publications, and local media keeps the program visibly connected to the institutional mission/purpose.

4. **Leadership**: The program takes an assertive leadership stance toward self-definition. For example, social work faculty can become active on major university committees and governance structures in order to further define and clarify the needs and goals of their program within the context of the institution. If faculty are asked to take on leadership roles within the institution, the program director can demonstrate support by adjusting faculty workload to accommodate new responsibilities. (Keeping a strong pool of qualified adjunct faculty who can teach across the curriculum will make it easier to adjust workloads of full time faculty and keep the program stable.)

5. **Fact-Finding**: The program makes an effort to know about the institution's organizational structure, services, and personnel. For example, before proposing a curriculum change it is prudent to find out what ramifications the change may have for other units. Study the catalog and the institutional academic handbooks to see what units are affected. Meet with representatives of those other units to discuss any issues pertinent to the curriculum change. Float the idea to field instructors, students, and graduates to gain their perspectives on the change before firmly deciding to move forward. Then, once a change is adopted, disseminate the information about the change to all stakeholders.

# Social Work Program Context

Using earlier work by Flax and Swaine (1995) as an organizing framework, administrative responsibilities in the academic affairs domain are divided into two categories: (1) curriculum development, evaluation, and improvement, and (2) instructional support and effectiveness. A review of the following responsibilities in academic affairs, organized in these two categories will be examined/described in detail from a program director's perspective.

# Curriculum Development, Evaluation and Improvement

Curriculum planning, development, organization, scheduling, presentation, and evaluation involve continuous efforts and structured processes within the domain of academic affairs. Academic program leadership requires a director to create and follow formal structures and processes to monitor and evaluate the relevance of the curriculum and the effectiveness of instruction within the context of the program's mission and purpose in relationship to the regional needs of the university service area. Maintaining curriculum relevance requires faculty to consistently engage in such evaluative oriented tasks as reviewing curriculum content in view of practice emphasis/competencies needed by social service agencies, organizations and systems served by the program, academic background/needs of students enrolling in the program, evolving knowledge base of the profession, accreditation standards for social work programs, and the feedback from agency-based field practicum supervisors, etc. Frequently meeting with faculty in purposeful work sessions to review program evaluation results, including curriculum content, delivery, and evaluations of curriculum areas in relation to desired educational objectives, is one way to use a team approach to curriculum review and planning. Using the time to consider curriculum structure, delivery, and results, then planning for needed changes is an effective way to continuously evaluate and improve a program's curriculum.

Administrative leadership in the realm of instructional effectiveness requires the director to focus on both the teaching performance of individual faculty members and on the overall quality of the faculty as an instructional team. Because a social work curriculum should be congruent with the program's mission, purpose and goals, the academic requirements and learning experiences for students must be carefully defined and structured to help insure that they have a clear understanding of such factors as the: (1) purposes, content focus and character of introductory and culminating requirements, (2) nature and rationale of the academic structure and requirements and (3) functional relationships between academic requirements and the realities of contemporary social work practice. In other words, the curriculum is a coherent whole rather than a collection of courses, which in turn requires each faculty member to function within this type of curricular and instructional orientation.

Academic instruction which is organized and functions as a collective requires the development and advance of faculty as an instructional team with each member bringing knowledge about and respect for each others' teaching and course expectations. The administrative tasks of a program director related to evaluating and developing teaching performance of faculty members is the focus of Chapter Six of this book, which uses a holistic orientation to academic program human resource administration.

## Curriculum Changes

Once a decision is made to modify the social work curriculum, it is critical that those modifications be coordinated and evaluated within the context of the college or university. Having a working relationship with the institutional academic officials and being knowledgeable about the institutions' policies and procedures for curriculum changes, remaining persistent about moving the proposed change/s through the system by observing deadlines, using appropriate forms, following up on the results once deadlines have passed, disseminating information about proposed (then, approved) changes, and anticipating consequences of proposed changes for social work students and faculty are important dimensions of coordinating and evaluating curriculum changes.

Monitoring current and proposed curriculum changes in competing and complimentary academic programs is quite important in the domain of academic affairs of a university. Curriculum changes are not developed, proposed, and implemented in a vacuum, rather they occur in the context of the institution and have an impact on more than just the social work program's stakeholders. Curriculum changes in other units may have relevance for the social work program, especially in relation to courses on which the program depends for its liberal arts perspective and those the program requires of its majors. Curriculum changes in the social work program in turn also affect other units. The social work program's decision to teach its own research courses, after years of relying on other disciplines for that content, will have an effect on the enrollment in those previously required courses, as well as such factors as faculty workloads, course schedules and sequencing in the social work program. Small programs in particular may find it necessary to rely on other disciplines to provide or supplement curriculum content. Such collaborations with faculty in other academic disciplines often require program faculty to request changes or modifications of content or assignments within those courses critical to the professional development of students in the social work program. Monitoring curriculum changes in the context of the program's institution is an ongoing process, one to be taken seriously and not ignored.

## Course Syllabi

Another curriculum activity for the program administrator involves reviewing syllabi for existing, new, and proposed courses. One approach to the task is to consider the following questions before approaching a review of program syllabi. What is the purpose of the course syllabus? Does the university have a standard format for course syllabi? Does the social work program have a standard format for course syllabi? What syllabi content, if any, is required by the college or university, the academic department, and the social work program? What expectations do accreditation standards place on social work program syllabi? One assumption in social work education circles is that course syllabi reflect, even document, how courses are delivered, how courses connect with curriculum content areas within the social work curriculum, how courses link to the program's educational objectives, and how students are evaluated in program courses. An effective program administrator will regularly review course syllabi and assist faculty in making modifications to course syllabi when needed. Exchanging course syllabi with program faculty for feedback and discussion can be the topic of a faculty development work session periodically. At such a session, faculty can develop a more comprehensive understanding of the total curriculum and its relationship to program goals and outcomes, how other faculty approach instruction, what assignments can cut across specific courses or curriculum sequences (e.g. a practice or case study example can be used to analyze practice, policy and research concepts), and how previous learning experiences of a student is built on in required sequential courses. Providing opportunities in group meetings for faculty to describe and demonstrate instructional approaches that have been particularly successful is another useful way for a director to promote both faculty develop and instructional effectiveness.

Another wise practice for the program director is maintaining a master file of program- approved current course syllabi and related course materials (hand outs, exams, class activities, reading list, etc.). Such a file will assist the program administrator to be prepared for situations in which an adjunct professor or colleague in the program is needed to fill in for another faculty member. Faculty illnesses, absences for short or long periods, professional development leaves, or death may cause a program administrator to implement contingency plans for covering courses within the social work program. Having approved, current course materials on hand facilitates that process for the program administrator and the clerical staff who often field course-related questions for students, program faculty, other university support staff such as librarians, etc., in the normal pace of an academic term.

Curriculum related tasks also include regularly reviewing the university catalog and other academic program promotional and academic materials for accuracy and making revisions as needed. All publications with references to the social work program, its faculty and the curriculum, should be routinely reviewed for content and accuracy by the social work program administrator regularly. Care should be taken to review and modify written material about the program when changes occur. Consistency among program documents is important and can be overlooked when curriculum changes occur. For example, changing a program's educational objectives requires changes to educational objectives in curriculum areas, courses, field instruction, and outcomes assessment tools. Academic advisement materials, freshmen and transfer orientation materials, recruitment brochures and pamphlets, and the college or university and program websites all represent examples of materials which may be updated routinely (annually, bi-annually, etc.) by units within the institution and which must be updated when changes to content in the printed or posted information occur in the social work program.

# Evaluate and Improve Curriculum

Involving faculty, students, field instructors and other stakeholders in periodic and systematic evaluation of curriculum strengths and needs is another administrative task within the curriculum area of academic affairs. As a team, program faculty should annually review student evaluations of courses and instruction, field instructor evaluations of student performance in field, field instructor and agency practitioner evaluations of program graduates and the program, and advisory board/committee feedback about the curriculum and program. A comprehensive approach to seeking insight into program curriculum strengths and needs provides a fuller evaluation of the curriculum and program, and expands the stakeholders' involvement with the program which is, of course, one avenue of program renewal.

When evaluations and reviews of curriculum are completed, the results of curriculum review and evaluation may indicate a need for curriculum revision. When curriculum evaluation reveals a need for change, plans must be developed, then implemented, to address that need. If, for example, the need revealed is that more macro practice content is needed in the curriculum and more macro practice opportunities in practice are needed by social work students in field practicum, the faculty should embark on planning to meet this identified need. Perhaps another course is needed, or perhaps additional macro practice content in an existing course will suffice if supplemented, for example, by requiring students to complete a carefully structured community-based, macro oriented experiential learning assignment to reinforce the theoretical practice content focus of the currently required course. If a new course is needed, how and when will it be delivered and sequenced with other practice courses and with field? Furthermore, how can field instructors be involved in the curriculum change so that they are committed to providing more macro practice opportunities for students in field practicum and meeting the other identified curriculum needs identified in the example above? Those are important questions to consider when evaluating the need for curriculum change and subsequently planning for that change.

## Instructional Support and Effectiveness

The second category in the domain of academic affairs is instructional support and effectiveness. Figure 2.3 identifies examples of administrative tasks that a program director may complete to foster effective program instruction.

## Instructional Responsibilities

The social work program administrator usually carries responsibilities which include providing course instruction and curriculum development in areas of professional/academic specializations, and supervising special student projects such as independent study, honors theses, senior projects, and providing academic advising to social work majors. The program administrator is generally viewed by the academic officials of the institution and program stakeholders as the academic leader of the program. As its leader, the program director is commonly expected to be knowledgeable about social work education and accreditation. The program director is expected to be the program's spokesperson and its primary academic advisor. The program administrator promotes and supports special projects and independent study opportunities for students, learning opportunities

## FIGURE 2.3

### Instructional Support and Effectiveness Activities in Academic Affairs

- Providing course instruction and development in areas of specialization
- Providing orientation and serving as a mentor for new faculty
- Supporting faculty efforts to enhance instructional quality and effectiveness, including faculty scholarship
- Assisting faculty in using new instructional technologies
- Procuring instructional supports for faculty and students
- Promoting extra-curricular experiential learning for students and assisting faculty with integrating cognitive, experiential, and affective oriented learning/course assignments
- Promoting continuing education/in-service training and professional development of opportunities for social work practitioners and faculty
- Monitoring program exams, grading procedures, student evaluations of faculty instruction, and instructional standards
- Using faculty and student input when developing class schedules for the program and teaching responsibilities for faculty
- Periodically and systematically reviewing instructional activities in the program as a whole to evaluate effectiveness, then making changes for improvement where needed

in community agencies, and other professional development opportunities that unfold during the academic year. Making the most of those opportunities enhances student learning and establishes the program administrator as a dynamic leader. If an agency needs assistance with a special project such a needs assessment, a survey of client services, an updated resource file, etc., the program director and faculty would be wise to work with the agency to develop the project into a learning opportunity for students. Projects such as these provide a platform for students to integrate interviewing skills, research knowledge, and macro practice foundation knowledge in an experiential opportunity mentored and supervised by program faculty and in collaboration with a community agency.

# Faculty Development and Support

Another activity of the program director in the area of instructional support and effectiveness involves providing orientation and serving as a mentor for new faculty, both full time and adjunct. Orienting new faculty, as discussed in Chapter 6, is an important task in the domain of academic affairs. New faculty need academic affairs information specific to the program and the institution. Those new to social work education will also need orientation to the faculty role, to the field of social work education, and to accreditation and other matters related to professional education in institutions of higher education. Once orientation is provided, new faculty need to be mentored for a time — maybe for a year, maybe longer. Some special type of mentoring may be provided by the program administrator, for example, teaching about routine activities, time-lines, and academic responsibilities of the social work program as a unit and the social work program faculty as a whole, including forms and reports specific to the program. Additional mentoring, such as sharing instructional approaches and technological information, linking new faculty with others in the community, can be provided by program faculty or other support staff. Mentoring can be enhanced by establishing relationships with other individuals and units within the university's academic affairs division in order to maximize the faculty development process. For example, universities typically sponsor new faculty orientation and offer professional development opportunities for all faculty. The program administrator should be familiar with the university's orientation and other faculty development offerings and support faculty participation in those activities.

Supporting faculty efforts to enhance instructional quality and effectiveness is another responsibility of the program administrator. To be their best, program faculty need ongoing professional development which must be supported by the program administrator. Making faculty aware of workshops and conferences which are relevant to their development as social work educators, securing funds to support faculty participation in those workshops and conferences, supporting faculty memberships in professional organizations, encouraging research and writing, making presentations with faculty at social work education meetings, and accessing additional funds to support faculty development are ways in which the program administrator can demonstrate support for faculty development The program administrator is ultimately responsible for periodically and systematically reviewing instructional activities in the program as a whole to evaluate effectiveness, and making changes for improvement where needed. CSWE Evaluative Standards have consistently required programs to have ongoing oversight of curriculum, continuous evaluation, and maintenance of program integrity. Faculty and other program stakeholders should be involved in this activity. As was noted earlier, new social work faculty in particular need mentoring and support to become social work educators and scholars. According to Flax and Swaine (1995), an important function of the program director is to identify, access, and link instructional resources to the social work program, and when necessary to develop new resources. Securing needed equipment, providing information about available resources, distributing new information about curriculum resources as they become available are just a few ways that the program director can support faculty to become effective educators.

There are numerous ways to assist faculty to improve their teaching skills and enhance the program's instructional quality. One such way, as previously discussed, is to establish a faculty mentoring program for newer faculty. Another way is to create faculty development opportunities for faculty within the program and/or for faculty across disciplines of similar interest. Setting a good example for faculty by being a good role model is also an effective way for program directors to assist faculty to improve teaching skills and enhance program quality. Another technique is team-teaching, which can encourage faculty collaboration and often contributes to teaching innovation. Professional associations such as the Association of Baccalaureate Social Work Program Directors (BPD), the Council on Social Work Education (CSWE), the National Association of Black Social Work Educators (NABSE), the National Association of Social Workers (NASW), NASW state chapters and regional units, and others offer workshops and conferences which provide opportunities to learn about new teaching technologies, skills, and methods, obtain teaching materials, and interact with colleagues who share similar professional interests or have experience in specific areas of the social work curriculum. Directors can encourage attendance at these conferences and workshops in many ways, particularly by providing adequate financial support which may require creative fund raising by the program director.

At times, for a variety of different reasons, certain faculty members may have difficulty with their teaching. Some faculty can improve their teaching on their own, while others need added support and encouragement. Because program directors evaluate faculty, they can be instrumental in offering assistance when necessary. A problem solving approach to supporting faculty with improving instruction is one offered by Creswell et al. (1990). The approach is essentially a five-step process to improve the teaching performance of faculty. The steps include (1) gathering information, (2) clarifying the problem, (3) observing teaching performance, (4) facilitating improvement and practicing new skills, and (5) monitoring progress and advocating for the individual.

Of course, faculty need time to implement this five-step process. Individual program directors who wish to try this method can adapt it as needed to fit their own administrative styles and program cultures. Student evaluations of courses and instruction over time, enrollments in courses over time, and student performance in field instruction and on other outcome measures offer ways to gather information for discussion with faculty. University resources such as instructional or teaching/learning centers, team teaching with more experienced instructors, instructional workshops, and reward systems for instructional accomplishments are a few ways to assist faculty with improving their instruction.

Faculty responsibilities include ongoing development as a teacher-scholar which, as described in the Faculty and Staff Resources in Chapter 6, requires that social work education programs provide the time and other supports necessary for faculty to engage in research, writing, publication, and other scholarly production. Supporting faculty in the responsibilities of "...the scholarship of discovery, of integration, of application, and of teaching..." as they strive to develop scholarly works is an important role for program directors (Boyer, 1990). Boyer notes that " Scholarship in earlier times referred to a variety of creative work" the integrity of which was measured by the ability to think, communicate, and learn (1990).

Boyer's report recognizes four interdependent responsibilities of scholarship:

1. Research which aims at the discovery of new knowledge.
2. Thought and inquiry which integrates the bodies of specialized knowledge.
3. Learning which applies knowledge to consequential problems.
4. Teaching which disseminates knowledge and promotes the critical and creative capacities of other learners.

Social work educators generally arrive in academia after a time in social work practice. They arrive as professional social workers, aspiring to be social work educators, with limited knowledge of the social work education field. They have been "doers and thinkers" in practice, now they must adapt to expand their repertoire of skills to include other scholarly activities. Equipped with the proper educational and practice credentials, new social work faculty now learn what it means to be a social work educator.

This, of course, takes time, support, and mentoring. Swaine and Flax (1995) note that beyond providing the time required to engage in scholarly activity, it is the program director's responsibility to develop the ways and means of supporting and promoting faculty scholarship. Hull (1991) suggests that perhaps the easiest task is to set aside time to talk about scholarship. Specifically, he suggests that regular discussion meetings be held to stimulate interest in research projects. A 1993 study of undergraduate social work faculty scholarship revealed that "...a majority participated in conference or workshop presentations and did not publish" (Mokuau, Hull, and Burkett, 1993). Even though CSWE accreditation standards require accredited programs to systematically contribute to the knowledge base of the profession, performance expectations of faculty related to scholarship vary according to a range of program characteristics such as size, resource support, unionization, promotion and tenure requirements, and release time from teaching responsibilities (Hull and Johnson, 1994). Keeping faculty informed of calls for papers for presentation and/or publication, securing funded research opportunities for collaborative projects with other faculty or practitioners and systematically assigning annual research time for every faculty member encourages their research involvement and demonstrates administrative support.

While the Creswell model cited above provides good advice on how to approach a problem situation in the area of faculty scholarship, adopting a strategy for preventing such an outcome is worthy of attention. Providing faculty support for scholarly activities early in the faculty member's employment and continuing that support over time may prevent problems from developing in the first place. High on the list is encouraging scholarly collaborations between experienced and new faculty including writing papers, making presentations, and engaging in research projects. This is a strategy worth considering as a matter of everyday practice in an undergraduate social work program.

Another way that program administrators support faculty development is by assisting faculty in using new instructional technologies. The program administrator should take the lead in learning new instructional technologies and arrange opportunities for faculty to see demonstrations to learn and use developing technologies. If one faculty member emerges as more interested than the others in developing new instructional skills, that faculty member could become a resource for others in the program. Circulating promotional materials which reflect information about new instructional technologies keep faculty apprised of opportunities to learn and develop new skills. These opportunities may be provided through the university's continuing education program, academic support services, workshops/conferences on or off campus, or organized for and delivered specifically to social work program faculty.

Program faculty and students need a program director who recognizes the importance of procuring instructional supports for faculty and students in order to enhance instructional support and effectiveness. This involves the procurement of equipment and technological supports for faculty and student use. Finding those resources within the context of the college or university may be challenging. For example, on one campus at the end of every budget year, in the months of August and September, new computer equipment and instructional supports are targeted for purchase. The wise program administrator is aware of what equipment the social work program needs and quickly presents the request through the appropriate channels in order to meet deadlines for procuring new equipment and technological supports for the social work program at the appropriate time within the context of the institution. Persistently pursuing instructional supports, keeping the list of needs current and updated, and acknowledging the acquisitions are requisite activities in support of instructional enhancements.

# Experiential Learning

The program director is responsible for promoting extra-curricular experiential learning for students and assisting faculty with integrating cognitive, experiential, and affective oriented learning/course assignments. Social work education is professional education and, as such, requires a different structure for learning than academic disciplines. For example, the student majoring in history studies history by attending required classes, completing assignments which typically involve reading, research and writing, and watching or listening to audio visual tapes or programs in support of learning history. The social work major, on the other hand, is expected to followed a sequenced curriculum plan in which social work courses often include assignments requiring the student to spend time in community social service agencies to meet a variety of education objectives in the program and in specific courses. Learning for the social work student occurs at the cognitive, experiential, and affective levels in order to socialize the social work student into the profession. Learning takes place in the classroom, in agencies, in volunteer activities, in attendance at professional social work and social work education meetings, at social work club meetings, in interactions with faculty, program stakeholders, and practitioners, and in reading, thinking, observing, and self-reflection. The effective program director understands the value of experiential learning for social work education and sets a standard as a role model for involving students actively, purposefully, and professionally in their learning.

# Continuing Education

As the program administrator and the recognized leader in social work education in the program, the director is expected to promote continuing education/in-service training and professional development opportunities for social work practitioners and faculty in the service region. Opportunities like this can be strategically planned so that programs for professional development are delivered regularly, such as annually during March, (Social Work Month), once a semester (fall, spring, and summer), etc. Linking with the local unit of the National Association of Social Workers (NASW) to provide continuing education programs and credits at unit meetings is one strategy which works well for several social work programs and the social workers who work in their regions. Surveying field instructors, advisory board members, and program graduates to determine training needs can give insight for planning professional development opportunities which are relevant to social work practice. One such survey revealed a need for training in the areas of malpractice and liability. To respond to that need, the program arranged for a workshop by NASW Trust to be included as part of an annual social work program or regional conference.

# Technical Activities

Another responsibility of the program director involves monitoring program exams, grading procedures, student evaluations of faculty instruction, and academic program standards. Posting final exam schedules, clarifying grading standards for the university, arranging for the administration of student evaluations of faculty, reviewing those results and discussing them with faculty during the annual conference or earlier if needed, are activities included in instructional effectiveness. Grading pattern reports are generated in some universities and can be used by the program administrator to monitor grading pattern in courses and of faculty. Working with faculty to problem-solve grading issues such as incomplete grades, make-up exams, assignment extensions, grade appeals, etc., is a routine activity for program administrators.

Planning the schedule of course offerings and assigning faculty workloads are other activities included in instructional effectiveness. To complete those tasks it is wise to use faculty and student input when developing course assignments and schedules for the program and teaching responsibilities for faculty. Universities have workload standards, usually defining the number of courses taught or a workload expectation, which must be followed in assigning faculty workload. On some campuses, faculty workload is established by a collective bargaining agreement which is honored by the university.

It is imperative that the program administrator knows the context of the university and its policy for workload standard, including any flexibility afforded the program administrator in assigning workload credit. For example, if the program needs someone to assume responsibility for outcomes assessment, could the program director adjust a faculty member's teaching load and grant one-course credit for outcomes assessment oversight and reduce the teaching load accordingly?  The ability to do so indicates that the program administrator has a fair amount of autonomy over workload assignment, within the standards of the institution.  The times that classes are offered are also set by the university, but within those specified time frames, a program administrator usually has flexibility in shaping the schedule for social work courses.  This is especially important considering that courses are sequenced, students have agency assignments and activities which support their instructional activities, some students are employed, and some students are in field instruction.

As programs grow, it becomes necessary to divide coursed into multiple sections and offer courses more often across the academic year.  The effective program administrator works with faculty to plan ahead for these growing program needs rather that react to crises situations as they occur.  One program, for example, with a number of students who need night classes, may find it necessary to offer a day section and a night section of the required social work courses.  University standards for course enrollments are considered when dividing courses into multiple sections.  Although a minimum number of twelve (12) undergraduate students per course may be required of the university for the course to be offered, sometimes such a rule can be waived if a strong rationale for offering the course is provided.  Knowing the scheduling needs of students and university policies for course scheduling is critical to making sound course schedule plans for the program.

## Summary

The role of the program director in the academic affairs domain is to provide leadership in developing, planning, implementing, and evaluating social work curriculum, as well as to provide instructional support and promote instructional effectiveness, including the development of faculty as educators. Using an ecological framework to assess the institution's organizational structure and services is useful in identifying, accessing, and linking institutional resources with the academic affairs needs and activities of the social work program. The ecological framework also directs attention to CSWE accreditation standards and the role of accreditation in academic affairs, which will be discussed in greater detail in Chapter Seven.  Needs of the profession and current and developing practice trends also affect the changing expectations of social work education for professional social work practice.  Developing and maintaining a high quality undergraduate social work program demands that the program administrator give continuous attention to tasks found in the domain of academic affairs.

# References

Boyer, E. L. (1990). Scholarship Reconsidered: Priorities of the Professorate. The Carnegie Foundation for the Advancement of Teaching. Princeton: New Jersey, 25.

Council on Social Work Education. (1994). Handbook of accreditation standards and procedures. Alexandria, VA: Author.

Council on Social Work Education. (1994). Curriculum policy statement for baccalaureate degree program in social work education in council on social work education. In Handbook of accreditation standards and procedures. Alexandria, VA: Author.

Creswell, J. W., Wheeler, D. W., Seagren, A. T., Egly, N. J., & Beyer, K. D. (1990). The academic chairperson's handbook. Lincoln, NE: University of Nebraska Press.

Flax, N., & Swaine, R. L. (1995). Academic affairs. In Macy, H. J., Sommer, V. L., Flax, N. & Swaine, R. L. Directing the baccalaureate social work program: an ecological perspective. Jefferson City, Missouri : Association of Baccalaureate Social Work Program Directors.

Hull, Grafton H., Jr. (1991, Winter). Supporting BSW faculty scholarship. ARETE, 16(2), 19-27.

Hull, G. H., Jr., & Johnson, H. W. (1994, Winter). Publication rates of undergraduate social work programs in selected journals. Journal of Social Work Education, 30(1), 54-62.

Mokuau, N., Hull, G. H. Jr., & Burkett, S. (1993, Spring/Summer). Development of knowledge by undergraduate program directors. Journal of social work education, 29(2), 160-170.

Reid, N. P., & Peebles-Wilkins, W. (1991, Spring/Summer). Social work and the liberal arts: renewing the commitment. Journal of social work education. 27(2), 208-219.

Sheafor, B. (1979). The social work program: Its place in higher education. In B. L. Baer & R. C. Federico. (Eds.). Educating the baccalaureate social worker. Boston: Ballinger Publishing Company.

Sheafor, B. (1996). Taking the mountain to Mohammed: Enhancing rural human services through distance education. Journal of baccalaureate social work, 1(2), 27-39.

Wheeler, B. R., & Gibbons, E. G. (1992). Social work in academia: Learning from the past and acting on the present. Journal of Social Work Education, 28(3), 300-311.

# Bibliography

Colby, I. (1998). Adjunct faculty in social work education. Journal of teaching in social work, 16( ), 133-147.

Epstein, W. M. (1995, Spring/Summer). Social work in the university. Journal of social work education. 31(2), 281-292.

Flax, N., & Swaine, R. (1996). Influence of administrative structure on BSW program objectives. Journal of baccalaureate social work, 1(2), 41-49.

Harper, K. V., Ramey, J. H., & Zook, L. J. (1991, Spring/Summer). BSW program administration: directors' perception of their power to manage. Journal of social work education, 27(2), 176-186.

McMurtry, S. L., & McClelland, R. W. (1997, Spring/Summer,). Class sizes, faculty workloads, and program structures: how MSW programs have responded to changes in their environments. Journal of social work education, 33(2), 307-320.

Menges, R. J., & Associates. (1999). Faculty in new jobs. San Francisco, CA: Jossey-Bass Publishers.

Pearson, P. G. (1998). The educational orientations of graduate social work faculty. Journal of social work education, 34(3), 427- 436.

Petracchi, H. (1998). The combined use of video and one-way broadcast technology to deliver baccalaureate education: a comparative assessment of student learning in a school of social work. Journal of baccalaureate social work, 4(1), 51-59

Poulin, J. (1989). Goals for undergraduate social work research: a survey of BSW program directors. Journal of social work education, 25, 284-289.

Skolnik, L., & Papell, C. P. (1994, Winter). Holistic designs for field instruction in the contemporary social work curriculum. Journal of social work education, 30(1), 90-96.

# Chapter 3

# Financial and Physical Resources

The purpose of this chapter is to identify and examine the major administrative tasks and responsibilities found in the financial and physical resources domain of academic program administration. Developing and managing financial and physical resources are critical to the successful administration of a high quality social work program in an academic unit of a college or university. Performing those tasks within the context of the institution is challenging to the program director. However, the significance of the program director's responsibility for financial and resource management cannot be overemphasized. Having adequate resources and the autonomy to manage program resources contributes to program quality in any social work education program.

## Resource Administration Responsibilities

Examples of the major administrative tasks in the financial and physical resource domain are listed in Figure 3.1. A complete listing of specific interrelated administrative responsibilities that compose the personnel domain is found in Appendix B. These responsibilities can be completed directly by a director or can be shared with or may be completed entirely by other administrative officials located within the formal personnel system of the institution. The tasks listed in Appendix B are arranged in a format that provides opportunity to assess the relative importance of the tasks within the context of a specific program and to locate the locus of assigned administrative responsibility. This administrative task assessment process provides a means to examine personnel management priorities and to identify personnel issues that are unique to a particular program.

Major tasks in the domain of financial and physical resources are found in the following figure.

## FIGURE 3.1

### Program Director Tasks in Financial and Physical Resources Domain

- Formulating the annual operating budget.
- Developing periodic fund raising initiatives.
- Administering the use of allocated financial/physical resources.
- Monitoring routine expenditures (such as telephone charges); preventing excessive expenditures.
- Authorizing the processing of receipts and disbursements by the institutional accounting office(s).
- Maintaining an inventory system of program resources.
- Formulating policies and procedures for the use of supplies, materials, space, resources, and equipment.

# Institutional Context

## 1. Budget Development and Administration

Regardless of the type of organizational structure that houses the social work program, the program is responsible for developing and administering its own budget. This includes financial allocations for fundamental program needs such as personnel, travel, equipment, and in-kind resources such as classroom and office space. Therefore, the program director needs and understanding of the formal procedures, required documentation, and administrative approval process for program-based financial matters which operate within the context of the university.

The figure above shows that the typical institution has separate specialized units within business affairs. The vice-president of business affairs may also serve as the treasurer. In this organizational chart, the divisions of business affairs include purchasing, auditing, contracts and grants, accounting and space management, and student financial aid. But organizational structures vary across

# FIGURE 3.2

## Financial Affairs Organizational Chart

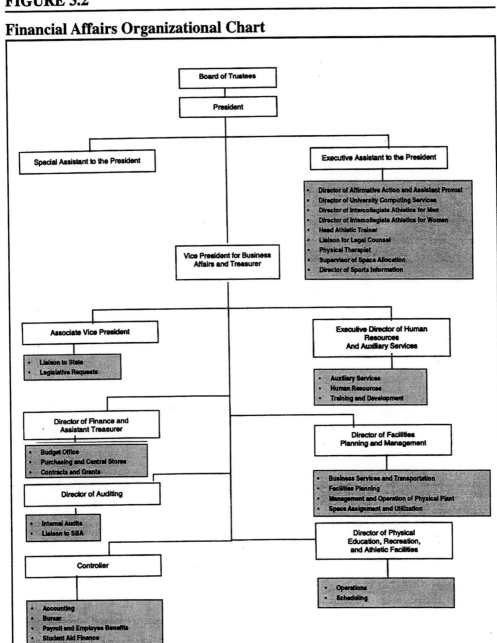

universities, so the prudent social work program director will learn well the organizational structure for his/her institution.

## 2. Linking Budget to Planning

As the resource manager for the program, the director links annual resource planning requests to program goals, objectives, and desired outcomes, explaining the need for resources and demonstrating that resources are being used effectively. The director often manages scarce resources for the current academic year, send long range resource requests to the institution's development office (or other designated unit within the institution), document current expenditures, justify current instructional equipment needs, and identify future resource needs of the social work program. Although level funding is common in academic programs, and is a common source of under-funding, the prudent program director seeks ways to defend resource requests and, when necessary, expand program resources with external funds. Such is the norm today when even traditionally state supported colleges and universities are calling themselves "state assisted", indicating a smaller share of state funding is available to universities and programs than in years past.

Managing this program area/administrative domain requires specialized information, language, and training for program directors to be effective. Although differences in program size and administrative auspices may lead to different management policies in universities and/or social work programs, some responsibilities in this program administration domain are typical of virtually all institutions. These tasks are not easy to complete. Program directors rank financial and resource management among their most demanding responsibilities (Creswell, Seagren & Henry, 1979; Macy, 1990; Swaine & Flax, 1992). Resource management at the academic program level includes four major activities: (1) planning, i.e., anticipating and developing sources of funding; (2) budgeting; (3) managing resources; and (4) reporting. Although these activities are interrelated, specialized offices in the institution may treat them as distinct operations, and thus this chapter presents them separately.

## 3. Managing Resources

Managing resources may raise institutional support and autonomy issues for a program director. The program's unique resource needs require understanding and support from institutional officials. The director finds ways to explain to institutional officials the unique needs of the program and maintain formal and informal collaborative relationships with these decision makers. In addition to formally scheduled gatherings such as quarterly meetings of academic program directors, institution-wide faculty meetings, and institutional governance meetings, the director should initiate periodic meetings with administrative officials to discuss program accomplishments, long-range resource needs, and the status of overall program operations. Informal contacts and program visability within the institutional community can reinforce formal administrative understanding of the program. Routine attendance by the director and faculty colleagues at campus social events, hosting campus receptions for students completing the social work degree, reporting faculty and student accomplishments in the institution's public information services, and providing leadership to campus-wide programs such as the annual United Way campaign, student recruitment initiatives, commencement ceremonies, and public social problem forums are examples of ways to promote the program's visibility. This visibility is important in developing an understanding of the program within the campus community.

## 4.  Annual Budgets and Strategic Planning

The formulation of an annual operating budget at a college or university requires a series of compromises among the competing personnel, programmatic, and physical resource needs of the institution. Each of the fundamental operational areas typically receives less than fully adequate resources. As a result, annual allocations made to competing academic units within the institution are also less than optimal. The annual budget allocation process can be viewed as a series of political compromises among competing interest groups, causing the program budget allocation over time to take on a marginal, incremental pattern (Wildavsky, 1964). Developing resource expansion strategies to obtain larger portions of budget allocations within the institution is an interesting, yet necessary, challenge for the program administrator. Strategic financial planning (at least annually) for three and five year periods includes the social work program's long range plans and resource needs, as well as those which are immediate. Strategic financial planning provides documentation of the program's resource needs for the short and long term and assists the university's administration with budget planning and resource allocation.

## 5.  University Policies and Budgets

Administration of social work program resources is linked to the resource management policies of the institution. The program director prepares an annual program budget request which is reviewed by administrative officials within the institution's decision hierarchy. Planning is a crucial first step that the director takes when preparing an annual budget proposal and identifying long-range program resource needs. To seek funding within the institution, the director fills out resource planning requests, develops budgets, then submits it through the appropriate channels. Technology makes is possible for planning budgets to be entered into the university's main computer system, then accessed, viewed, and approved by other units in the administration. On one campus, four planning budgets are requested of all budget managers; one at level funding, one at a five per cent reduction, one at a five per cent increase, and one which includes all resource needs and wants. Using this model provides budget managers with an opportunity to purposefully reflect on budget possibilities in the context of the university, for the next year. Ultimately, central administrators in collaboration with the institution's financial office determine the annual budget for the institution as a whole, as well as units within the institution, including the social work program. If strategic planning documents are used, linking planning to budgeting, then the program's financial resource needs may be addressed over time.

## 6. Incremental Budget Changes - the Norm

As a rule, funding changes from one year to the next, if any, tend to be incremental for several reasons:

- The most readily available information used by administrative officials in determining funding allocations is related to current program offerings.

- Budget determination is a shared administrative process within the institution.

- The centralized institutional budget priorities represent a political compromise among competing institutional constituencies (Wildavsky, 1972, pp. 286-287).

## 7. Political Realities

The budgeting process, therefore, is inextricably linked to the political system of the institution. Significant budget increases for a social work program would require the director to not only provide a clearly documented justification for increased resources, but to also mount a strategic administrative effort to shift the embedded political and administrative support for current institutional financial priorities. Otherwise, annual program budget allocations are based on a percentage of the operating budgets used during the past year or two. The program director is left to manage an insufficient annual allocation, which is determined by officials who are generally unfamiliar with the day-to-day operations of the program and may not appreciate its value. The following Figure 3.3, illustrates on BSW program's annual budget allocation ($355,997), its current month expenditures ($39,092.68), the amount of funding currently committed or encumbered ($372.35), and the balance available ($186,388.55). Salaries, wages, and benefits are found in object codes 1000 - 2210 and total $344,675 or 96.8% of the total program budget. The remaining $11,322 of this program's annual budget is for all expenses other than personnel.

## 8. Documenting Resource Needs

While the illustrated budget represents the university's budget allocation for the BSW program, programs may need additional funds to operate a high quality program. Separate accounts such as foundation accounts, grants, and contracts can supply additional funding. Consistently documenting the program's accomplishments, plans, and resource needs provides administrators with information essential for budget allocation. For example, one social work program director included the need for an additional faculty line in the program's strategic plans for five-year periods every year, using the program's steady enrollment growth over its history as one justification for additional program resources. Persistently including a resource need in the program's strategic plan, year after year, yields the needed funding for that resource in time. On the other hand, omitting that needed but unfunded resource request from the program's strategic plan year after year will likely guarantee that the resource will not be funded. A little patience combined with persistence will carry the program director forward in the direction of resource procurement.

## 9. External Funding

Because all units receive funding at a less than preferred level, administrators of the budgetary units develop resource expansion strategies to obtain larger portions of the finite annual budget allocation. The difficulties of administering an academic program that receives less than adequate resources and the continuing need to increase its funding base are compounded by the high expectations of constituents inside and outside the program. Students,

# FIGURE 3.3

## Annual Program Budget and Monthly Expenditure Report

| OBJ CODE DESCRIPTION | BUDGETS ORIGINAL | REVISED | ACTUALS CURRENT MONTH | FISCAL YEAR | OPEN COMMITMENTS | BALANCE AVAILABLE | PERC USED |
|---|---|---|---|---|---|---|---|
| 1000 PROFESSIONAL. FISCAL | 309,475.00 | 183,095.41 | | 34,516.25 | | 183,095.41 | 0 |
| 1120 FACULTY - FISCAL YR | | 34,516.25 | 8,903.25 | 34,516.25 | | | 100 |
| 1220 PROF INSTR - ACAD YR | | 88,285.34 | 22,863.60 | 88,285.34 | | | 100 |
| Prof/Ade-Flec & ACad | 308.47500 | 305.897.00 | 29,566.85 | 122.80159 | | 183,095.41 | 40 |
| 1250 PROF-TEMPOR FACULTY | | | 4,463.10 | 17,862.40 | | 17,862.40- | 0 |
| 1300 PROFESSIONAL, SUMMER | | 10,934.00- | | | | 10,934.00' | 0 |
| 1320 PROF INSTR - SUMMER | | 7,803.00 | | 7,802.00 | | | 100 |
| 1340 PROF INSTR - 2N0 5S | | 3131.00 | | 3,131.00 | | | 100 |
| Prof/Adm-Summer | | | | 10,934.00 | | 10,934.00- | 0 |
| 1600 STAFF AND SERVICE PE | 30,185.00 | 18,725.85 | | | | 18,725.85 | 0 |
| 1610 STAFF PERSONNEL | | 10,952.05 | 2,291.08 | 10,952.05 | | | 100 |
| 1650 STAFF PERS BI-WEEKI--Y | | 507.10 | | 507.10 | | | 100 |
| Staff Pers/Serv Staf | 30,185.00 | 30,185.00 | 2,291.09 | 11,459.15 | | 18,725.86 | 37 |
| 1900 WAGES. STUDENT | 5,015.00 | 3,126.20 | | | | 3,126.20 | 0 |
| 1910 STUDENT - REGULAR | | 1,888.80 | 508.86 | 1,888.80 | | | 100 |
| Student Personnel | 5,015,00 | 5,015.00 | 508.86 | 1,888,80 | | 3,126.20 | 37 |
| Salaries | 344,675.00 | 341,097.00 | 36,830.90 | 164,935.94 | | 176,161.06 | 48 |
| 2000 STAFF BENEFITS | | 44.74 | | | | 44.74 | 0 |
| 2110 GP INS LIFE AD & 0 | | 2.94- | | 2.94- | | | 100 |
| 2120 OP INS SASIC HEALTH | | 36.09- | | 36.09- | | | 100 |
| 2140 OP INS SALARY CONT | | 2.39- | | 2.39- | | | 100 |
| 2210 ANNUITY & PENSIONS | | 3.32- | | 3.32- | | | 100 |
| Staff Benefits | | | | 44.74- | | 44.74 | 0 |
| 3000 ACCOUNT POOL | 11,322.00 | 8,145.34 | | | | 8,145.34 | 0 |
| 3210 SUPPLIES | | 1,311.10 | 566.86 | 1,038.75 | 272.35 | | 100 |
| 3219 | | 593.09 | 253.70 | 593.09 | | | 100 |
| 3610 EQUIP MAINT & REPAIR | | 25.00 | | 25.00 | | | 100 |
| 3630 EQUIP MAINT CONTRACT | | 435.30 | 92.87 | 435.30 | | | 100 |
| 3710 PRNTNG A OU' ON CAMP | | 86.15 | | 86.15 | | | 100 |
| 3720 PRINTING-OFF CAMPUS | | 25.33 | | 25.33 | | | 100 |
| 4120 COMP SOFTWARE-PURCH | | 420.90 | 27.00 | 430.90 | | | 400 |
| 4230 PSTG- 1ST & PRIORITY | | 172.95 | | 172.95 | | | 100 |
| 4231 PSTG- 1ST PRESORT | | 73.03 | | 73.03 | | | 100 |
| 4232 PSTG- MISC. | | 23.67 | | 23.67 | | | 100 |
| 4236 PSTG- EXPRESS DELVRY | | 22.27 | | 22.27 | | | 100 |
| 4238 PSTG BUSINESS REPLY | | 3.78 | | 3.78 | | | 100 |
| 4310 LONG DISTANCE SHOS | | 201.80 | 148.70 | 301.80 | | | 100 |
| 4330 TELEPHONE EQUIP CHGS | | 1330.75 | 286.15 | 1,330.75 | | | 100 |
| 4870 MEALS & LODGING | | 7.46 | | 7.46 | | | 100 |
| Supplies & Other Exp | 11,322.00 | 12,876.72 | 1,353.28 | 4,450.03 | 272.35 | 8,145.34 | 36 |
| 6160 COMPUTER EQUIPMENT | | 6,068.36 | 508.00 | 8.06636 | | | 100 |
| 8700 UNIV MOTOR VEHICLES | | 670.51 | | | | 670.51 | 0 |
| 8710 MOTOR POOL MILEAGE | | 5.51- | | 5.81- | | | 100 |
| 8720 MTR POOL DAILY USAGE | | 35.00 | | 35.00 | | | 100 |
| Motor Pool ChArgie | | 700.00 | | 29.48 | | 670.81 | 4 |
| 8800 TRAVEL POOL | | 1,363.90 | | | | 1,363.90 | 0 |
| 8810 TRAVEL-PROF UNIV BUS | | 1,636.10 | 402.50 | 1,636.10 | | | 100 |
| Travel | | 3.000.00 | 402.50 | 1.636,10 | | 1,363.90 | 54 |
| Tot Non-Salry Relatd | 11,322.00 | 22,645.00 | 2,261.78 | 12,192.90 | 272.35 | 10,179.75 | 55 |
| Total Expenses | 355,997.00 | 363,742.00 | 39,092.68 | 177,064.10 | 272.35 | 186,385.55 | 48 |
| Account Total | 355,997.00 | 363,742.00 | 39,092.68 | 177,084:10 | 372.35 | 186,388.55 | 48 |

| | | | OPEN COMMITMENTS STATUS | | | | |
|---|---|---|---|---|---|---|---|
| ACCOUNT | REF. NO. DATE | DESCRIPTION | ORIGINAL AMOUNT | LIQUIDATING EXPENDITURES | | ADJUST-MENTS | CURRENT AMOUNT |
| 1-65700-32100001721 | 08/10 | STAPLES | 83.89 | | | | 83.89 |
| 1-65700-32100005283 | 11/05 | STAPLES | 308.68 | | | | 208.86 |
| 1-65700-41200004883 | 10/26 | BELL INDUSTRIES | 27.00 | | | 27.00 | COMPLETED |

faculty, field instructors, program graduates, agency supervisors and administrators, and other program stakeholders have expectations for a social work program's performance, including the quality of its graduates, faculty, and products such as conferences, workshops, manuals, papers, and publications. Adequate resources are essential to deliver a high quality program and produce high quality outcomes.

Planning for external funding is becoming more and more critical as budget dollars are stretched and tested. External funding may include applying for grants, developing contracts for external funding, and looking for community-based projects which can bring resources into the social work program. Some program directors have relied on their advisory boards to assist with fund-raising, some have established businesses to feed funds into the program, some have established foundations, others have set up scholarships and bequests as creative ways to bring external funding to the program. Learning what potential funding resources are available to the program, securing those resources, and managing those resources responsibly is critical. External funding enhances and expands what programs do and improves the program's quality. For example, some external funding supports field practica, some supports faculty salaries, some supplements faculty travel, some supports equipment upgrades and purchases, and some supports curriculum development. The beauty of external funding is that it is generally provided to achieve specific purposes or meet certain goals of the social work program, hence is tailored to address program specific needs and/or goals. It is with the support of external funding that many social work education programs sustain high quality programs over time. Some well-tested funding sources for baccalaureate social work education programs are Title IV-E and IV-B Child Welfare Training Grants. Partnering with child welfare systems, social work education programs receive funding to prepare social work students for child welfare practice. The source of this funding is the Department of Health and Human Services, Children's Bureau. Their web site is http://www.acf.dhhs.gov/programs/cb.

## 10. **Foundation Accounts**

Figure 3.4, Quarterly Foundation Account Expense Report, shows how one program's university reports on foundation accounts. In this case, the social work foundation account has $3,429.61 available and spent $234.54 on office supplies during the period of time covered by the report. Sources of funding for foundation accounts include program alumni, students, faculty, agencies, and corporations. In addition, funds generated from workshops, conferences, and other program-sponsored events can usually be placed in the program's foundation account.

## FIGURE 3.4

### Quarterly Foundation Account Expense Report

| | |
|---|---|
| DEPARTMENT/COLLEGE/AREA: | SOCIAL WORK PROGRAM |
| ACCOUNT AUTHORIZATION:<br>SUPERVISORY AUTHORIZATION: | SOCIAL WORK PROGRAM DIRECTOR<br>CHAIRPERSON, DEPARTMENT OF SOCIAL WORK<br>SOCIOLOGY AND ANTHROPOLOGY<br>DEAN, COLLEGE OF SCIENCES & HUMANITIES |
| ACCOUNT NUMBER: | 008999 |
| TITLE: | SOCIAL WORK PROGRAM |

| ACCOUNT BALANCE | COMMITTED | AVAILABLE |
|---|---|---|
| $3,651.65 | | $3,429.61 |

ACTIVITY FOR THE MONTH

| TRANS DATE | TRANS CODE | DESCRIPTION | AMOUNT |
|---|---|---|---|
| 01/15/00 | WITHDRAWAL | OFFICE SUPPLIES | $ 234.54- |
| NET ACTIVITY FOR THE QUARTER | | | $ 234.54- |

## 11.  Financial Reporting

The process of requesting and reporting financial information is a required responsibility of a program director and represents a significant opportunity to lobby for the resource needs of the social work program. Communication with a number of key institutional administrators occurs within the budget cycle of the institution. This cycle begins with the director making a resource request, which typically includes the following information:

- an annual operating budget;

- financial statements showing status at the beginning of the cycle;

- activities completed during the budget year;

- a year-end institutional audit showing that policies and regulations were followed; and a justification of the resource request.

# Program Context

## 1. Resource Management

The director has the task of spreading scarce resources effectively, efficiently, and economically among competing program needs. To effectively manage resource allocations, address unmet resource needs, and develop information and technical support networks needed in this program domain, the program director fully comprehend the administrative budgetary structure and the specialized financial offices of the institution. A beginning point in understanding financial operations is a review of the institution's administrative structure. For example, the operational areas and their respective officers under the administrative direction of the Vice President for Business Affairs and Treasurer in the organizational chart in Figure 3.2 should be familiar to most program directors.

A budget is a mechanism for making choices among alternative expenditures. It links financial resources and human behavior to accomplish policy objectives (Wildavsky, 1964). Because the institutional budgeting process shapes the program budget, the director should understand the financial cycle and elementary budgeting practices. Access to technical consultation from the director's administrative superior and collaboration with the specialized financial offices should be available if needed.

Program faculty who support the hiring or appointment of a colleague to serve as the program director have the implicit, although often unexpressed, expectation that the director will successfully expand the program's resource base as well as the program's degree of autonomy in controlling its resources (Tucker, 1984). Resource adequacy and autonomy are key factors in a program's survival (Johnson & Hull, 1992), important indicators of administrative authority (Harper, Ramey & Zook, 1991), and significant requirements for Council on Social Work Education (CSWE) program accreditation.

## 2. Resource Adequacy

For a social work program to be one of high quality, it needs adequate funding. Adequacy of program-based financial resources was noted by Gibbs (1995) as a significant CSWE program accreditation compliance issue. However, it is program quality which establishes the financial and physical resource needs of a social work program and CSWE accreditation standards, representing the profession's current beliefs about what minimum resources are needed for quality social work education programs, which underscore and support a program's need for adequate resources.

For a variety of reasons, the resource needs of a social work program are substantive. The delivery of field-based education, the need for small skill-oriented classes, and the need to maintain accreditation all translate into budgetary needs. The need for adequate resources to deliver professional social work education can create tensions between the college or university and program. For example, funding is required for travel related to field instruction, annual professional membership dues, and program accreditation, which requires initial fees, reaffirmation fees, and site visitation costs. Classroom space and furnishings must accommodate small group instructional methods. The program may need special resources such as computer-based training, internships, and instructional videos. Special student and field instruction advising manuals represent another extra cost. These manuals are important because they provide academic and professional program information to advance students through a highly structured professional development and educational experience.

## 3.  External Influences and Resources

Administration of program resources is also subject to external influences such as CSWE accrediting standards which historically have defined the types, stability, and quantity of resources an accredited program must have in order to deliver a high quality social work education program. Within the context of program goals, CSWE sets standards for fundamental resources such as space, equipment, library, and secretarial support. These standards are priorities that a program director keeps in mind when requesting and monitoring resources. Four categories of major provisions related to program resource needs and administrative control requirements are identified in CSWE accreditation Evaluative Standard 2 (CSWE, 1994, pp. 82-83). According to Evaluative Standard 2, the program should:

- Have primary responsibility for planning, administering, and evaluating budget and program resource requirements.

- Receive from the institution sufficient and stable financial, equipment, personnel, library, and operating resource allocations to permit program planning, implementation and achievement of goals.

- Participate in developing and administering policies related to hiring, retention, and use of program personnel to achieve program goals.

- Have jurisdiction over sufficient physical space to achieve program goals.

Social work, unlike some other disciplines, has considerable potential to generate external funding because of its relationships with professional, consumer, governmental, and political entities. Opportunities exist to develop contractual arrangements to complete community-based projects, such as needs assessment studies, sponsored programs, staff development offerings, continuing professional education workshops, and technical assistance to social welfare delivery systems. Such revenue-generating arrangements can produce a number of benefits, including additional funds to support faculty travel, faculty development opportunities, work enrichment options, and effective student-instructor collaborations. Program initiatives of this kind, however, shift valuable faculty resources away from academic responsibilities, thereby requiring the department to employ contract or part-time instructors. The director is wise to plan carefully when assigning faculty to external initiatives, so as to avoid jeopardizing the overall quality of the baccalaureate degree program.

# Program Needs

## 1. Identifying Needs

A program director determines the program's needs by assessing seven critical decision areas:

- **Financial**, including the operational budget (for basic program expenditures such as personnel, supplies, telephone, and travel) and designated or restricted funds used for special expenses and projects (such as receptions for program guests and the faculty development initiative).
- **Human Resources**, including faculty, staff, technical support.
- **Student Enrollment**, including the number of majors, class standing, field placement requests.
- **Academic Activities**, including resources for instruction, professional service, scholarship.
- **Student Affairs**, including student association support, experiential learning.

- **Program Advancement**, such as development activities, alumnae/ alumni association, student recruitment, and fund raising.

- **Physical**, such as instructional space and materials, office space, equipment, and travel support.

Ideally, these decision areas should conform to the governance policies and procedures of the university while addressing the needs of the social work program.

## 2. Matching Needs with Allocated Resources

- **Annual Budgets**

    The director uses three major sources of information to make and implement decisions in the seven critical areas listed above (Hyatt, 1989). An *annual budget* that reports the institutional allocations to the program for a financial year is one source of confirmation. This budget shows annual institutional or general fund allotments for basic program resources such as faculty salaries, wages of staff, secretarial, and technical support personnel, operating expenses, and faculty travel. Figure 3.3 shows an example of a fiscal year budget for a social work program housed in an academic department. The annual budget may also include allowances for summer instruction, temporary, adjunct or non-tenure track instructors, memberships, cost-sharing commitment on grants or sponsored projects, and equipment maintenance.

- **External Funding**

    Federal state and foundation grants, corporate gifts, technical service contracts are examples of ongoing external funding streams used by programs to supplement annual institutional budget allocations. Value added program initiatives such as recruiting exemplary students by providing scholarships, creating endowed faculty positions and developing collaborative partnerships with social service systems to prepare students for specific practice settings are examples of program initiatives that may be supported by supplemental funding streams. As was mentioned earlier, Federal Title IV-E grant funds, for example, have been used by programs to fund child welfare agency partnerships that provide continuing education for practitioners, financial stipends for students, and specialized curriculum content to prepare students for entry into children/youth/family service settings (Zlotnik and Cornelius, 2000). These external funds supplement program budgets and assist programs in meeting its needs.

- ## Policies and Procedures

    The annual budget should also follow the institution's official budget guidelines, policies for the use of various types of funds (such as petty cash, honorariums, etc.), and a set of standard forms used in all financial and resource transactions should be available for use by office personnel. Examples of institutional financial requirements that a program director may be required to use include procedures and standardized forms for completing internal budget transfers among budget categories, contracts for payments to invited lecturers, computer equipment and supplies, library acquisitions, and petty cash purchases.

- ## Monthly Program Financial Report

    A second source of information is the *monthly program financial report.* This report should show the annual budget amounts for each operating expense, expenditures by operational item for the month and year-to-date, open commitments, balances available in all operating areas, and percentage of allocation used to date. If program activities are grant-supported, the director should also receive financial reports on these activities on a monthly basis. This information is needed to monitor all expenditures and revenue transactions and to avoid financial emergencies. Figure 3.4 is an example of a monthly financial report for a social work program.

- ## Quarterly Reports on Restricted Accounts

    In addition, the director should receive *quarterly reports on restricted accounts, sometimes called foundation accounts.* Restricted accounts include allocations to alumnae/alumni affairs, student scholarships, program advancement, and other special program projects. Figure 3.4 shows an example of a quarterly report of a restricted social work program account used to supplement social work program expenses. Scholarship, field instruction stipends, and student organization accounts are other examples of restricted accounts found in social work program budgets.

- ## Creating and Using an Information Network

> The director receives and analyzes large amounts of data to monitor resource usage, document needs, and request program development funds. At the program level, financial and resource information should flow to the director from the appointed official in the financial affairs area of the institution. It is important that this information network provide timely and accurate data on the fund balances and current operating budgets. The director can create an information network that collects a variety of data on events that can have a long-range financial impact on the program. Information about projected social work student enrollments or changes in academic requirements of the state's social work licensing provisions are examples of non-financial data that the director can analyze to define the programs funding needs and to provide documentation required for program-based decision making.

## 3. Ecological Framework

Resource management can be viewed as a complex communication process among the director, faculty, staff, and administrative officials. This view of resource management fits well within an ecological framework that focuses on promoting cooperation between program and institutional operations. Program faculty have an important role in the preparation of a program's budget including defining resource needs, completing program resource forms and reports, and wisely consuming program resources. Faculty can also be leaders in procuring external sources of funding to support the program. Involving faculty in resource development, managing, reporting, and consuming resources builds stronger BSW programs whose faculty understand resource needs and allocations and are invested in its resource development and use. Resource management is a continuous, time-consuming process that requires persuasive strategies, wisdom, competence, and documentation of needs to generate administrative, financial, and political support for the program.

## 4. Reporting Financial Information

The director is responsible for reporting on the department's financial status, both for reasons of accountability and to support proposals for additional resources. Financial reports are written specifically for an intended audience — typically an official whom the director hopes to persuade. Clearly written summaries, supplemented by graphs, comparative listings, and diagrams, are used to report technical data. In general, data used in decision- making becomes less specific as information flows up the administrative hierarchy. Program directors need very specific data about day-to-day operations, such as enrollments for each current and upcoming course. Administrative superiors need data on projected resource needs for the academic year and projected needs based on historical trends. Central administrators want summaries that identify historical and future trends for social work programs within the institution.

An effective working relationship with the various constituencies makes it possible for the director to provide each group with the right kind of information. Understanding the program's resource needs helps these groups remain active in decision making. Faculty, for example, is informed of program revenue patterns with quarterly financial reports if the director expects their cooperation in controlling expenses. About ninety per cent (90%) of a program budget goes to fixed and unavoidable costs (salaries, wages, telephone, equipment service contracts). As a result, cost containment efforts can only succeed with more flexible expenses such as copying, audio-visual rentals or purchases, long-distance telephone charges, postage, and supplies. If the program is to be able to acquire supplemental funds for major equipment purchases or to provide additional travel funds, all faculty members should be prudent in their use of those discretionary resources.

## Summary

The ecological framework can help the director effectively manage the technical, informational, and planning tasks inherent in this program domain. Appendix F, Influencing Entities, identifies the internal and external environments of an accredited social work program and entities within these environments that affect the financial and physical resources domain. A program director can complete an environmental scan of his/her program in order to identify influences on short-term and long-range program resource needs, as well as potential opportunities for program advancement. Completion of the Self-Evaluation Inventory found in Appendix B will assist the director in determining the relative importance of the twenty-four (24) specific administrative responsibilities related to the financial and physical resource affairs domain of a specific social work program. A thorough understanding of the financial and resource allocation policies, procedures, forms, and reports of a university is imperative for the program director to manage in this administration domain. The director is responsible for diverse technical, informational, and strategic planning tasks in financial and physical administration. These responsibilities require the creation of an information system, a technical support infrastructure, program-based decision-making processes, and an administrative support network to effectively define, document, allocate, and develop the fundamental financial and physical resources required by a resilient and high quality social work program.

# References

Council on Social Work Education. (1994). Handbook of accreditation standards and procedures. Alexandria, VA: Author.

Creswell, J. W, Seagren, A., & Henry, T. (1979, Winter). Professional development training needs of department chairpersons: A test of Biglan model. Planning and Changing, 224-237.

Gibbs, P. (1995, Winter). Accreditation of BSW programs. Journal of Social Work Education 31(1), 4-16.

Harper. K. V., Ramey, J. H., & Zook, L. J. (1991). BSW program administration: Directors' perceptions of their power to manage. Journal of Social Work Education, 27, 176-187.

Hyatt, T. A. (1989). Presentation and analysis of financial management information. Washington, DC: National Association of College and University Business Officers.

Johnson, H. W., & Hull, G. H. (1992). Autonomy and visibility in undergraduate social work education. Journal of Social Work Education, 28(3), 312-320.

Macy, H. J. (1990). Role analysis study of chairpersons in academic departments offering accredited baccalaureate social work degree programs. Unpublished doctoral dissertation, Ball State University, Muncie.

Macy, H. J., Sommer, V. L., Flax, N., & Swaine, R. L. (1995). Directing the Baccalaureate Social Work Program: An Ecological Perspective. Jefferson City, Missouri: Association of Baccalaureate Social Work Program Directors.

Swaine, R. L., & Flax, N. (1992). BSW program directors: Characteristics and role experiences. ARETE, 17(2), 16- 28.

Tucker, A. (1984). Chairing the academic department: Leadership among peers (2nd ed.). New York: ACE/Macmillan.

Wildavsky, A. (1964). The politics of the budgetary process. Boston: Little, Brown and Company.

Wildavsky, A. (1972). Political implication of budgetary reform. In Francis E. Rourke (Ed.), Bureaucratic power in national politics. Boston: Little, Brown, and Company.

Zlotnik, J.L. & Cornelius, L. F. (2000). Preparing social work students for child welfare careers: The use of title IV-E training funds in social work education. The Journal of Baccalaureate Social Work, 5(2), Association of Baccalaureate Social Work Program Directors.

# Bibliography

Zeiger, S., Hobbs, R., Robinson, M., Ortiz, L., and Cox, M. J. (1999). The impact of expansion: Adding an MSW program to an existing BSW program. Journal of Baccalaureate Social Work (5)1, 27-44. Fayetteville, AR: Association of Baccalaureate Social Work Program Directors.

# Chapter 4

# Academic Program Governance

Governance, a cornerstone of academic program administration, is comprised of the official institutional policies, regulations, and decision procedures among all employees and stakeholders of the education enterprise. The purpose of this chapter is to (1) identify the administrative responsibilities of a program director within an academic program-based governance structure, (2) examine influences from institutional governance structures and cultures, collective bargaining agreements, legal requirements, administrative guidelines, and accreditation standards on the process of academic program governance, and (3) identify administrative guidelines and program decision structures designed to promote governance effectiveness and facilitate basic program operations.

## Program Governance - A Definition

The following definition, provided by the Carnegie Foundation, reflects the spirit and aim of governance at the academic program level:

> Governance is the process by which people pursue common goals and, in the process, breathe life into otherwise lifeless forms. The best measure of the health of a governance structure at a college is not only how it looks on paper, but the climate in which it functions. Do those involved see some point to what they are doing? Do they believe their efforts can make a difference? Is there a sense of

excitement? Is the leadership confident of its aims and goals, without being isolated from either the larger society or the particular institutional community on whose behalf leadership is being exercised? (Carnegie Foundation for the Advancement of Teaching, 1982, p. 40)

Governance may be viewed as a shared administrative process between the program and the institution as policies and decisions flow between these organizational units; therefore, a program director administers within this partnership or organizational context. As noted throughout this publication, college and universities are increasingly being subjected to administrative oversight and review by externally located legal, regulatory and governmental entities that are in general are requiring more stringent levels of accountability in the use of scarce resources and documentation of academic program effectiveness (Greenberg, 1993; Boyer, 1990; Finn, 1987).

Governance touches every aspect of the program, defines the level of decision making autonomy enjoyed by the program, and shapes the daily administrative practices related to each operational domain including academic affairs, resources, personnel and student affairs. Examples of major administrative tasks related to program governance are listed in Figure 4.1. It is noteworthy that more than one-half of the generic administrative responsibilities identified in Figure 4.1 are program-based governance tasks.

## FIGURE 4.1

### Program Governance Responsibilities

- Apply decision-making practices that adhere to institutional, legal, and ethical regulations.
- Maintain relationships with financial, advancement, and administrative officers to promote efficient, accurate decision-making practices that promote the program's reputation, interests, and resource base.
- Promote the operation of governance structures and use by representatives of key program constituencies and stakeholders (students, faculty, staff, and field instructors, etc.).
- Resolve conflicts among competing constituencies; seeking to promote effective governance processes.
- Represent the program in personnel, program, curricular, legal, and administrative matters.
- Maintain records of meetings and correspondence to provide factual information for timely decision making.

A more complete list of generic administrative tasks that comprise the governance domain of a social work program is found in Appendix C. Please note also, that a program director can add additional governance tasks to this list based on a review of the governance structure of one's institution.

# Institutional-Based Governance Structures

The academic program and its institution share the responsibility for governance and policy development as previously stated. The official decision-making and policy formulation structure of the institution is generally found in the faculty and professional staff handbook. Governance systems also serve as legislative structures in colleges and universities designed to address personnel welfare, academic matters, and student life policies. These faculty-dominated structures represent a formal means for faculty members to examine policies and proceeds in concert with the formal bureaucratic administrative authority of the chief executive officer of the institution.

Figure 4.2 shows an example of a university senate-type institutional governance structure. This particular institutional decision hierarchy is made up of appointed officials, elected faculty, staff, and student representatives. The specialized decision-making committees, comprised of representatives from each of the stakeholder groups, staff both the standing and ad-hoc committees created to formulate policy recommendations. A review of the titles of "standing committees" that comprise each of these three "councils" identified in Figure 4.2 provides a glimpse into the range of stakeholder matters that receive ongoing attention by committee members.

The illustrated example of a governance system in Figure 4.2 also exemplifies a kind of "hybrid" system since membership of a "university senate" model includes elected representatives from the faculty, administrative officers, graduate and undergraduate students and professional staff. In contrast, college and universities widely use a "faculty senate" model which has membership limited to faculty members who serve along with a small number of ex-officio administrative officers.

A thorough understanding coupled with an ability to use the governance or legislative structure, along with that of the administrative hierarchy of the institution (see Figure 4.2) to promote the interests and needs of the program is helpful. Program faculty should supplement academic program leadership efforts by actively serving within the governance structure; because over time about every fundamental issue impact the faculty, staff and student welfare, program quality and academic affairs are formulated, discussed and evaluated prior to becoming administrative policy of the institution.

## FIGURE 4.2

### Governance Organizational Structure

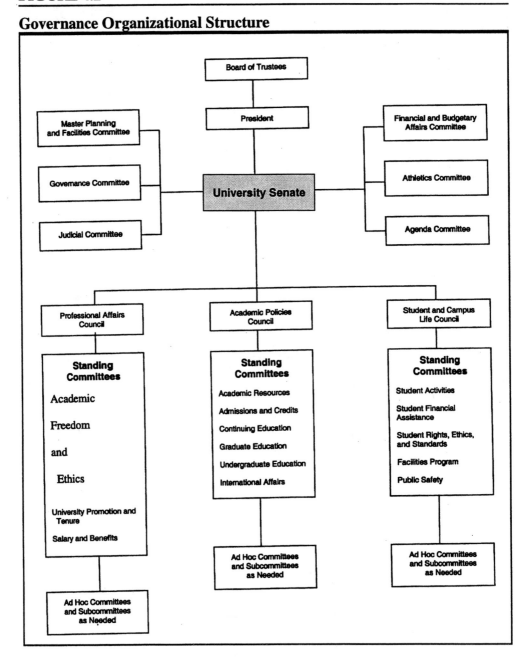

# Institutional Decision Making Structures - Program Governance

As noted in Chapter 8, the decision processes in post-secondary institutions differ significantly from those in public and private social welfare, businesses, government offices, and industry. Four different, co-existing decision structures or frameworks overlap at an academic program level, each of which adds a unique dimension to the governance process.

## 1. <u>Bureaucratic Decision Structure</u>

The *bureaucratic* decision structure is often used in decisions related to such responsibilities as financial operations, staff appointments, equipment requisitions, and program operating expenses including supplies. According to Stroup (1966) and Baldridge, et al. (1977), the bureaucratic process has the following basic characteristics:

- Authority is centralized, within a formal vertical administrative hierarchy

- Communication among appointed officials occurs within formal channels. The program director is defined as an administrative official with authority over faculty and staff.

- Decision-making is clearly defined by rules and regulations and formally coordinated to follow the administrative authority hierarchy of the institution; authority centered at top of administrative hierarchy.

- Conflicts arise within the organization from the need to integrate complex programming operations, coordinate human resource specialists, and control finite resources.

- Values include rationality, centralization, control, standardization, stratification, and predictability; specialized competence is the basis for appointment, compensation, and stature.

## 2. <u>Collegial Decision Structure</u>

The *collegial* or "community of scholars" decision structure is always used in faculty selection, performance evaluations, curricular and other academic matters (Hobbs & Anderson, 1971). Its characteristics include:

- Authority is decentralized and is linked to academic expertise and formal administrative appointment; faculty members are equals, and the program director is seen as a "first among equals."

- Decision-making is consensus-oriented, with emphasis placed on participation, thorough analysis, and discussion of issues.

- Conflicts arise from tensions between academic disciplines and from the tension between academic-based authority and institutional formal authority and conformity

- Values include equality and consensus of opinion; faculty rely on expertise, informal relationships, and normative behavior standards to promote conformity. (Bimbaum, 1988)

## 3. **Anarchical Decision Structure**

The *anarchical* decision structure appears in large colleges and universities. According to Cohen and March (1974), its characteristics include

- Authority within the institution is dynamic and fragmented; different special interest groups compete for scarce resources and control.

- Decision-making is decentralized, tend to be fluid and situationally oriented; different constituencies and interest groups move in and out of direct involvement in the decision continuum.

- Conflicts arise when the organization adapts to new external constraints and shifts in program priorities.

- Values include autonomy, diversity and participation.

Baldridge (1971b) noted that the bureaucratic, collegial, and anarchical structures do not fully explain the decision processes and outcomes of complex higher educational institutions. He noted, for example, that the bureaucratic structure does not allow for the informal forms of authority that shape program priorities, nor does the collegial structure adequately explain how decisions are made when faculty members do not reach a consensus. He concluded that a political decision process emerges as institutions of higher education evolve from small, collegiate organizations into large, complex institutions and that an informally oriented political process infuses with the other formal co-existing structures. The characteristics of the political decision structure include:

## 4. **Political Decision Structure**

- Authority is fragmented among competing, pluralistic coalitions, which are comprised of representatives of internal and external stakeholder groups affiliated with the institution. Administrators hear claims from multiple groups that articulate their value-laden interests in different ways and compete for control, visibility, and resources.

- Decision-making is decentralized, and frequently includes bargaining, "behind the scenes" maneuvering, and coalition building. Groups use power, influence and force whenever possible to influence policies.

- Conflicts arise from divergent interest groups that share common interests and points of view; yet disagree on specific issues. Policy formation and administrative procedures cause conflict within the institution.

- Values include organizational change. (Baldridge, 1971b)

The importance of a program director to apply a political framework to analyze interactions and decision processes within the institution cannot be overstated. This factor is underscored by Bolman and Deal (1984) who argue that it is in the political arena of organizations where coalitions of institutional stakeholders who have different and enduring preferences and values compete for scarce resources and control. Governance dynamics such as shifting power group alignments, group conflict, and continual maneuvering are essential features of organizational life (p. 109).

Since the values, goals, and cultural orientation of these four coexisting structures differ, a program director understands and strategically administers program policies and procedures within the contexts of each of the four co-existing decision structures that flow across the five program domains. If the institution is unionized, as described later in this chapter, yet another significant decision structure is present. Therefore, a program director is faced with the need to adapt administrative practices in order to apply appropriate leadership strategies according to the types of decisions, situational priorities, and the official governance process of the institution. Consequently, a contingency oriented academic program administrative approach evolves from the application of differing decision structures across the program domains.

# Institutional Influences That Shape Governance Responsibilities of a Program Director

As previously noted, the specific range and types of position responsibilities for a program director are shaped by such institutional factors as the organizational structure of the program and by external entities that regulate professional social work practice. The overall results of these influences require a program director to define the administrative parameters of the position which even includes extending the range of position responsibilities beyond the institution in order to, for example, oversee the field practicum component of the program. Three significant sources of direct influences (institutional sanction, context and structure - organizational structure - and method of appointment), on position responsibilities have been selected for description in terms of how position responsibilities of a program director related to program governance are shaped to form the administrative ecology of the administrative role. Each of these three direct influences is described from the administrative perspective of a program director. Position responsibilities, role parameters, and administrative practices are also indirectly influenced by a number of characteristics inherent in higher education institutions; these are examined in Chapter 8.

## 1. Institutional Sanction, Context and Structure

As a new program director examines the institutional structure of a program, consideration of the official sanction of the college or university is the third significant source of influence that shapes the governance dimensions of the administrative position responsibilities. A large, public land-grant public University when compared, for example, to an institution sanctioned by a religious denomination created to serve a very distinct student population provides a very different administrative environment and climate for a program director.

Figure 4.3 illustrates, for comparison purposes, an institutional structure of a social work program housed in a public, state-assisted university. The social work program is one of twenty separate academic departments that comprise the College of Sciences and Humanities, which is one of the seven colleges that, in turn, comprises the university. This institutional context and administrative hierarchy form the organizational environment for the social work program and represents a major dimension of the administrative governance framework or context for the program director. In contrast to this large, formal, bureaucratically-oriented institutional structure, a social work program housed in a smaller private

# FIGURE 4.3

## Institutional Administration Structure

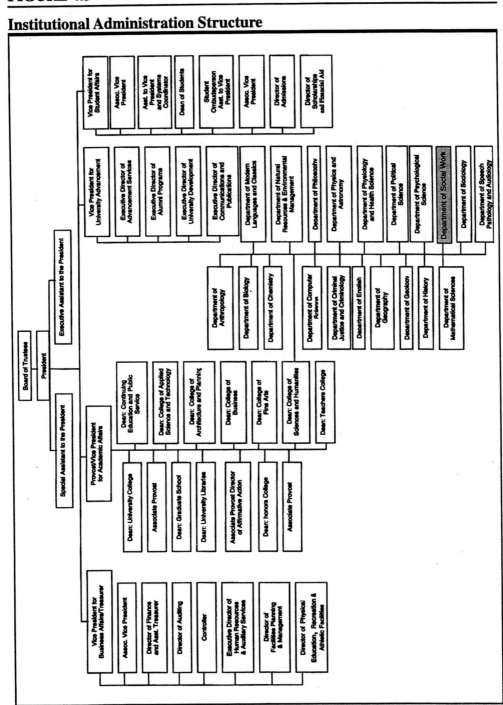

institution might have a less complex, formal decision, operational and administrative governance structure, and may be co-located with a number of other allied disciplines.

Understanding the institutional-based governance environment of the social work program, developing working relationships with key officials in offices that provide resource, technical, and administrative supports for the program operations, and selecting administrative strategies that are "institutional appropriate" or complementary to institutional mission and norms are among the leadership challenges faced by a new director (Gutierrez, GlenMaye, & DeLois, 1995; Bracy & Cunningham, 1995; Icard, Spearmon & Curry-Jackson, 1996). Therefore, an organizational assessment of the director's location, and implications of that location of that position within the academic administrative structure and decision hierarchy of the institution is a useful step for identifying the officials who help form the management context, decision hierarchy, and resource access points within the institution.

## 2. <u>Organizational Structure</u>

The size and structure of a social work program as previously noted is a fourth significant source of influence that shapes the scope and locus of a director's position responsibilities including program governance. Such position responsibilities as personnel, financial and curriculum matters in combined BSW and MSW degree programs may be assigned to a dean or director of the entire academic enterprise. In contrast, a baccalaureate social work program located in an academic structure that offers a number of allied disciplines such as sociology, criminology and anthropology may have an academic unit division director who would assume financial management of the entire division. The dominant organizational structures that house baccalaureate social work programs according to Flax and Swaine, 1996 include.

- The baccalaureate social work degree is offered as the only academic major offered by an independent or freestanding academic department.

- Under the administrative auspices of another multi-disciplinary independent department, the social work program is offered, along with a number of other allied academic majors, such as criminal justice and criminology, psychology, sociology, or anthropology.

- A graduate level administrative structure such as a school of social work offer both a baccalaureate and graduate social work degree.

Even though all three types of structures are found within the over 400 accredited baccalaureate programs, the 1998 CSWE survey reveals that the dominant BSW program administrative structure and auspices for BSW social work education programs, were separate BSW or stand alone academic units with typical faculties located in public state institutions had less than 10,000 full-time enrollments that employed nearly two-thirds of all social work faculty. (Lennon, 1999)

**FIGURE 4.4**

**Organizational Chart - Sample Small College**

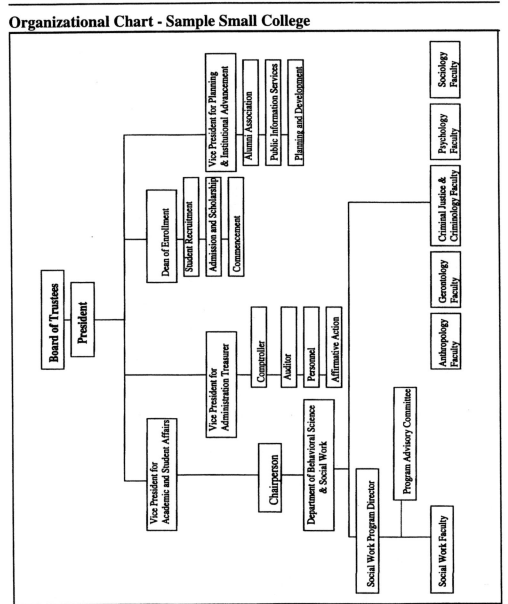

Program quality dimensions such as the level of autonomy, identity and visibility, formal program linkages with other academic disciplines located within the institution, are shaped by the type of administrative auspice, along with the location of the social work program within the organizational governance hierarchy of the institution and the relative size of the institution the program-based governance participation and resource allocation equity. The significance of each of these overarching program-based quality factors is defined by Sheafor (1979):

First, it is essential that the identity of social work as a unique discipline with its own knowledge, values, skills, purposes and professional culture be recognized. ...Second, the social work program must be visible on the campus and in the public information released by the university. ...Third, there must be recognition of the autonomy required to maintain an effective social work program. ...Fourth, the faculty of a social work program must have opportunities for participation in the governance of the college or university. ...Fifth, a social work program should have available, and where possible, be in control of the necessary resources (e.g., money, staff, time, and space) for the maintenance of that program. ...The last major issue facing baccalaureate social work programs is that of building linkages to other social work programs. (p. 43)

The relationship between program autonomy, visibility, and resource access as perceived by program directors, administrative practices, and self reports of role performance satisfaction, have been a focus of a number of research studies. A review of research findings may be helpful as a new program director sets administrative and planning priorities (Harper, 1985; Johnson, 1990; Harper, Ramey & Zook, 1991; and Swaine & Flax, 1992).

The issue of program auspice was also identified as a factor in a study by Johnson and Hull (1990) who surveyed 31 baccalaureate social work degree programs that had either been discontinued by the college or university or had lost CSWE accreditation. In an examination of the relationship between CSWE Evaluative Standards related to program autonomy, visibility, student enrollment, and adequate financial resources were found to be program continuance factors influenced both by the program's type of administrative auspices and the degree of complementarity between program goals and those of the institution.

Researchers have found increased tensions, complexities, restraints, and opportunities inherent in multidisciplinary academic units which influence position responsibilities of a director (Sheafor, 1979; and Potter-Efron, 1985). In view of research findings related to such quality program measures as autonomy, resources, personnel, and governance, a program director should determine where the formal administrative responsibilities are placed for each of the sixteen position administrative tasks identified in Figure 1.1.

## 3. Methods Used to Select the Program Director

Role responsibilities and parameters are influenced by the methods used by a college or university to select and appoint a faculty member to the position of a program director. The dominant pattern is for institutions to fill the position with faculty members who have distinguished themselves as strong visible teachers, researchers, and campus leaders. Rarely do institutions place the highest emphasis on academic program administrative experience and demonstrated competencies in completing such significant program leadership tasks as faculty development, curriculum improvement, financial management, student recruitment, strategic planning, and educational outcome evaluation processes.

The methods used by the institution to fill the position of program director are a fifth source of influence that shapes overall role performance parameters of a program director. An adaptation of findings by Mobley, 1981, state the three major methods used to select the faculty member as a program director include:

1. Appointment by an administrative official such as the academic dean with input from program faculty members. Applicants may be appointed after the completion of private individual conferences with each faculty member of the program or after a faculty-based search and screening committee process has been completed which then forwards a ranked list of recommended internal and external applicants.

2. Election of the program director from internal candidates by the program faculty with an administrative official such as the dean of the academic unit retaining the option to either approve or disapprove the elected faculty person.

3. Position is filled on a rotation basis among faculty members; rotational appointments specify such factors as length of term, and option to be appointed for successive terms.

The method used to fill the director position is a governance guideline and may also influence the amount of administrative creditability, authority, status, and support by program faculty held for the director. For example, when one compares being elected by colleagues as compared to being appointed with limited faculty input, the level of faculty support for the director may be different. The length of term assigned to the position influences the perceptions and expectations held by a director and program personnel. A three-year term limit, with no option to succeed oneself in the position, or a mandatory rotational model of selection may help define the position as temporary program management responsibilities with a "don't rock the boat" type role expectation. In contrast, appointment for an indefinite term may foster the view that the director position is a formally designed administrative leader of the program with responsibilities to engage in major program development, and the authority to tackle such sensitive issues as faculty development, curriculum changes, and resource development. A careful consideration of the methods and terms of appointment, options for successive terms and the image or informal expectations of the position held by program faculty are factors that shape role performance and administrative posture, and governance responsibilities of a director.

## Accreditation Standards—Program Governance

A detailed examination of program accreditation is the specific focus of Chapter 7, consequently, only a summary overview of the relationship between program governance and accreditation is provided in this chapter. Two categories of CSWE accrediting standards shape program governance which are consistent with promoting academic program quality. Eligibility standards are factual institutional and program requirements that the program must meet before it can become a candidate for accreditation or submit a self-study report to seek reaffirmation of accreditation. The requirement that the institution must have a written equal opportunity/affirmative action plan has been a long-term key Eligibility Standard related to program governance.

In addition to Eligibility Standards, there are also a set of Evaluative Standards related to governance that a program must address. A program must have, for example, sufficient authority and resources to achieve its goals. The level of program autonomy is evaluated in the context of the policies, decision-making procedures, and resources of the institution. To assess autonomy, an evaluation of such factors as the program's ability to establish goals, control financial resources, acquire physical resources, determine curriculum content and structure, manage human resources, and formulate policies within a governance process is completed (Johnson & Hull, 1992). Nondiscrimination and affirmative action practices related to program-based faculty, staff, students, and administrative practices are other categories of governance-related CSWE Evaluative Standards.

Faculty rights and responsibilities are also specified in the governance provisions of Evaluative Standards. Faculty and program-based administrators must participate in formulating and implementing policies and procedures related to program personnel, curriculum, and tangible resources, and they are to be afforded opportunities to participate in institutional governance. In addition, faculty are to have all rights specified in the institution's employment standards, including affirmative action, civil, and constitutional protections, and professional development guarantees.

Program governance standards associated with the rights, responsibilities, and opportunities of social work students are another category contained in CSWE Evaluative Standards. Policies and procedures related to student admission, advising, course registration policies, performance evaluations, and formal opportunities for students "to organize and participate around their self interests" as a program stakeholder group is provided. The program documents methods used to inform students of its admission, retention, advising and performance standards and provide a grievance appeal procedure based on due process procedures.

A review of CSWE Eligibility and Evaluative Standards illustrates the level at which accreditation standards are found in the governance domain of a social work program. CSWE program accreditation standards, in turn, are referenced by the National Association of Social Workers (NASW) to identify and enforce national practice standards of baccalaureate practitioners. NASW, for example, currently identifies completion of, or enrollment in, a CSWE-accredited/recognized program as a requirement for its "regular" and "student" membership categories, anchors the entire profession in the NASW Code of Ethics, and cites graduation from a CSWE-accredited program in its public information monograph titled "Legal Regulation and Professional Credentials for Baccalaureate Social Workers (BSWs, 1997)." In addition, NASW periodically publishes practice policy monographs (such as *NASW Standards for the Classification of Social Work Practice Policy* Statement 4, September, 1981) and dedicates issues of its professional journal, *Social Work,* to focus on practice with selected client populations (such as the homeless), service methodologies (such as family preservation), practice settings (such as public welfare), conceptual frameworks (such as ecological), and social policy issues (such as privatization of social welfare services). Therefore, it is important that a program director develop information networks to keep up with changes in standards and influences originating from both CSWE and NASW; each of these regulatory entities shape program governance priorities and administrative practices.

A key reference for defining the administrative responsibilities of a program director is found in the program quality standards established by the

Commission on Standards and Accreditation of CSWE. As previously noted, the Eligibility and Evaluative Standards, along with the Curriculum Policy Statement, represent a collection of quantitative and qualitative oriented standards for the total academic enterprise and thereby provides defining administrative parameters for the program director. Evaluative Standards that directly relate to administrative tasks, for example, include:

- Operationalizing the program's mission, goals and objectives

- Promoting program advancement based on a formal, systematic evaluation process

- Developing, managing and evaluating formally allocated financial, physical, and human resources

- Operationalizing, in collaboration with the faculty, a competence-based academic enterprise.

Identifying where, within a particular administrative program structure, the administrative responsibilities inherent in each of the accreditation standards have been placed is a position orientation step for a new director. One could, for example, specifically determine the institutional officials who are responsible for each of the administrative governance functions (see Figure 1.1) related to the program to determine with whom a director administratively collaborates; and to locate locus of institutional governance controls. In other words, an assessment of the position parameters helps define the administrative governance environment of the position. For example, a director's governance responsibilities in a combined BSW and MSW degree program that has a college of social work organizational structure within a university as compared to a social work program located within a baccalaureate sociology degree program has significant differences in administrative structure and governance operations.

## Collective Bargaining—Program Governance

The basis for the continuing growth of collective bargaining in higher education has been examined by Johnstone (1981), who identified a set of overlapping influences that combine to promote the use of collective bargaining to define employer-employee work relationships within the institution's governance structure, policies and procedures. The factors include

- Decline of trust, respect, and confidence between institutional administrators and faculty, which has reduce the quality of a unified collegial partnership.

- Fragmentation of faculty members interests associated with the expansion of campus-based academic specialization increased specialization of faculty with loyalties linked to external associations rather than with institutional-based colleagues, institutional mission and interests.

- Erosion of the economic security as perceived by the faculty because of rising inflation, loss comparable annual salary increases paid to central administrative and unionized staff achieved through collective bargaining.

- Rise in the number of white-collar unions whose use of collective bargaining is increasingly viewed as an appropriate method to address employer-employee relations.

- Increased institution bureaucratization and the application of corporate or business-oriented administrative models in higher education which exacerbate the fragile partnership between faculty and administration and reduce the clarity about common or management and faculty employment interest.

- Growth of enabling legislation that fosters the use of collective bargaining by public employees whose professional and union membership organizations advocates for improved employment rights and benefits coupled with the increasing litigious nature of American society (Johnstone, 1981).

The combined influences of these trends fostered a rapid growth in the use of collective bargaining by an increasing number of colleges and universities and by stakeholder groups within these institutions.

Collective bargaining agreements in colleges or universities may explicitly define employer-employee rights, responsibilities, and benefits, and thereby dictate the administrative governance responsibilities of a program director. Contemporary higher education administration researchers such as Lucas (1994); Johnstone (1981); and Tucker (1984) conclude that collective bargaining agreements are becoming more detailed and comprehensive regarding faculty and staff employment provisions and decision procedures. Examples of provisions commonly found in higher education agreements include the following (Johnstone, 1981):

- **Rights of Faculty as Members of the Academic Community** - personnel matter such as affirmative action, nondiscrimination, academic freedom, composition of personnel files, grievance procedures, and regulations, mandated negotiations, and arbitration.

- **Academic Personnel Decisions** - provisions that specify such matters as initial appointments, annual reappointment, tenure and promotion, discipline and dismissal, retrenchment, retraining, and rehabilitation of personnel due to illness or injury.

- **Faculty Compensation** - matters such as salary increments, meritorious performance compensation, equity adjustments, promotion in academic rank, and compensation increases based on completing additional or specialized assignments such as serving on thesis committees, overload teaching assignments, or program administrative appointments.

- **Fringe Benefits** - matters such as insurance protection for medical and hospitalization, disability, dental, life, and other types of specialty coverage such as for eye care and professional liability, short term leaves for such occasions as jury duty, funerals, and expert witnessing, long-term absences for such occasions as medical/sickness, maternity/ family, and sabbatical leaves, retirement benefits that include such provisions as institutional payments to individual accounts and early retirement bonuses, and a variety of other types of specialty-type benefits such as tuition waiver for faculty and dependents, and faculty discount programs to purchase such personal items as discount computer equipment, books, supplies, daycare provision for dependents, and tickets to campus events.

- **Workload Assignments** - provisions that define such factors as course load, student-to-faculty ratios, student advising loads, office hours, class size, number of course preparations, defined working conditions that include secretarial support, office/lab facilities, and furnishings such as furniture, telephones, personal computers, access to student assistants, provision of motor vehicles to complete work assignments, recreational facilities, and other work related conditions such as adequate lighting and noise control.

- **<u>Professional Conduct and Role Performance</u>** - specifications for faculty performance requirements such as the documentation of effective discharge of teaching and related instructional responsibilities; demonstrated commitment to maintaining mastery of subject matter, professional competencies, and instructional effectiveness; participation in professional societies and institutional-based programs, committees, and initiatives designed to promote quality education and student development; maintenance of sound professional and ethical work relationships; engagement in the completion of scholarly and creative works; worthy representation of the institution in public affairs; and contributions to the mission of the institution by fully and faithfully performing the duties of a faculty member.

- **<u>Academic Program Performance Expectations</u>** - matters related to a cluster of specific performance requirements, responsibilities, and duties such as being available to students by adhering to specified office hours, serving on institutional committees, maintaining full-time employment with the institution, conducting student academic and thesis advising, adhering to the institution's grading standards, attending official institutional ceremonies such as commencements, and scheduling of courses to realistically accommodate student academic needs.

These seven provisions of a faculty contract agreement represent an example of major factors in a faculty contract which represent significant administrative parameters for program governance practices that a director completes in colleges or universities which bargain collectively.

# Nature of Grievances That a Director May Face

On both union and non-union campuses, academic program directors identify personnel and governance as major sources of administrative conflict and the basis for formal grievances (Swaine and Flax, 1992; Carroll, 1974; Macy, 1990; Gmelch, 1992). A set of common types of grievances that confront an academic program director have been identified by Tucker (1984); Ward Mulaney & March Timberlake (1994). These have been placed into three categories listed below.

1. **Compensation and Employment Practices**

   • Claims that existing status or classification did not reflect training, experience, or responsibilities

   • Claims that inequities were due to discrimination against race, sex, religion, or handicap

   • Claims that employees were not notified of nonrenewal within contractual time limits, that reasons for nonrenewal were not provided on request, or that reasons provided were in violation of the contract, the law, or university rules or constitution

   • Claims of failure to follow contractual guidelines for layoff or failure to pursue actively recall and placement procedures

   • Objections to: negative letters placed in personnel file; suspension or termination of employment

   • Claims that administrators failed to observe time lines, to conduct impartial meetings, or to make good faith efforts to reach a settlement or to issue decisions based on the merits of the grievance. (Tucker, 1984; Ward Mullaney & March Timberlake, 1994).

2. **Evaluation of Performance**

   • Claims that evaluations were biased, supervisors failed to notify employees of the results of their observations, evaluation procedures and instruments used were in violation of the contract, that the evaluation file was stacked with negative information, or that the evaluation was based on materials not contained in the evaluation file.

   • Claims of failure to conduct peer reviews so that administrative decisions would be based on consistent criteria and procedures established by the contract, the federal law, or university policies/ procedures

   • Claims that decisions were not based on established criteria, were arbitrary and capricious, or contradicted supportive materials in the evaluation folder

   • Claims of unwillingness to overturn an erroneous review on its merits; or there was total disregard for a favorable peer review

- Disagreements over administrative use of "relevance" or "privilege" arguments to regard access to records, documents or information

3. **Work Assignments and Procedures**

- Colleagues, administrators, students or community disagree over teaching methods, course content, research design, or subject matter

- Claims that assignment was made late, represented an undesired overload, constituted disciplinary action, or was made arbitrarily and capriciously

The number of governance and personnel conflicts can be minimized if a director follows sound administrative practices that are based on strict adherence to all policy and procedure provisions specified in the institutional personnel handbook, the current governance structure and in the current union contract, apply personnel practices that are objective, systematic, fair and equitable, provide means to resolve dispute and change arbitrary or capricious directives, and focus on effective use of conflict resolution to promote employer-employee work relationships. Additional administrative guidelines are found in the legal requirement context examined next in this chapter and in the information related to human resource management found in Chapter 6.

# Legal Requirements - Program Governance

It is not possible to overstate the importance of the influence of federal laws and regulations on academic program governance. Boyer (1989) noted an increasing shift in influence from government to the courts as more individuals seek resolution of their civil and legal disputes outside the institution. This trend towards litigation requires a program director to become more formalistic, systematic, exact and knowledgeable regarding significant case and legal statutes that affect higher education administration.

The broadening legal dimension of baccalaureate program administration is commonly viewed by most directors as unfamiliar, treacherous, and an area of stressful position responsibility. A review of the generic position description provided in Chapter 1 reveals that the advocacy, evaluation, decision-making and oversight responsibilities inherent in such program operations as student admission assessments, faculty tenure reviews, personnel performance evaluations, administrative approval of program academic standards publications, and enforcement of academic standards all have intrinsic legal risks and obligations for a director.

From these position responsibilities and types of management decisions, legal issues might arise even though judicial review of academic program administrative decisions is very limited. This judicial restraint is based on the courts' presumptions that academic program-based decisions are uniformly made on behalf of the institution by an academic program director, are consistent and reasonable, comply with official institutional policies and procedures, and are made in good faith for motives consistent with the bonafide purposes of the program and the institution. Furthermore, courts view academic decisions made by the director as the types of decisions that require an expert assessment of cumulative information and tend to be qualitatively oriented evaluations. On the other hand, administrative based decisions that tend to be more adversarial in character such as personnel decisions must have a factual or quantitative base. Consequently, personnel-type decisions are conducive to legal standards of proof and verification.

Even though courts have been reluctant to intrude into reviewing higher education administrative decisions, there is a growing rate of judicial reviews of an increasing number of fundamental operations of academic programs. This growing litigious trend further adds to the potential use of resources, time, and efforts required to respond to investigations or even possible litigation with accompanying punitive damages; all of which can be avoided if the program director adheres to basic legal principles and follows institutional policies and procedures as delineated in such publications as the faculty and professional staff handbook. It is imperative, therefore, that a program director routinely completes in-service training that focus on the changing legal requirements for academic program administration to supplement a thorough understanding of the administrative and governance policies and procedures of the institution.

# Constitutional Amendments - Overview of Federal Acts

Even though case laws and new statutes continually modify the legal context of academic program administration, a director maintaining a fundamental understanding of federal and state administrative guidelines that form the beginning of a legal context of academic program management. A cornerstone of this context can be represented by a set of U.S. Constitutional amendments and federal acts, which directly shape administrative practices of a program director. Examples of significant federal constitutional and statutes which define legal parameters for administrative practices are provided in Figure 4.5.

## FIGURE 4.5

### Constitutional Amendments and Federal Acts -
### Legal Administrative Parameters*

| | |
|---|---|
| **Federal Constitution** | |
| Article I Section 10 | Relates to faculty contracts, curriculum requirements, and any contractual relationship between the state and a constituency. |
| First Amendment | Relates to use of public funds and freedom of speech, including written, spoken and symbolic expression. |
| Fourth Amendment | Relates to concept of privacy and the concept of liberty found in the Fourteenth Amendment. |
| Fifth Amendment | Relates to due process and the right of privacy associated with the concept of liberty in the Fourteenth Amendment. |
| Tenth Fourteenth Amendment | Defines protections for the rights of individuals. Amendment This relates to rights of citizens, due process and equal protection provisions. |
| **Federal Statutes** | |
| Rehabilitation Act of 1973 (Section 504) as amended by the Rehabilitation Act Amendments of 1974 | The "general welfare" clause of the constitution provides the basis for setting conditions for states that accept federal funds to serve the "public good." This act relates to civil rights for individuals with disabilities. Provisions of the Rehabilitation Act of 1973 (Section 504) were supplemented by the Americans with Disabilities Act of 1990 which also defines minimum guidelines for procedures related to accommodation and non-discrimination. |
| Education for All Handicapped Children Act of 1975 | The "general welfare" and "public good" provisions cited above are the basis for this act, which relates to special education rights of persons with disabilities. |
| Civil Rights Act of 1866 | Relates to equal rights protections guaranteed in the constitution. |
| Civil Rights Act of 1871—Section 1983 | Provides the basis for a federal court to pass on a school regulation where deprivation of a federal constitutional right is alleged. |
| Civil Rights Act of 1964 | Prohibits employers in public and private sectors from engaging in discriminatory practices, including discrimination based on race and gender |
| Family Medical Leave Act 1993 | Provides federal Department of Labor job protection leave to enable employees to care for family members. |

*Moll (1998) provided this legal framework overview of a social work program.

# Risk Management Practices - Administrative Guidelines

A program director stays informed about the legal standards that govern administrative practices. In general, a program director is obligated to act in the best interests of the institution, its faculty, staff and students, and the citizens of the state where the program is commissioned. Legal liability issues such as breach of contract, denial of constitutional rights, arbitrary and capricious actions, and discrimination can arise unexpectedly. The director has access to legal consultation when formulating program standards, writing program publications, or making decisions on the status of faculty, staff, and students. Higher education institutions have staff attorneys or contracts with legal firms to provide an array of specialized legal services to the governing board and to administrative personnel. Access to the institution's legal counsel usually requires both administrative approval and a review of the specific request by the Affirmative Action officer of the institution. A director should discuss with the administrative superior the institutional policies and procedures governing the request for and use of legal assistance.

A basic understanding of common law principles is important to program administration. Common law statutes related to property rights, parental responsibilities and rights, and tort issues (which include injury, liability, duties, and contracts) are relevant to academic program administration. Reutter's *The Law of Public Education* (1985) provides an excellent overview of higher education administration legal standards that are anchored in common law principles. In the area of social work student admissions, for example, the *Journal of Social Work Education* routinely publishes timely articles that provide administrative guidance related to this important administrative responsibility such as academic dismissal of students, academic tenure procedures, and personnel practices.

In addition, the program director is responsible for many quasi-legal administrative issues. These may range from enforcing the provisions of the Family Educational Rights and Privacy Act (which governs information dissemination, such as grade posting and letters of reference) to monitoring the storage and handling of hazardous materials, to overseeing computer and physical security and enforcing personnel training and compliance with universal precautions regulations.

A thorough, detailed examination of the legal context of academic program administration is beyond the scope of this publication, consequently, a summarized set of nine administrative guidelines (Bennett & Figuli, 1990; Edwards, 1992; Glenny & Dalglish, 1973; Hecht, Higgerson, Gmelch & Tucker, 1999; Lucas, 1994; Tucker, 1984; Ward Mullaney & March Timberlake, 1994; Cobb, 1994; and Cole & Lewis, 1993) is provided as follows:

## 1. Adhere to Official Position Responsibilities and Authority Limitations

Directors should understand and confirm the limits of their administrative responsibilities and authority when completing position tasks. By virtue of the delegated authority and officially assigned position responsibilities that occur at the time, the institution formally appoints a faculty member as the program director; all role or position-based decisions are defined in a legal context as actions taken as an institutional agent, not as an individual. Consequently, the decisions of a director, whether done intentionally or not done through omissions or delayed by failure to respond in a timely manner, are viewed as actions committed within the scope of employment and therefore are attributable to the employing institution. This scope of decision responsibility extends to providing administrative oversight of actions by employees affiliated with the program and to monitoring of compliance with formal institutional policies and procedures.

## 2. Inform Administrative Superiors and Key Institutional Officials

Whenever a program director is faced with an academic program decision that has high potential for a legal review, it is prudent that administrative and legal consultations be completed. In addition, it is important that a director informs appropriate officials and stakeholders when such an administrative decision is made. Administrators do not like surprises, and those that have an inherent legal issue are particularly troublesome. Consultation and routine collaboration with administrative superiors is a sound administrative practice and helps to prevent the director from overstepping position authority and responsibilities. Additionally, it is important that a program director understand the specific source, amount and nature of institutional legal support available when a situation occurs.

## 3. Adhere to Federal Constitutional Rights

As previously stated, the likelihood of judicial review of a program director's academic program decision making and administrative procedures is generally remote since courts, in an exercise of judicial restraint, tend to avoid intervening in higher education institutional administrative practices. However, clear exceptions to judicial restraint are in matters related to actions that are:

- **Arbitrary or Capricious Administrative Actions** - the failure, for example, to systematically apply formal, uniform unambiguous program-based academic standards for completing student admission, evaluation, dismissal, and approval for graduation. Admission criteria, are a particularly challenging area of oversight responsibility because social work programs not only evaluates the academic record of candidates, but also assesses behaviorally-specific personal attributes and demonstrable competencies commensurate with the ethical, values, and skill performances of the social work profession.

- **Failure to Respect the Federal Constitutional Rights of Students, Staff, and Faculty** - failure, for example, to systematically apply due process procedures regarding adverse administrative decisions regarding faculty, staff and student property rights, liberty interests, resources entitlements, or avoiding actions that would result in a negative stigma for an employee related to such issues as tenure, salary equity, dismissal, and admission is an essential administrative action.

- **Violations of the Prohibition Against Discrimination Contained in the Equal Protection Clause of the 14th Amendment** - Administrative actions taken, for example, when the decision violates an individual's equal protection rights based on such factors as age, religion, gender, handicap, right to free speech, and exercise of association is thereby discriminatory.

## 4. • Keep Confidences

The information flow through the position of program director is considerable, and as a result, a program director routinely acquires a large number of confidences. These confidences are discretely managed and kept confidential. Consequently, the use of a "need-to-know" rule in all communication and the practice of keeping confidences are essential. A useful practice is to complete regularly scheduled conferences with one's administrative superior in order to benefit from consultation and have opportunities to "talk through" confidential program-based matters. This administrative official is also required to keep confidences but must be kept alert to program-based matters that might require administrative attention at other institutional levels.

## 5. Understand, Comply and Document Adherence to the Official Policies and Procedures

The officially approved policies and procedures of the college or university that govern practically every academic program-based decision made by a director and by faculty committees are ordinarily found in a faculty and professional personnel handbook. This institutional policy and procedure manual is routinely updated, published and distributed to administrative officials to help ensure that there is consistent adherence to current policies and procedures. The manual informs a program director of policies and procedures that govern program-based operations and decision-making in each of the five program domains as defined in Chapter 1 and are routinely reviewed as a decision-making step. In addition, a program director should maintain an accurate understanding of contemporary higher education issues such as student admission, faculty dismissals, and affirmative action practices that are receiving legal review by monitoring the outcomes of major federal court rulings and by reading such weekly publications as *The Chronicle of Higher Education.*

## 6. Know and Protect Student Rights

Academic advising occurs under the umbrella of academic affairs. As previously stated, the courts have always hesitated to enter the academic arena and substitute their judgement for that of the academician. In doing so, they have recognized the academic freedom that protects academic decisions, and that their repeated presence in the academic community possibly could cause deterioration in the otherwise beneficial student-faculty relationship. Thus, if academicians do not abuse their discretion in dealing with students, they need not fear judicial intervention. The courts will intervene, however, if evidence exists of arbitrary or negligent treatment of students or a denial of their protected rights. The increasing number of court decisions dealing with classroom and academic matters attests to the growing judicial sensitivity to students' rights in academic affairs.

In academic affairs, a contractual relationship exists between the student and the institution. The basic provisions of the college catalog, recruiting brochures, various bulletins and the student handbook become part of the contract. The institution sets forth certain requirements for passing courses and for successful completion of programs and subsequent graduation. If students fail to meet the required standards they can be penalized through such action as dismissal, suspension, or failure to graduate on schedule. If the institution fails to respect its own regulations, the student may seek judicial relief.

## 7. **Provide Accurate Program Information and Administrative Documentation**

An institution may create certain contractual obligations through statements in its publications. Courts consider college bulletins, program guides, and brochures as contracts that create mutual obligations between institution and student. Fundamental fairness to the parties involved in a lawsuit requires that the court consider the extent to which a contractual relationship did exist between parties and the potential harm when one party has breached a duty under terms of the contract. As a consequence, the oral representations of faculty advisers and deans have been relied upon as a basis for initiating a suit for beach of contract. However, courts do not appear to apply contract standards rigorously, choosing to resolve many ambiguities in favor of the institution and often abstaining from resolving substantive matters of academic policy.

## 8. **Faculty Advising Supervision and Oversight**

Faculty advising responsibilities represents a contractual relationship between a student and the college or university. Obligations and responsibilities usually appear in an advisor's handbook and often in publications readily available to the student. An increasing emphasis on quality advising to enhance retention brings added responsibilities to the advisor. More and more faculty advisors not only are expected to understand such things as scheduling and registration procedures and degree and program requirements, but also they may be expected to function as a referral service or possibly as career counselors. Thus, institutions should be conscious of an advisor's obligations, which might be created by unequivocal statements regarding advisor responsibilities.

Most institutions' catalogs state that the ultimate responsibility for knowing degree requirements rests with the student. This type of statement normally would protect advisors if they commit an advising error. Generally, the advisor is not going to be held personally liable for erroneous advising in the absence of gross negligence, irresponsible behavior, or arbitrary or capricious treatment of the student. Advisors should keep notes of their discussions with students during advising sessions. An accurate record of advising sessions would help solve any disputes over the content of previous advising and also serve as a legitimate protection against claims of erroneous advising. In today's litigious atmosphere, the advising function is more critical than ever.

When legal issues arise and there is formal challenge to a director's reasonableness, consistency, and adherence to institutional policy decision, it is very helpful to have written documentation that corroborates administrative action. Even in a written evidentiary record such as copies of memoranda, letters, and even management notes compiled by a director, though tedious to consistently complete and available to all parties if legally obtained, are a very welcome resource and aid to resolve administrative disputes.

## 9. Administrative Oversight of Program Representatives

Administrative oversight of the decisions by employees affiliated with the program is monitored to ensure that legal regulations and official institutional policies and procedures are followed. This compliance extends to information provided by program personnel. This guideline, anchored in contract law, governs a range of program based operations that includes such matters as inducements offered for enrollment, representation of degree requirements, the implied rights and responsibilities inherent in course syllabi used by students, accuracy of documentation cited in student recruitment literature, academic program descriptions published in the institutions catalog, and salary offers to prospective faculty members.

These nine broad guidelines represent only an introductory set of recommended administrative guidelines that comprise the complex, legal landscape of academic program administration. Each guideline, along with the legal parameters of the various program operations represented in each of the five program domains, receive on-going study by a director through such professional development activities as completing additional research and readings, using legal consultation, and securing specialized in-service training.

# Field Practicum Liability

The field instruction program represents a particularly challenging area of legal and administrative oversight (Gelman, Pollack, Auerbach, 1996). The field practicum is an important program operation that is designed to promote student learning and professional development while simultaneously providing quality services to social service clientele. Each field practicum placement requires the design of a formal relationship between representatives of the educational program and the field practicum agency, which involves such individuals as the practicum student, social work faculty liaison/instructor, agency or field-based supervisor/instructor, agency consumers/clientele, and multidisciplinary collaterals located throughout contiguous human service delivery systems. The differing goals of each stakeholder within a field practicum configuration coupled with the complexity of the instructional and service provision responsibilities supplemented by increasing litigious levels of human services combine to represent an arena in which there is considerable potential for ethical and legal risks for all parties (Zakutansky and Sirles, 1993). Administrative issues related to the field practicum include, but are not limited to, the following:

- Informing faculty about the institution's indemnification of personnel policies.

- Identifying, in the field instruction handbook for students, personal risks (i.e., physical health), appropriate protections (i.e., knowledge about universal precautions), and risk protection/information resources (i.e., institutional liability coverage that includes property damage, personal injury protection, bodily injury and intern liability protection).

- Providing formal memoranda of field instruction agreements that identify all rights, responsibilities, protections, and waivers afforded every participant.

- Including in the student handbook appeal procedures for students who are involuntarily removed from a field work agency.

As a result of the increasing array of personal and professional hazards that field practicum stakeholders face, risk management practices must be correspondingly increased (Gelman, Pollack and Auerback, 1996; Alexander, 1993; Bullis, 1990; Jacobs, 1991; Kutchins, 1991; and Reamer, 1992).

An increasing level of liability is a growing inherent dimension of the administrative oversight policies, procedures, and governance processes related to each of the five program domains. Decisions by federal courts create a continuing source of legal regulations for academic programs to follow. There are many significant judicial decisions that guarantee individual rights and protections. For example, Cole and Lewis (1991) identified 36 federal and state court decisions dealing with student conduct, grades, attendance standards, catalog information, and student dismissal procedures relating to student admission and retention; an entire section of a publication edited by Gibbs and Blakely (2000) examined legal perspectives related to the "gatekeeping" or admission and retention procedures in baccalaureate programs. Aspects of every program domain include student admission and termination, faculty hiring, tenure and dismissal, academic honesty, and student performance evaluations subject to conflicts that are receiving legal review. (Cobb, 1994; Cole, 1991; Cole and Lewis, 1993; Gelman and Wardell, 1988; Moore and Urwin, 1991; Koerin and Miller, 1995; Moore, Dietz, and Jenkins, 1998; Gibbs, 1994; and Saunders, 1993).

# Program Information - Governance

Information management is a significant governance activity in an accredited social work program. This sub-section examines how information management can be used to complete the management tasks found in the governance domain. It is necessary to keep the various program constituencies informed and to promote understanding of the program goals. Effective information management can also promote participation in decision making and create an educational milieu that fosters excellence. An accredited social work program provides information about academic and professional standards, policies, and procedures beyond that provided by an academic program that does not prepare students for entry into a profession. Accreditation standards, for example, require the program to disclose its outcomes to faculty, students, institutional administrators, field instructors, and social work professionals affiliated with the program. It is recommended that a social work program should provide six types of printed information:

## 1. Catalog Information

A means to help potential students be attracted to and make informed decisions about seeking admission to a baccalaureate social work degree program is to have an accurate description of the educational program published in the institution's official undergraduate catalog. In addition to the stated purposes of the program, this description should clearly explain the mission and purposes of the social work degree program, and include other information such as the admission standards and procedures, curriculum structure and course descriptions, means to contact the program, names of faculty members, and the title of degree awarded.

Because the catalog serves as an official program description as well as an important program marketing publication, the program description should include unique features, such as part-time degree options, financial assistance opportunities, unusual field settings, or opportunities for study abroad.

## 2. Student Handbook

This publication supplements the institution's catalog and general student advising manual by providing specific information about the social work program. It may include such as information a description of:

- The program mission and purposes, development and accreditation history

- Social work curriculum

- Required course descriptions

- Admission and retention standard and detailed procedures

- NASW Code of Ethics

- Financial aid resources

- Illustrated plan of study for completing the degree

- Experiential learning opportunities

- Biographical data about faculty

- Academic registration procedures

- Program advising resources for students

- The current CSWE Educational Policy Statement and Evaluative Standards

- A list of institutional resources such as academic support, career assessment, career/placement services, computer resources, and student organizations

## 3. Practicum or Field Work Handbook

This handbook, which explains the social work practicum, is needed because of the significance and the administrative and curricular complexities of this curriculum component.

The Field Work Handbook may contain:

- Curriculum and prerequisites for the practicum

- Field placement procedures

- Rights and responsibilities of students, practicum faculty, and field instructors

- Placement policies and procedures

- Practicum course objectives

- Field practicum teaching and learning structures

- Performance evaluation procedures

- Program agency affiliation agreement form

- Policies regarding legal liability

- Grievances and conflict resolution procedures

- Performance evaluation standards and forms

- Learning contracts to individualize field practicum assignments

## 4. Social Work Career Information Document

In order to effectively recruit and inform individuals wanting a four-year baccalaureate degree, transfer students from two-year Associate degree programs and adults who are seeking a second career, a program provides accurate social work career related information in both printed and electronic formats. An effective program marketing "career fact sheet" should have such categories of information as:

- Contemporary responsibilities of professional social workers as defined by NASW and compared to allied human service professions such as criminal justice and criminology, psychology, educational counseling and guidance, nursing and to such allied academic disciplines as sociology, anthropology, and health science.

- Employment trends for social workers along with other comparative human service professions as identified by the U.S. Department of Labor and by state-level workforce development projections.

- Information related to employment profiles and salaries of social workers nationally, along with consumer satisfaction, employment rates, and salary profiles of program graduates, identified by the systematic program outcome survey.

- Electronic information sources and addresses should be developed to supplement the availability of program-based printed information. The development of a professionally designed homepage, linked to the homepage of the institution, to related social work information sites, and to human service aptitude assessment sites, is needed to accommodate a growing use of electronic information by individuals to learn about and compare degree options offered by competitive programs. Undoubtedly, the Internet will continue to expand as the method of choice for individuals to learn about the increasing number of human service career options and to match individual interests.

## 5. Social Work Program Advising Manual

Academic and professional advising by full-time faculty members is an essential social work program component that promotes overall quality. Student centered advising should be designed to promote such basic academic and professional development purposes as:

- Orientation and initial assessment of interests, aptitudes, values, and abilities for professional social work practice.

- Integration of liberal arts perspective with the professional foundation content contained in the professional curriculum areas.

- Systematic self-appraisal of professional values, knowledge, and competencies.

- Development of a life-long orientation towards professional growth.

- Integration of the cognitive, affective, and experiential learning components of the structured curriculum.

- Effective use of campus and community-based academic and personal improvement services to facilitate professional development.

- Selection of elective courses and field work settings that meet professional development needs and career interests.

All faculty advisors should receive a specialized manual that identifies all of the program's current policies, procedures, and basic academic and professional resources in order to provide students with accurate information. The manual explains the purposes of social work advising and the responsibilities of both advisor and student. Specific academic procedures such as course registration, withdrawal, and repetition should be included, along with copies of sample forms. Catalog information regarding institutional requirements for academic degrees (such as degree credit hour and time limits, residency requirements, course load policies, grading system, and withdrawal policies) are reprinted in the manual along with the current social work curriculum, liberal arts requirements, and a list of elective courses classified, for example, by client populations. A listing of special student information (for example, students with disabilities, non-traditional, and multicultural) and student services (such as psychiatric counseling, addiction treatment, and job placement) is included along with procedures for completing referrals.

The advising manual is continually updated as faculty members learn about new resources, or the institution changes academic policies, procedures, and personnel, academic, and professional supports for social work students evolves.

## 6. Admission Application

Because of the importance of the selective social work admission procedures, a separate document or packet related to admission standards, policies, and procedures is recommended. The social work admission and retention packet can be distributed in a required lower-division course, for example, and be included along with a class discussion of professional standards, licensing requirements, and characteristics of a professional, and a discussion of NASW student membership benefits. Copies of the forms and materials used in the admission and retention procedures, along with instructions for completion, are included.

The process of requiring each student to complete a formal social work admission procedure can be designed to also serve as a useful professional development learning opportunity. Such procedures as completing a scheduled evaluation conference with a faculty admission committee to:

(1) Discuss the contents of a submitted word-processed written application.

(2) Present writing and scholarship examples to demonstrate academic abilities.

(3) Identify strengths and professional development goals as related to the purposes of social work.

(4) Explain career goals including clientele and practice settings of interests.

(5) Completing a self-assessment of professional attributes and limitations coupled with a definitive plan to remedy and/or strengthen are examples of admission procedures are useful learning opportunities.

They can be applied to subsequent field practicum placements, and provide a firm basis for professional advising.

The social work program might also develop and distribute a range of informal publications designed to tell students about the program, useful institutional resources and the information related to the social work profession. In addition to the career "fact sheet," used to describe social work career opportunities, fact sheets or internet address of sources for information on professional trends, alumnae/alumni employment information, evolving legal standards, and the unique qualities of social work practice across service systems and clientele may be used to inform students in the introductory courses. Such handouts or information sources are useful in student recruitment and orientation and in advising students who are considering a change of major to social work. Information about social work employment, campus activities, professional development events and workshops, NASW activities, and program deadlines can be displayed on a bulletin board in a frequently visited area. Printed or electronic newsletters distributed periodically to all social work majors are a method to inform students about program events and opportunities, academic information, and for students to provide evaluative feedback to the program.

## Program-Based Governance Committees

The teaching, scholarship, and professional service responsibilities of a faculty member combined with the number and scope of position responsibilities required of a program director necessitates the formal delegation of some administrative responsibilities to program committees. Standing and ad-hoc committees, comprised of both elected and appointed faculty along with student and practice representatives, are invaluable sources for policy development, technical assistance, and completing time-limited administrative tasks. Completing a faculty search, evaluation of program outcomes, formulating curriculum revisions, and revising student-advising materials are examples of committee-based task assignments in which the results are then submitted for administrative review and implementation. Programs might create additional standing committees that focus on a delegated administrative function such as faculty evaluation or identifying the most viable off-campus course offerings, along with a number of time-limited committees that complete such specialized tasks as completing faculty searches, examining governance issue, hosting invited speakers, recommending library acquisitions, or planning social events. Effective programs develop goals, policies, and procedures for the operation of all standing and ad-hoc committees and require minutes to record the actions or outcomes of these work groups.

If clear guidance, instructions, and deadlines are given to program-based committees, the director is better able to provide effective organization, coordination, and leadership of the academic enterprise because of the policy development, technical advice, and service provision benefits of the committee process. A key responsibility related to the committee process is the need for the director to fully integrate and coordinate the work of each specialty committee with the corresponding specialty office or staff employed by the institution. For example, program-based student recruitment efforts and strategies would be fully integrated with the office of admission to efficiently and accurately contact, inform, and meet with prospective students. A supply of program information such as social work career information sheets can be provided to admission staff who actually visit high schools, represent the institutions at college admission workshops, or complete telephone contacts.

The size of the program determines the number and types of committees needed. Programs with fewer than five faculty members might function largely as a committee-of-the-whole and have very few formal committees, whereas larger programs may routinely use many of the governance related committees from the following representative list:

- **Curriculum Committee** - Comprised of selected faculty, students, and practitioners, this committee evaluates and recommends curriculum content and structure including both required and elective course options for the social work major with a focus on enhancing content relevancy, integration, and compliance with program goals, the Curriculum Policy Statement of CSWE, and the emerging knowledge base of the profession.

- **Student Admission and Retention Committee** - Comprised of faculty members, this committee might assist a faculty member who administers the program admission process, reviews applications, and makes admission recommendation, provides assistance and consultation regarding students who, because of unsatisfactory performance, become ineligible to remain in the social work major, and assists with an evaluative updating of admission and retention standards. One result of this type of unified evaluation is that faculty members can link the student with the most appropriate remedial academic and personal development resources (Moore & Urwin, 1991, p. 13).

- **Planning Committee** - Comprised of faculty, appointed social work practitioners and invited students, this committee provides assistance to the director in assessing the future needs of the program, analyzes program evaluation reports, develops short and long term development priorities, and formulates planning recommendations for consideration by the entire faculty.

- **Student Recruitment Committee** - Comprised of faculty, invited students, and appointed practitioners, this committee develops and implements various information and marketing methods to contact and inform prospective students about social work career opportunities and program offerings.

- **Promotion and Tenure Committee** - Comprised of tenured faculty members, this committee creates an institutional-approved social work performance-based promotion and tenure document that defines standards, procedures and policies, evaluates the performance records of faculty seeking performance reviews, and makes formal recommendations to the academic review governance offices and official of the institution.

- **Faculty Development Committee** - Comprised of faculty members, the committee plans, implements, and evaluates approved performance development opportunities that contribute to the professional enhancement of teaching, scholarship, and professional service competencies.

## Program Advisory Committee

An assurance of maintaining program relevancy is enhanced if there are channels for systematically exchanging information with professional practice communities. A program advisory committee, as exemplified in Figure 4.4, is invaluable in increasing curriculum relevance, strengthening instructional resource materials, marshaling political support, increasing program visibility, and an advisory group might also be created to address specific program issues such as field instruction, or it may be a standing committee composed of representatives from the constituencies involved in the baccalaureate program.

Other governance processes that can occur at the program level include annual performance reviews and regularly scheduled faculty meetings. A formal performance evaluation of each faculty and staff member occurs at the program level. One purpose of this evaluation is to determine an annual salary amount.

However, it can also foster communication between the director and individual faculty members, integrate program objectives and faculty performance goals, promote professional development, provide an opportunity to affirm each faculty member's contributions to the program, and create a more harmonious work environment. For more information on annual performance evaluations, refer to Chapter 7.

# Faculty Meetings - Program Governance

Regularly scheduled faculty meetings are a useful forum for discussing program operations. For example, a meeting might examine issues in the field program, such as unusual trends, problems, or the number of students enrolled. The director might use faculty meetings to communicate about library holdings and acquisitions, student applications for admission, the number of acceptances and rejections, and the budget status of the program.

In addition, the program director reports on institutional issues such as changing policies, enrollments, and administrative procedures that will affect the program. Delegates to the institutional governance structures makes reports to the rest of the faculty. For example, faculty representatives to institutional-based government committees such as Academic Affairs, Professional Affairs, and the University Senate reports on issues under consideration and any recommended policy decisions that will be forwarded for formal consideration by the governing board of the institution.

Faculty meetings also provide a forum to report unusual program or individual accomplishments, discuss common issues such as the revised Curriculum Policy Statement, or examine the implications of a significant publication. Opportunities for more informal exchanges among faculty can strengthen the quality of the academic and professional community.

# Social Work Student Association - Program Governance

The student association functions within the student affairs policies and procedures of the institution. The program director assists in its formation and provide support in the form of copying services, telephone services, and space for meetings. A faculty liaison may be assigned to provide administrative and technical guidance and to facilitate communication between the program and the student association.

To promote student involvement in program governance, the program can invite student representatives to attend routine faculty meetings, report on student association activities, and help plan program-based initiatives that promote student development. Formalized student involvement in the governance process provides a valuable source of information and consumer perspective for the overall development of the program.

## Summary

Higher education governance is a complex decision-making and policy formulation process that permeates all levels of the administrative hierarchy of the institution and intrudes into every responsibility of a social work program director. Applying the ecological approach to this domain helps the director identify the internal and external institutional and program entities that influence the governance process, gain an understanding of institutional policy and decision structures that a director shares with other administrative officials, and manage the information required by the program's constituents.

The ability of a baccalaureate social work program to make and carry out decisions related to personnel, curriculum, and operational resources is the essence of governance, according to CSWE accrediting standards. To achieve this type of program autonomy within the bureaucratic structure of the institution, the director provides effective leadership and perform numerous technical, informational, and strategic planning tasks. A periodic review of administrative responsibilities in the governance domain, an evaluation of the priorities given to competing administrative tasks, and an evaluation of the director's information needs is recommended. The Self-Evaluation Inventory at the end of this publication is designed to assist a program director in conducting an ecologically oriented assessment.

# References

Alexander, R. (1993). The legal liability of social workers after DeShaney. Social Work, 39(1), 64-68.

Baldridge, J. V. (1971b). Power and conflict in the university: Research in the sociology of complex organizations. New York: John Wiley & Sons.

Baldridge, J. V., Curtis, D. V, Ecker, G. P., & Riley, G. L. (1977). Alternative models of governance in higher education. In J. V. Baldridge and T. E. Deal (Eds.). Governing academic organizations. Princeton, New Jersey's Carnegie Foundation for the Advancement of Teaching. McCutchan Publishing Co.

Bennett, J. B., & Figuli, D. J. (1990). Enhancing departmental leadership: The roles of the chairperson. New York, NY: Macmillan Publishing Company.

Bolman, L. G., & Deal, T. E. (1984). Modern approaches to understanding and managing organizations. San Francisco: Jossey-Bass.

Boyer, E. L. (1990). Scholarship reconsidered: Priorities of the professorate. Princeton: Carnegie Foundation for the Advancement of Teaching.

Boyer, E. L. (1989). Governing the campus: A national perspective. In J. H. Schuster & L. H. Miller (Eds.). Governing tomorrow's campus. New York: ACE/Macmillan.

Bracy, W., & Cunningham, M. (1995). Factors contributing to the retention of minority students: Implications for incorporating diversity. The Journal of Baccalaureate Social Work, 1(1), 85-95.

Bullis, R. K. (1990). Cold comfort from the supreme court: Limited liability protection for social workers. Social Work, 35(4), 364-366.

Carnegie Foundation for the Advancement of Teaching. (1982). The control of the campus. Washington, DC.

Carroll, A. (1974). Role conflict in academic organization: An exploratory examination of the department chairman's experience. Education Administration Quarterly, 710, 61.

Cobb, N. H. (1994). Court-recommended guidelines for managing unethical students and working with university lawyers. Journal of Social Work Education 30(1), 18-31.

Cohen, M. D., & March, J. G. (1974). Leadership and ambiguity: The American college president. New York: McGraw-Hill.

Cole, B. S. (1991, Winter). Legal issues related to social work program admissions. Journal of Social Work Education 27(1), 18-24.

Cole, B. S., & Lewis, R. G. (1991, September). Gatekeeping: A comparative overview of administrative models. Paper presented at the Ninth Annual Conference of the Association of Baccalaureate Social Work Program Directors, Orlando, Florida.

Cole, B. S., & Lewis, R. G. (1993, Spring/Summer). Gatekeeping through termination of unsuitable social work students: Legal issues and guidelines. Journal of Social Work Education 29(2), 150-159.

Edwards, R. (1992). How to avoid litigation. Academic Leader, 8(7), 1.

Finn, C. E., Jr. (1987). Context for governance: Public dissatisfaction and campus accountability. In J. H. Schuster & L.H. Miller (Eds.). Governing tomorrow's campus. New York: ACE/Macmillan.

Flax, N, & Swaine, R. L. (1996). Influence of administrative structure on BSW program objectives. The Journal of Baccalaureate Social Work, 1(2), 41-50.

Gelman, S. R., Pollack, D., and Auerbach, C. (1996). Liability issues in social work education. Journal of Social Work Education, 32(3), 351.

Gelman, S. R., & Wardell, P. J. (1988, Winter). Who's responsible? The field liability dilemma. Journal of Social Work Education, 24(1), 70-78.

Gibbs, P. (1994). Screening mechanisms in BSW programs. Journal of Social Work Education, 30(1), 63-74.

Gibbs, P., and Blakely, E. H. (2000). Gatekeeping in BSW programs. New York, NY: Columbia University Press.

Glenny, L. A., & Dalglish, T. K. (1973). Higher education and the law. In J. A. Perkins (Ed.). The university as an organization. New York: McGraw-Hill.

Gmelch, H. (1992). The department chair as mediator. The Department Chair, 3(1), 1 & 16.

Greenberg, M. (1993, October 20). Accounting for faculty members' time. The Chronicle of Higher Education, XL(9), A68.

Gutierrez, L., GlenMaye, L., & DeLois, K. (1995). The organizational context of empowerment practice: Implications for social work administration. Social Work, 40(2), 249-258.

Harper, K. V. (1985). Social work education: Do female coordinators have the power to direct undergraduate programs? Unpublished paper presented at the Women's Issues Symposium, Council on Social Work Education, Washington, DC.

Harper, K. V., Ramey, J. H., & Zook, L. J. (1991, Spring/Summer). BSW program administration: directors' perception of their power to manage. Journal of Social Work Education, 27(2), 176-186.

Hecht, I.W.D., Higgerson, M.L., Gmelch, W.H., & Tucker, A. (1999). The department chair as academic leader. Phoenix, AZ: The Oryx Press.

Hobbs, W., & Anderson, L. (1971, December). The operation of academic departments. Management Science, 18(4), Part 1: B134-B143.

Icard, L. D., Spearmon, M., & Curry-Jackson, A. (1996). BSW programs in black colleges: Building on the strengths of tradition. Journal of Social Work Education, 32(2), 227-235.

Jacobs, C. (1991). Violations of the supervisory relationship: An ethical and educational blind spot. Social Work, 36(2), 130-135.

Johnson, H.W. (1990). Baccalaureate social work education consortia: Problems and possibilities. Journal of Social Work Education, 26(3), 254.

Johnson, H. W., & Hull, G. H. (1992). Autonomy and visibility in undergraduate social work education. Journal of Social Work Education, 28,(3) 312-321.

Johnson, H. W., & Hull, Jr., G. H. (1990). The rest of the story: Baccalaureate social work programs no longer accredited. Journal of Social Work Education, 3, 244-253.

Johnstone, R. L. (1981). The scope of faculty collective bargaining: An analysis of faculty union agreements at four-year institutions of higher education. Westport, CT: Greenwood Press.

Koerin, B., & Miller, J. (1995). Gatekeeping policies: Terminating students for nonacademic reasons. Journal of Social Work Education, 31(2), 247-260

Kutchins, H. (1991). The fiduciary relationship: The legal basis for social workers' responsibilities to clients. Social Work, 36(2), 106-113.

Lennon, T. M. (1999). Statistics on social work education in the United States: 1998. Alexandria, VA: Council on Social Work Education.

Lucas, A. (1994). Strengthening departmental leadership: A team building guide for chairs in colleges and universities. San Francisco: Jossey-Bass.

Macy, H. J. (1990). Role analysis study of chairpersons in academic departments offering accredited baccalaureate social work degree programs. Unpublished doctoral dissertation, Ball State University, Muncie, Indiana.

Mobley, T. (1981). Selecting the department chairman. Educational Record, 52, 322.

Moll, J. (1988, October). Legal guidelines for academic department chairs. Paper presented at a Meeting of University Heads, Muncie, Indiana.

Moore, L.S., Dietz, T. J., & Jenkins, D. A. (1998). Issues in gatekeeping. The Journal of Baccalaureate Social Work, Association of Baccalaureate Social Work Program Directors, 4(1), 37.

Moore, L. S., & Urwin, C. A. (1991, Winter). Gatekeeping: A model for screening baccalaureate students for field education. Journal of Social Work Education, 27(1), 8-17.

National Association of Social Workers, Inc. (1981, September). NASW standards for the classification of social work practice: Policy statement 4. Prepared by the NASW Task Force on Sector Force Classification.

Potter-Efron, R.T. (1985). Cooperation and conflict between social workers and sociologists in combined undergraduate departments. Journal of Sociology and Social Welfare, 21(3), 27-37.

Reamer, F. G. (1992). The impaired social worker. Social Work, 37(2), 165-170.

Reutter, E. E. (1985). The law of public education. Mineola, NY: The Foundation Press, Inc.

Saunders, E. J. (1993). Confronting academic dishonesty. Journal of Social Work Education, 29(2), 224-231.

Sheafor, B. W. (1979). The social work program: Its place in higher education. In Betty Baer and Ronald Federico (Eds.), Educating the baccalaureate social worker (pp. 49-53). New York, Ballinger Press.

Stroup, H. H. (1966). Bureaucracy in higher education. New York: Free Press.

Swaine, R. L., & Flax, N. (1992). BSW program directors: Characteristics and role experiences. Arete, 17(2), 16-27.

Tucker, A. (1984). Chairing the academic department: Leadership among peers. (Second Edition). New York, NY: Macmillan Publishing Company.

Ward Mullaney, J., and March Timerlake, E. (1994). University tenure and the legal system: Procedures, conflicts, and resolutions. Journal of Social Work Education, 30(2), 172-184.

Zakutansky, T. J., & Sirles, E. A. (1993, Fall). Ethical and legal issues in field education: Shared responsibility and risk. Journal of Social Work Education, 29(3), 338-347.

# Chapter 5

# Student Affairs

The realm of student affairs concerns the administration of activities that enhance students' personal, academic, and professional development. The purpose of this chapter is to examine the administrative practices that a program director can use to promote the effectiveness of this program domain. Students affairs begins with the program's effort to recruit enough quality students to meet its enrollment and academic goals and concludes with the successful completion of the academic program. During the students' academic careers, faculty advisors provide guidance for personal and career aspirations, and serve as role models of professional social work behavior. In this chapter, the administrative domain of student affairs is cast within an adult learning model which is consistent with the professional development model of professional social work education. Through this model students actively participate in their learning which occurs at cognitive, affective, and experiential levels and expands to include extracurricular activities designed to supplement and extend professional development opportunities for students to integrate theory and practice, enhancing the students' academic experience. Routinely structured reviews of student and program performance ensure that students continue to meet the program's academic and professional standards and that the program fulfills its gatekeeping function for the social work profession.

# Student Affairs Administrative Responsibilities

Figure 5.1 lists the 12 administrative tasks found in this program administration area. The twelve tasks are clustered into three categories: (1) recruitment and admission; (2) retention and advising; and (3) gatekeeping, which collectively reflect the program director's administration of program-based student recruitment, admission assessment, advising and discharge practices.

## FIGURE 5.1

### Student Affairs Domain Tasks

**Recruitment and Admission**

- Assure the availability of catalogues, handbooks, and other materials that accurately state the program's and institution's academic/ professional standards, policies, and procedures.

- Evaluate student enrollment, attrition, registration, and advising procedures; recommend policies, practices and procedures to improve current procedures.

**Retention and Advising**

- Maintain a student information system that provides academic, professional, program admission, personal, and employment reference data.

- Maintain academic, professional, and career advising services for students.

- Promote a student registration process that permits qualified program matriculates to efficiently register for required sequential courses and provide assistance to resolve academic and financial issues.

- Evaluate career services to assure career and advanced/continuing education information is distributed, assistance is available for students seeking employment and that the policies, procedures and information is accurate.

- Oversee procedures to notify students of encumbrances (e. g., unpaid parking violations) that jeopardize academic standing; directing students to appropriate institutional resources and personnel to resolve such matters

- Facilitate extra-curricular activities that enhance the education process and professional development of students.

**Gatekeeping**

- Oversee the administrative structures, policies, and procedures designed to systematically evaluate students' academic and professional development; utilize institutional and community resources to address deficiencies.

- Evaluate the program's student admission, selection and retention policies and procedures to assure compliance with professional, institutional, legal and accreditation standards.

- Ensure that academic, professional, and personal behavior infractions are addressed in a timely and equitable manner and in compliance with all academic, legal, professional, accreditation, and institutional requirements.

- Support faculty advisors to assist students with a range of matters including academic, psychological, personal, medical, and legal; develop collaborative agreements with institutional and community-based specialized service systems.

Organizational factors such as program size, governance procedures, and academic disciplinary structure determine which personnel responsibilities are direct, formal position responsibilities of a social work program director. These responsibilities can be completed directly by a director or can be shared with or may be completed entirely by other administrative officials located within the formal personnel system of the institution. A complete listing of generic interrelated administrative responsibilities that compose the personnel domain is found in Appendix D. The tasks listed in Appendix D are arranged in a format that provides opportunity to assess the relative importance of the tasks within the context of a specific program and to locate the locus of assigned administrative responsibility

# Institutional Human Resource Administration Organization and Development Structure

Academic, training, technical support and student financial assistance offices located throughout the institution must be linked to program-based student services administration. An institutional-based example is provided in Figure 5.2 to illustrate the director's coordinated use of the student recruitment, admissions, development, support, and evaluation responsibilities.

The student affairs structure, illustrated in Figure 5.2, shows that the institution's student affairs administrative decision responsibilities under the direction of the Vice President for Student Affairs, who provides a range of student support services such as registration and academic progress, ombudsperson assistance, scholarship assistance and counseling services. These administrative and student development/support offices directly control student affairs administration at the academic program level and represent institutional-based resources for development, collaboration, evaluation, compensation and recognition. An understanding of the specialized purpose of each office that controls, supports, rewards, and evaluates program-based student services, along with having a working relationship with the personnel who function within this program domain of the institution contributes to effective program administration.

Effective human resource administration requires a program director to develop working relationships with a number of campus-based officials and to routinely involve the services provided by these officers when completing administrative tasks in this program domain. Administrative accountability begins with a thorough understanding of the human resource structures, policies, and procedures of the institution; consequently, a review of the institution's personnel

# FIGURE 5.2

## Student Affairs Administrative Responsibilities

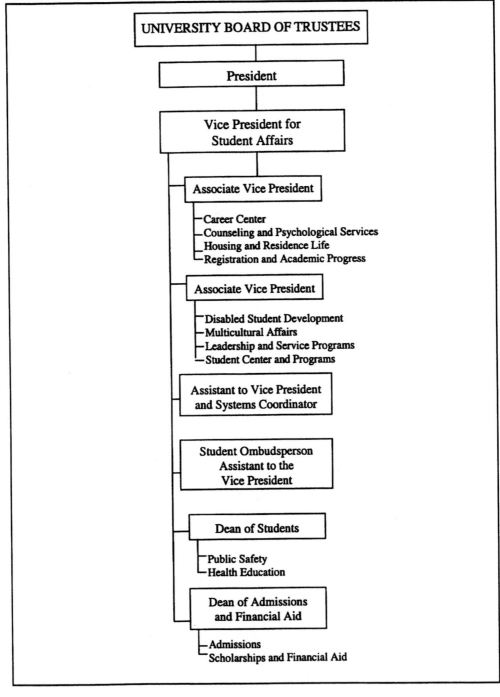

structure, responsibilities of personnel officials and the human resource policies is a useful beginning point for a program director.

The ecological framework as described in chapter 8 provide a context for the work of the program director in student affairs. These components include (1) the organizational structure and services of the institution, (2) Council on Social Work Education (CSWE) accreditation standards, (3) professional standards for social work practice, and (4) compatibility issues between the university and the social work program. To understand the structure and resources of the institution, the program director is advised to read institutional publications and form working relationships with key administrative personnel in areas such as academic advisement, student recruitment, student activities, counseling and health services, disability support services, financial aid, and career services. Establishing and maintaining these relationships links the social work program administrator to institutional resources dealing with student needs and opens avenues for developing new resources when necessary. Council on Social Work Education (CSWE) accreditation standards regarding admissions and retention, advisement, recruitment, and diversity help to shape the program's policies. In areas where differences between the policies, procedures, and goals of the institution and those of the social work program affect student affairs, the director is recommended to develop strategies to improve the complimentarity of the program and the institution (Sheafor, 1979). Student affairs issues often stem from fundamental differences between academic and professional programs, such as differences in criteria for admission and retention, emphasis on academic learning vs. holistic professional development, emphasis on academic vs. professional advising, and recruitment issues.

# Recruitment

By establishing systematic recruitment activities, the director helps the program to attract a sufficient number of qualified and diverse social work students for professional development. As a professional gatekeeping function, undergraduate social work education programs have the responsibility to recruit students who are capable of professional development and have the values orientation requisite for entry-level social work practice. According to Bogo, Raphael, and Roberts (1993), as keepers of the gate, "... social work education needs to develop new strategies for recruitment and admission of students most likely to be committed to the continuity of the traditional professional (social work) paradigm." Initially, the director can begin by scanning the institution's environment to learn as much as possible about the methods that the institution uses to recruit students. Most universities and colleges engage in a variety of recruitment activities including campus visitations, informational fairs, distribution of printed material, media advertising, and correspondence with potential students as methods or approaches to recruitment. Awareness of the institution's total recruitment system can enable the program director to develop strategies that link institutional recruitment resources to the specific recruitment needs and goals of the social work program, according to Swaine and Flax (1995).

A multi-tiered approach to recruitment seems advisable and is adaptable to the institutional and regional context of each social work program. For example, some programs may have a strong linkage to professional organizations like NASW and may use organizational meetings as opportunities for recruitment. Strong advisory boards may also be considered as having members who are potential recruiters for the social work program. Program graduates are potential recruiters as well, purposefully, by word, and unintentionally, by action/behavior in practice. Linking the social work program with allied minors in the university may be another avenue for recruiting social work majors. Nursing, criminal justice, and family and consumer science are three examples of allied programs where a potential pool of social work majors exists. While these seem casual, even natural, approaches to recruitment, they can be methods which are part of an overall recruitment plan. Program administrators " ... need to encourage faculty to develop a more planned recruitment", one that is "... a targeted, developed recruitment program. Vague and unprofessional recruitment is an ineffective use of professional skills. A well-developed and focused recruitment

## FIGURE 5.3

### Recruitment Activities

- Campus visitations

- Informational fairs

- Distribution of printed material (university recruiters, potential students, etc.)

- Media advertising

- Program web site

- Outreach programs for high school and community college students

- Articulation agreements with other colleges and universities

- Linkages with professional organizations like NASW (host meetings, chapters, provide continuing education programs, etc.)

- Involving social work program advisory boards, alumni, students, faculty, field agencies program of 4 % can have a significant impact." (Frost, Anderson, & Sublette, 1987). They present a recruitment model which offers guidelines for social work programs to shape a recruitment plan, unique for a program's context. Their recruitment model includes the following components:

- Utilize students and alumni in a targeted manner

- Enhance communication between social work schools and employers (regularly scheduled meetings, focus groups)

- Establish regular feedback from the consumer (applicants, current students, graduating students, alumni)

- Assign specific responsibilities to faculty (especially those interested in recruitment; reward accordingly)

Having a recruitment plan which suits the needs of the social work program and utilizes all available resources to strengthen and extend its potential for success is a critical first step in accomplishing the tasks found the student affairs domain. Having no recruitment plan yields no measurable results in the recruitment dimension of the student affairs domain. For example, suppose faculty agree that the social work program needs more minority students to expand and enhance its diversity. How to approach this recruitment goal is a matter for study and reflection, according to Berger (1991) and Raber, Tebb, and Berg-Weger (1998). Berger suggests targeting previously untargeted groups for potential students, such as social service agency employees who are in contact with clients but are in clerical or other non-social work positions. This target group may have minority staff among its composition who may be motivated and have the capacity and value orientation to succeed in a BSW program. For minority recruitment efforts to be successful and produce qualified minority students who will succeed in the BSW program, they must... "provide counseling, financial assistance, curriculum flexibility, and alternative scheduling opportunities", according the Raber, Tebb and Berg-Weger (1998). They contend that for programs ... " to be successful in recruiting and retaining a diverse student body, programs need a support structure for faculty and staff, specialized student and academic policies, and the commitment of the entire social work department and university to the recruitment and retention of culturally diverse students." If a social work program is truly committed to developing a diverse student pool, then including some of the following implications for recruitment and retention of minority students (summarized from the writing of Raber, Tebb, and Berg-Weger, 1998, pp. 44-45), in a social work program's recruitment plan is suggested.

# Implications for Recruitment and Retention of Minority Students

- In universities with diverse student populations, those who transfer from general studies and arts and science may offer a pool of potential social work students. Feeder community colleges may offer additional pools of minority students who may be potential social work majors.

- Active involvement with alumni and community agencies where a potential pool of minority social work students may be found in non-social work staff interested in professional development such as that afforded a BSW program.

- Active involvement with community colleges, including extending articulation agreements to include human services and mental health programs. This is not to imply that educational standards will be compromised, rather that clear understanding about those standards and the curriculum's organization and implementation will be established and maintained.

- Student involvement in recruitment and retention can be an asset. Involving minority students formally and informally in the recruitment plan can produce positive results.

The program director is ultimately responsible for ensuring that recruitment practices are not discriminatory and that they promote a diverse student body. CSWE accreditation standards include non-discrimination policies and procedures as requirements for social work programs. This requirement is based on the proposition that social work requires a diverse student body as an integral part of its educational milieu and mission. To attract a diverse student body, recruitment efforts may take a variety of forms, as stated above. Internally, the program director is expected to make sure that personnel in the institution's admissions and advisement systems understand the social work program's need for a culturally diverse student body and for contemporary social work students to increase cultural competence (Gross, 2000). Externally, many programs have articulation agreements with community colleges in order to attract and recruit a diverse student population. The use of resources in this broader recruitment effort may raise compatibility issues with the university, particularly in small programs and those with limited resources. If the university does not support the recruitment activities required by the social work program, the director is challenged to secure that support. This support can be achieved by producing a minority student recruitment plan which yields positive results for the social work program and offering that plan as a model for other programs on campus which have similar goals for a diverse student population. As a member of the university's "team" of middle managers, the social work program director may emerge as a resident expert and leader in the area of minority student recruitment and may become a resource for other middle managers or other university administrators seeking to expand diversity.

A task related to recruitment is the preparation and distribution of written materials about the program and profession. For example, a program might develop a fact sheet with information about the profession (salaries, job potential, and range of opportunities) and about the program (academic requirements, extracurricular activities, accomplishments, and financial aid, scholarships, and training grants). All individuals (faculty, staff, students) in the recruitment system should have copies of these fact sheets to distribute to prospective students and social work program stakeholders. Most programs have brochures and program handbooks which may be excellent recruitment tools. Those printed materials can be supplemented creatively by developing program websites, videos, or formal presentations using current computer technology to strengthen recruitment efforts.

## Admissions

Since every program is unique and has somewhat different program and educational objectives, an important administrative task in the student affairs domain is the development of an admissions plan which meets the program's goals of recruiting, retaining, and developing social work students for competent entry-level social work practice, and satisfies the program's responsibility for professional gatekeeping. Cast in the context of the college or university and using knowledge about their potential and current students and feedback from alumni, field instructors, students, faculty, and other stakeholders, social work programs establish their own criteria for admission. Articulation and transfer agreements with other colleges and universities facilitate and formalize the transfer of credit from one university to another. They also clarify the social work program's curriculum, admission standards, and requirements for graduations so that transfer and native students are held to the same social work education standards.

Because these criteria may differ from the university's admission policies, it is important to clarify those differences with the university administration and secure institutional support for the program's professional admissions criteria. A common theme noted throughout this publication is the contextual relationship

# FIGURE 5.4

## Sample Initial Admission For the Social Work Major

For initial admission, students must have:

- Submitted a completed social work major application to the department.
- Earned a minimum grade point average of 2.3 in 100- and 200-level required courses completed for the major.
- Upon completion of SOCWK 220 and 230, completed assignment conferences with faculty instructors of these courses and submitted faculty reference forms to the department.
- Completed approved volunteer assignments of a minimum of 25 clock hours and submitted Performance Evaluations to the department.
- Completed application interviews with the Coordinator of Student Services and received from this Coordinator positive recommendations for admission to the major.

When completing the initial Admission step, it is recommended that students prepare an academic plan of study using information from your University Degree Analysis Progress Report issued each academic term and conferences with the Social Work Department Faculty Advisor in order to schedule the practicum during the semester of preference.

### Admission to Senior-Level Required Practice Courses

For admission to senior-level required social work practice courses, students must have:

- Earned cumulative grade-point averages of 2.5 in the major in order to register for SOCWK 424 and 426.
- Successfully completed the University writing competency exam.

### Admission to Social Work Practicum

For admission to social work practicum, students must have:

- Submitted completed applications for the practicum to the department.
- Earned grades of C or better in SOCWK 424 and 426.
- Submitted completed University applications for graduation.

University is an equal opportunity/affirmative action institution in accordance with Civil Rights legislation and does not discriminate on the basis of race, sex, religion, color, national origin, physical or mental handicap, age, or status as a Vietnam era veteran in any of its education programs, activities, admissions, or employment policies. Concerns regarding this policy should be referred to the Office of the Director of Affirmative action, University Administration building. The Title IX Coordinator and the 504 Coordinator may be reached at the same address.

between the institution and a social work program. Relational factors such as resource adequacy, organizational autonomy, educational outcomes and governance processes may represent tension arenas that a director must address. Selective student admission is a key quality program advancement operation in which there may be inherent tensions between the program and the institution. Gatekeeping issues such as the need for faculty to complete a labor-intensive operation of screening, advising and dismissing students, the application of admission and retention criteria beyond traditional academic standards to assess professional attributes of students, the rejection of program admission candidates translates into loss of institutional fees, and the lack of complementarity between a professional degree discipline and the goals of a liberal arts institution are examined by Morrow (2000).

An illustration of one program's admissions guidelines appears in Appendix I. As with student recruitment, discussed earlier, an initial step in developing an admissions plan involves environmental scanning to determine institutional resources, services, personnel, activities, and responsibilities related to student admissions and retention. For example, the administrative chart in Chapter 1, Figure 1.2, indicates what position/office/unit is responsible for admissions and other related services in the area of student affairs. Using this chart, the social work program director's goal is to identify which resources within the institution are available to assist with the program's admission plan, then make use of institutional resources such as legal counsel, financial assistance, career services, disability support services, and others to assist with the selection and subsequent retention of those students who are best qualified.

External influences, such as CSWE accreditation standards for undergraduate social work education, require admissions plans. Programs are expected to clearly articulate and implement criteria and processes of student admission. That a social work program have admissions criteria and a process for implementing that plan is required, but defining the criteria and admissions plan is left to the social work program. Gibbs (1994) surveyed BSW over two hundred programs regarding formal admissions criteria for entry into the social work major. One hundred forty programs specified that their admission criteria required an overall GPA of at least a C but less than a B. Other formal admission requirements included a minimum GPA in social work courses, a minimum number of completed credit hours, an introductory social work course, a written essay, and completion of "the liberal arts foundation". Gibbs (1994) further discovered that programs with formal admissions procedures (N=159) applied other admissions criteria which did not appear in printed admissions material: evidence of sound writing skills and oral communication skills, selective use of interview, consistency between personal values and social work values, adherence to social work ethics, and evidence of emotional/mental stability. An earlier national study by Constable (1977) found similar sources of admissions information: (a) written application, (b) interviews, (c) field experiences prior to admission, and (d) assessment through an entry-level course.

Admissions policies and criteria, once they are defined and agreed upon, are made publicly accessible through the institution's catalogues, student handbooks, and other publications, in addition to the social work program's own documents. Posting admissions criteria and procedures on bulletin boards in common areas of academic buildings, repeating them in program and university newsletters, and posting them on the program's website are additional ways to disseminate social work program admissions criteria and the related procedures. A sample application form for admission to a social work program is found in the Appendix.

Once students apply for admission to the social work program, the next step is to review the application, evaluate the application, and make a decision about the potential student's suitability for social work. Born and Carrol (1988) see this step as the first one in a multi-tiered approach to gatekeeping in the profession. To admit a student to the social work program is the first critical decision program faculty make in their roles as guardians of the gate to the social work profession. However, social work programs and their faculty often have difficulties making admissions selections (Dinerman, 1982), perhaps because personal characteristics and competencies are difficult to evaluate. Familiarity with legal guidelines can assist the program director and faculty in the admissions process and assist educators in avoiding legal difficulties (Cole, 1991, Cole and Lewis, 1993, and Cobb, 1994). Programs may choose to establish an admissions committee whose composition includes faculty, students and stakeholders, while others may elect to assign admissions to one faculty member as part of his/her workload, and still other programs may assign program admissions to the program director. As stated previously, social work programs are responsible for developing their own processes and criteria to select the best qualified students for social work education. In developing admissions criteria and establishing an admissions plan, the program director (and faculty) is advised to remember that "three areas are particularly relevant for admission into a social work program: (1) academic ability, (2) personal attributes, and (3) professional potential" (Swaine and Flax, 1995).

## Academic Advising in Social Work

The social work program needs an advising system which includes a systematic review of each student's academic and professional progress toward completing the BSW. Evaluative Standards have historically required that the program's advisement policies and procedures be clearly explained to both faculty and students. To meet this accreditation standard, many programs include descriptions of their advisement system in their student or program handbooks. An example of one program's advisement process is found in Appendix H. Components of a social work program's advising process are found below.

- Academic advising provided by full time social work faculty

- Using forms and program records to facilitate and formalize the process.

- Regularly scheduled and mandatory advising to monitor student progress

- Linking with university services to support student progress and meet student needs

- Counseling out those students who fail to make progress or are unsuitable to social work

- Career counseling; serving as employment reference

Assigning advisement responsibilities to full time social work faculty meets the requirement in CSWE Evaluative Standards which have required that

## FIGURE 5.5

### Sample Student Advising Procedures

Student Instructions:

1. To declare social work as your major field, you must complete a "declaration of major" card in the Dean's Office. Following the declaration of your major, your records will be forwarded to the social work department.

2. Upon receipt of your file, the social work department will assign you to an advisor. The department secretary can give you the name of your advisor.

3. You and your advisor meet to prepare an academic advising plan leading to your degree.

4. It is required that you meet with your advisor at least once each semester to review your educational program and progress and to obtain permission to register for classes.

advisors must be full-time or permanent faculty who have either the MSW or the BSW degree and a social work doctorate, and who are fully knowledgeable of the program. In some programs, student advising is the responsibility of one faculty member, while in other departments advising is shared equally among all faculty, or advisement is divided according the class standing. There is no one best model for organizing advising responsibilities, but each program is left to develop a method of advising its students in manner which works best or which best meets the program's educational objectives and contributes to a high quality social work program.

Advisors contribute to early and periodic evaluations of each student's performance. Traditionally, according to CSWE Evaluative Standards, the advisor's responsibility is to orient students and help them assess their aptitude and motivation for a career in social work. This responsibility requires that faculty advisors understand their students, including backgrounds and cultural frames of reference, academic preparation, demographics, motivation for social work practice, and resource needs (personal and academic). A student's interest in social work as a profession is personal, individual, and may be explained by life experiences, personal values, career goals, personal attributes, as well as other factors. An advisor's task is to facilitate the social worker student's self-awareness concerning his/her motivation for social work education and the professional practice of social work. A part of professional development process, advisors also guide students in selecting courses, required or elective, and in choosing field, volunteer, and employment settings that best meet their educational and career goals.

Many programs conduct periodic reviews of students' performance after their initial admission, a program activity in which advisors have an important role. Figure 5.5 on the following page provides an example of a review process in which students are evaluated at various stages of their progression through the program. After each review, a decision is made to continue the student (with or without conditions) or to discontinue the student from the program. CSWE accreditation standards require programs to have criteria in place for evaluating student performance, including procedures for terminating a student's enrollment.

# Administrative Oversight of Program-Based Advising

In social work, regular advising is required because understanding each aspect of the program is dependent upon a good understanding of the entire program. The advising process is designed to help students plan their programs logically and thereby enhance educational progress. In large programs, the advising may be formalized and students required to schedule time for faculty advisement. In small programs, informal procedures may prevail. In such a setting students may drop in for advisement without an appointment and that process may work well for that program. Whatever the program size, each program director and faculty decide how advising can be accomplished in the best way for their program, its students, and university.

However, these advising steps tell only one part of the story. Imbedded within the steps are qualitative issues of professional development and student progress toward educational and professional goals. Professional social work education takes place within the walls of academe and outside its walls in the communities, the agencies, the organizations, the activities, and the interactions which occur spontaneously and by design during a student's professional educational experience. The focus of this educational process is professional development, not academic mastery in the classroom alone. Academic performance in professional programs includes professional behavior in class, field instruction, and in all interactions. The advising process is an ideal place to address professional behavior issues, situational factors which may affect a student's performance, as well as course grades as students make progress toward degree completion. In some instances, it may be prudent to advise a student to take a semester off from school to deal with personal issues (the loss of a family member, a physical illness, divorce, etc.). Making that decision may be difficult for a student, but a faculty advisor can support the student's need to attend to personal matters first, then return to school with a stronger sense of competency.

## Student Organization and Participation

The program which encourages extracurricular activities pertinent to student interests and, in fact, purposefully organizes activities to support the program's educational objectives, is making wise use of the vast array of educational experiences available. Programs assist students in developing and maintaining a student social work association, which may become an official campus organization. Goals of such associations may include providing feedback to the social work program for review and improvement, making arrangements for additional educational experiences, providing leadership opportunities for students, and providing social support for social work students who are members. For an example of student association activities, see the sample schedule in Figure 5.6 which follows.

**FIGURE 5.6**

## Student Social Work Association Activities Schedule

**September**

Welcome party for new students

**January**

Food drive
Information panel for new social

**October**

Homeless rally and panel presentation
Urban "plunge" weekend
Legislative forum

**February**

Bake Sale
Employment Seminar

**November**

Bake sale
Car wash
Employment seminar
Red Cross flood relief project

**March**

Alternative "spring break" work
project
Bowl-A-Thon
Speaker on human diversity

**December**

Child abuse panel presentation
End of semester party

**April**

"Rural plunge" weekend trip
Child welfare panel presentation
Picnic

Since social work education is professional education and affiliation with professional organizations is recognized as one mark of a profession, social work students are encouraged to participate in professional organizations while pursuing their degree. Some programs require students to join NASW prior to admission to field practicum, some require NASW membership of all majors, and others simply recommend student membership in that professional organization. Two programs known to the authors, have NASW chapters or units at their campuses and students carry leadership roles. Communication with other students and professionals will assist students in refining their career objectives, developing an identity with the social work profession, and establishing relationships with others in their field. Other organizations which might be beneficial for students with special interests include the National

Association of Black Social Workers or the American Association of Christians in Social Work. In addition, some campuses have women's centers, African-American cultural centers, gay student organizations, religious student organizations, and other facilities or groups that social work students can join to satisfy special interests or expand experiential learning, which may enhance students' professional development.

Student participation in program and university decision-making and governance are important activities in a social work program whose goal is professional development. Experiences such as sitting on university committees, program committees, etc., give students a voice and strengthen their educational experiences. It is recommended that students be represented on all faculty search committees, on program admissions and scholarship committees, and that students have opportunities, both formal and informal, for involvement in program governance. Where standing committees exist, regularly assign student representation. When ad hoc committees are formed for particular activities, seriously consider the placement of students on such committees.

# Dismissals

The program director provides oversight to administer program-based advising and discharge practices that complement the academic policies, procedures, and standards of the university while meeting CSWE accreditation standards and social work practice expectations. Social work programs, as gatekeepers of the profession, are expected to dismiss students who fail to meet standards or criteria established for continuous enrollment or for completion of program requirements. Suspending or dismissing a student from the program can be handled in a number of ways. Sometimes the student can simply change majors. Faculty should be aware of this option and assist students or refer them to appropriate sources for degree planning (Moore & Urwin, 1991). Cole and Lewis (1993) suggest the following guidelines for academic and disciplinary dismissals (p. 157).

Compatibility issues, which may cause tension between the program and its institution, can arise from admission and retention decisions. For example, if the university's goal is to increase student enrollment, the social work program which controls student enrollment may find itself at odds with central administration over the issue. Social work programs, as professional educational programs, may be called upon to justify admissions and discharge policies regularly to administrators whose primary focus is enrollment growth.

While academic achievement is the major criterion for admission into most academic majors, the social work major requires certain personal characteristics and competencies in addition to satisfactory academic performance. The individual assessments conducted by social work programs require more resources than usual admission procedures do. Additionally, termination of students from the program can lead to tensions within the program and within the institution. As a result, the social work program director disseminates and explains the program's admission, retention, and dismissal policies and procedures to personnel in the university, whose support is secured.

Baccalaureate social work programs that are small in size (e.g. three or fewer full-time faculty positions) are generally much more informal in providing academic and professional advising services to students since there are many opportunities for faculty to observe, monitor and interact with students. The informally oriented advising process may also be the basis for the selective program admission and retention procedures, but according to Morrow (2000), small programs face three types of challenges related to the gatekeeping responsibility. These include:

- Faculty size requires these personnel to have a broad range of program responsibilities that include teaching, advising, service, scholarship and program and field practicum administration assignments which leaves limited time for developing, implementing, and monitoring comprehensive gatekeeping policies and procedures.

- Rigorous gatekeeping policies and standards for social work students may conflict with the need to compete with other academic majors enrolled at the institution and thereby jeopardize the continued development or even the survival of the program.

- Institutional support for small programs, which are commonly located in small liberal arts colleges, may remain unstable based on a continuing level of uncertainty about the appropriateness for the inclusion of professional academic degree programs in the institutional offerings since these programs have different educational outcomes, admission standards and academic standards (pp. 68-69).

**FIGURE 5.7**

**Guidelines for Academic or Disciplinary Dismissals**

- Clearly explain to students criteria for evaluation in classroom and field placement, including such requirements as attendance.

- Make academic decisions, including professional practice appraisals, in good faith. They must not be arbitrary or capricious. For example, a panel or committee might make decisions about practice skills insufficiency or incompetence, because the group decision would promote uniformity and add credence to the decision-making process. The program should be able to show that subjective grading is a rational exercise of discretion by the graders.

- Advise students, whose class or field performance makes his or her continuance in the program unwise, of deficiencies before dismissal from the program.

- Have in place a system of review and reevaluation for students who challenge academic decisions.

- Constitutionally guaranteed due-process rights must be afforded students in cases in which disciplinary action will result in termination from the program.

- Academic, ethical, and behavioral standards should be clearly stated, along with consequences for misconduct. The NASW Code of Ethics could be modified for this purpose. All appropriate university and social work program publications, such as student handbooks, program brochures, and university catalogues, should contain these standards and rules.

# Summary

For a social work program to be one of high quality, it needs to successfully address dimensions found in the domain of student affairs. This chapter explained the director's major responsibilities in student affairs: recruitment, admissions, advisement (including retention), student organizing and participating, and dismissals. Four components of the ecological framework provided a context for the work of the program director in each of the areas of major responsibility. Application of the ecological framework discussed in greater detail in chapter 8 enables the program director to identify and link institutional resource systems with student needs; to ensure that the program conforms to CSWE accreditation standards regarding admissions, retention, advisement, and recruitment; and to address compatibility issues in student affairs which may arise from fundamental differences between academic and professional programs in universities.

# References

Berger, R. (1991). Untapped sources for recruiting minority BSW students. Journal of Social Work Education, 27(20), 168-175.

Bogo, M., Dennis, R., & Roberts, R. (1993). Interests, activities, and self-identification among social work students: Toward a definition of social work identity. Journal of Social Work Education, 29(3), 279-292.

Born, C. E., & Carroll, D. J. (1988, Winter,). Ethics in admissions. Journal of Social Work Education, (1), 79-85.

Cobb, N. H. (1994). Court-recommended guidelines for managing unethical students and working with university lawyers. Journal of Social Work Education, 30(1), 18-31.

Cole, B. S. (1991, Winter,). Legal issues related to social work program admissions. Journal of Social Work Education, 27(1), 18-24.

Cole, B. S., & Lewis, R. G. (1993). Gatekeeping through termination of unsuitable social work students: Legal issues and guidelines. Journal of Social Work Education, 29, 150-159.

Constable, R. T. (1977). A study of admissions policies in undergraduate education. Journal of Education for Social Work, 13(3), 19-24.

Council on Social Work Education. (1994). Baccalaureate evaluative standards and interpretive guidelines. Alexandria, VA- Author.

Council on Social Work Education, Commission on Accreditation. (1999). Guidelines for termination for academic and professional reasons. Supplement to the handbook of accreditation standards and procedures (1994). Alexandria, VA.

Dinerman, M. (1982). A study of baccalaureate and master's curricula in social work. Journal of Social Work Education, 18, 84-92.

Frost, C. H., Anderson, M. F., & Sublette, S. (1987, Spring/Summer,). How to increase enrollment in undergraduate and graduate schools of social work. Journal of Social Work Education, (2), 75-87.

Gibbs, P. (1994). Screening mechanisms in BSW programs. Journal of Social Work Education, 30(1), 63-74.

Gross, G. D. (2000). Gatekeeping for cultural competence: Ready or not? Some post and modernist doubts. The Journal of Baccalaureate Social Work, 5(2), Association of Baccalaureate Social Work Program Directors.

Moore, L. S., & Urwin, C. A. (1991, Winter). Gatekeeping: A model for screening baccalaureate students for field education. Journal of Social Work Education, 27(1), 8-17.

Morrow, D. F. (2000, Spring). Gatekeeping for small baccalaureate social work programs. The Journal of Baccalaureate Social Work, 5(2), 67-80.

Raber, M., Tebb, S., & Berg-Weger, M. (1998). Recruitment and retention of minority students in bachelor of social work programs. The Journal o f Baccalaureate Social Work, 3(2), 31-49.

Sheafor, B. (1979). The social work program: Its place in higher education. In B. L. Baer & R. C. Federico (Eds.), Educating the baccalaureate social worker. Boston: Ballinger Publishing Company.

Swaine, R. L., & Flax, N. (1995). Student affairs. In May, H. J. , Flax, N., Summer, V. L., & Swaine, R. L. Directing the Baccalaureate Social Work Program: An Ecological Perspective. Jefferson City, MO: Association of Baccalaureate Social Work Program Directors (BPD).

# Bibliography

Berger, R. (1992). Student retention: A critical phase in the academic careers of minority baccalaureate social workers. Journal of Social Work Education, 28 (1), 85-97.

Black, P. N., Jeffreys, D., & Hartley, E. K. (1993). Personal history of psychosocial trauma in the early life of social work and business students. Journal of Social Work Education, 29(2), 171-178.

Butler, A. C. (1990). A re-evaluation of social work students' career interests. Journal of Social Work Education, 26(1) 45-56.

Cobb, N. H., & Jordan, C. (1989). Students with questionable values or threatening behavior: Precedent and policy from discipline to dismissal. Journal of Social Work Education, 25(2), 87-149.

Cole, B. S., Christ, C. C., & Light, T. R. (1995). Social work education and students with disabilities: implications of Section 504 and the ADA. Journal of Social Work Education, 31(2), 261-268.

Darnells, M., & Stuber, D. (1992). Mandatory psychiatric withdrawal of severely study and policy recommendation. NASPA Journal, 29(3), 163-168.

Delworth, U. (Ed.). (1989). Dealing with the behavioral and psychological problems of students. New Directors for Student Services. San Francisco: Jossey-Bass, Inc.

Fortune, A. (1987). Multiple roles, stress and well-being among MSW students. Journal of Social Work Education, Fall(3), 81- 90.

Gibbs, P., and Blakely, E. H. (2000). Gatekeeping in BSW programs. New York, NY: Columbia University Press.

Gibbs, P. (1992). Gatekeeping in BSW programs. Paper presented at the Council on Social Work Education Annual Program Meeting, Kansas City, MO.

Heyward, S. M. (1992). Access to education for the disabled: a guide to compliance with Section 504 of The Rehabilitation Act of 1973. Jefferson, N. C.:McFarland & Company.

Home, A. C. (1997). Learning the hard way: Role strain, stress, role demands, and support in multiple-role women students. Journal of Social Work Education, 33(2), 335-346.

Jones, E. F. (1984). Square peg, round hole: The dilemma of the undergraduate social work field coordinator. Journal of Education for Social Work, 33(2), 335-346.

Kaplan, W. A. (1985). The law of higher education, 2nd edition. San Francisco: Jossey-Bass publishers.

Kilpatrick, A. C., & Holland, T. R. (1993). Management of the field instruction program in social work education. Journal of Teaching in Social Work, 7(1), 123-136.

Knight, C. (1996). A Study of MSW and BSW students' perceptions of their field instructors. Journal of Social Work Education, 32(3), 399-414.

Koerin, B., & Miller, J. (1995). Gatekeeping policies: terminating students for nonacademic reasons. Journal of Social Work Education, 31(2), 247-260.

Koerin, B. B., Harrigan, M. P., & Reeves, J. W. (1990). Facilitating the transition from student to social worker: Challenges of the younger student. Journal of Social Work Education, 26(2), 199-207.

Koeske, R. D, & Koeske, G. F. (1989). Working and non-working students: Roles, support and well-being. Journal of Social Work Education, 25(3), 244-256.

Kramer, H., Mathews, G., & Endias, R. (1987, Fall). Comparative stress levels in part-time and full-time social work programs. Journal of Social Work Education, (3), 74-80.

McClelland, R. W., Rindfleisch, N., & Bean, G., Jr. (1995). Rater adherence to evaluative criteria used in BSSW admissions. Arete, 16(2), 10-18.

Meinhert, R. G., & Dubansky, B. (1989). A comparison of accelerated and traditional MSW students: Twenty years later. Journal of Social Work Education, 25(2), 160-167.

Meier, M., & Long, D. D. (1998). Student disclosures in social work education: Does your program need a policy? The Journal of Baccalaureate Social Work, 4(1), 27-36.

Mokuau, N., & Ewalt, P. L. (1993). School-agency collaboration: Enriching teaching, scholarship, and service in state hospital placements. Journal of Social Work Education, 29(3), 328-337.

Moore, L. S., Dietz, T. J., & Jenkins, D. A. (1998). Issues in gatekeeping. The Journal of Baccalaureate Social Work, 4(1), 37-49.

Moore, L. S., & C. A. Urwin. (1990). Quality control in social work: The gatekeeping role in social work education. Journal of Teaching in Social Work, 4(1), 113-128.

O'Connor, I., & Dakgleish, L. (1986, Fall). The impact of social work education: A personal construct reconceptualization. Journal of Social Work Education, (3), 6-21.

Peterman, P. J., & B. Richard. (1986). The inappropriate BSW student. Arete, 11(1), 27-34.

Potts, M. K. (1992). Adjustment of graduate students to the education process: Effects of part-time enrollment and extracurricular roles. Journal of Social Work Education, 28(1), 61-76.

Reeser, L. C. (1992). Students with disabilities in practicum: What is reasonable accommodation? Journal of Social Work Education , 28(1), 98-109.

Rompf, E. L., & Royse, D. (1994). Choice of social work as a career: Possible influences. Journal of Social Work Education, 27(3), 290-296.

Schwartz, S., & Robinson, M. M. (1991). Attitudes toward poverty during undergraduate education. Journal of Social Work Education, 27 (3), 290-296.

Solas, J. (1990). Effective teaching as construed by social work students. Journal of Social Work Education, 26 (2), 145-154.

Thomas, R. (1987). Systems for guiding college student behavior: Punishment or growth? NASPA Journal, 2.5 (1), 54-61.

Zakutansky, T. J., & Sirles, E. A. (1993). Ethical and legal issues in field education: Shared responsibility and risk. Journal of Social Work Education, 29 (3), 338-347.

# Chapter 6

# Faculty and Staff Resources

The purpose of this chapter is to examine, from the perspective of a program director, the basic responsibilities that comprise academic program-based human resource administration. Basic human resource administrative responsibilities such as personnel recruitment, evaluation, and development will be examined within the organizational and governance framework of the college or university that houses the social work program, along with selected contemporary human resource administrative issues related to promoting program quality. An examination of environmental influences on human resource administration will need to emphasize the program personnel accrediting standards of the Council on Social Work Education.

One cannot overstate the importance of human resources in determining the effectiveness of the total academic enterprise and the need for administrative excellence in this program domain. The significance of this domain within the total academic enterprise is represented by the fact that funding for faculty, staff, and technical personnel, irrespective of program size or academic discipline configuration, represents approximately 80 percent of the total annual operating budget of a program. A review of the faculty and staff resources domain identified in Figure 1.1, reveals three generic position responsibilities directly related to program-based personnel responsibilities. These responsibilities are viewed as the basis for the personnel administrative tasks that permeate throughout each of the five interconnected program domains.

The significance of the human resources domain is also understood by research findings related to studies focused on program administration and development. Directors consistently reveal that the position responsibilities inherent in the human resources program domain are the administrative tasks in which training needs are the greatest, a significant source of role conflict, and is the program component in which a significant number of non-compliance factors related to CSWE program accreditation standards have been identified (Gibbs, 1995; Flax and Swaine, 1995; Gmelch and Miskin, 1995).

# Fundamental Human Resource Responsibilities

Institutional factors such as governance procedures, official sanction, and academic disciplinary structure or organization that houses the program, determine the personnel responsibilities that are the direct, formal position responsibilities of a social work program director. Some examples of the fundamental human resource responsibilities are listed in Figure 6.1. A complete listing of specific interrelated administrative responsibilities that compose the faculty and staff personnel domain is found in Appendix E. These responsibilities, as noted above, can be completed directly by a director or can be shared with or may be completed entirely by other administrative officials located within the organizational structure that houses the program and collaboration with other officials located within the formal personnel system of the institution. The tasks listed in Appendix E are arranged in a format that provides opportunity to assess the relative importance of the tasks within the context of a specific program and to locate the locus of assigned administrative responsibility. This administrative task assessment process provides a means to examine personnel management priorities and to identify personnel issues that are unique to a particular program.

Because of the significance and complexity of the personnel management process, a program director is functionally linked to human resource officials located throughout the college or university. Examples of administrative oversight responsibility that these officials have include personnel recruitment, employment, development, compensation, evaluation, and dismissal. Therefore, a review of the personnel responsibilities identified in Appendix E and the personnel handbook of the institution is a useful position orientation step for a new director.

## FIGURE 6.1

**Personnel Responsibilities - Examples**

- Planning and documenting short and long-term personnel needs.

- Conducting recruitment, selection, appointment, and development of all program-based academic and non-academic personnel in compliance with institutional, professional, and accreditation standards.

- Assigning faculty responsibilities such as teaching, research and student services in a manner that promotes work effectiveness, individual strengths/ interests, and program goals.

- Conducting annual performance evaluations of all employees; identifying performance goals and activities; providing orientation, training, and supervision of all personnel; and coordinating the provision of professional development programming.

- Approving documented personnel compensation reports to obtain timely payroll and benefits payments.

- Identifying unsatisfactory faculty and staff performance in a timely manner; initiating appropriate actions to rectify performance issues; evaluating outcome of administrative efforts.

- Maintaining a personnel file system that documents administrative decisions.

- Maintaining position descriptions for each academic and non-academic position, including position title, responsibilities, education and skill requirements, compensation ranges, and evaluation procedures.

# Institutional Personnel Administration Organization and Development Structure

Responsibility for human resource recruitment, selection, supervision, management and performance evaluation is delegated to the program director by the college or university, who must administratively collaborate with academic, training and technical support offices located throughout the institution. Administrative accountability requires a thorough understanding of the human resource structures, policies, and procedures of the institution; consequently, a review of the institution's personnel structure, responsibilities of personnel officials located within the administrative hierarchy and the personnel policies is a useful beginning point for a program director. A program director will want to develop a working relationships with a number of campus-based officials and to routinely involve the services provided by these officers when completing administrative tasks in this program domain. Offices such as employment, affirmative action/equal opportunity, personnel orientation and training, or legal counsel, for example, are key sources of specialized information and support services for a director.

An institutional-based example of a human resource structure is provided in Figure 6.2 to illustrate the director's coordinated use of the faculty and staff hiring, development, support, and evaluation responsibilities. This structure, illustrated in Figure 6.2, shows that the institution's human resources office responsibilities under the direction of the Office of the Provost, who provides administrative oversight of the Social Work program, along with the College of Sciences & Humanities, Human Resource Office, and Affirmative Action and Equal Opportunity Office. Employment oversight of students in positions of part-time program secretaries, for example, is found under the administrative auspices of the Office of Human Resources and Student Financial Aid.

It is also important to note that the administrative structure links a number of human resource assessment and development offices under the administrative oversight of an Associate Provost. These administrative and personnel development offices directly control human resource administration at the academic program level and represent institutional-based resources for development, collaboration, evaluation, compensation and recognition. An understanding of the specialized purpose of each office that controls, supports, rewards, and evaluates program-based human resources, along with having a working relationship with the officials that function within this program domain of the host institution, is necessary for effective academic program administration.

## Program Personnel

A quality baccalaureate program requires an array of academic, secretarial, technical, and administrative specialists who are supported by part-time student employees that provide a broad range of support services. Therefore, the personnel employed in a social work program may include full-time tenure-eligible faculty, full-time contract (non-tenure) faculty, part-time contract faculty, full-time and part-time professional staff such as secretaries and technicians, and part-time student employees.

The different categories of program-based personnel are subject to different personnel policies within the college or university and the manner in which the director works with them.

# FIGURE 6.2

## Institutional Human Resource Administration Organization and Development Structure

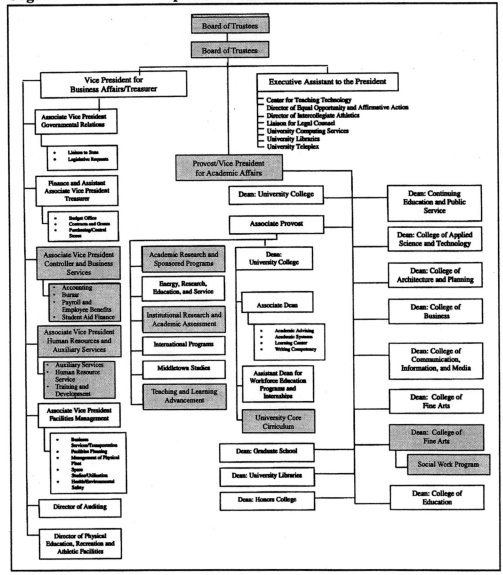

Student employment, for example, can be offered by the host institution as a form of financial assistance. Employment regulations determine the maximum number of hours a student can be employed, as well as the allowable tasks, and procedures for documenting the completion of work. New payroll regulations are different for full-time faculty personnel. For example, annual employment appointments are extended to tenure-eligible faculty members who have successfully completed a mandatory annual evaluation to determine acceptable progress in the performance areas of teaching, scholarship and professional service. The employment contract, usually approved by the institution's governing board, stipulates that a successful annual performance review has been completed. The review results in documentation of satisfactory performance, the salary for a specified academic year or calendar year, and identification of the person who will make position assignments and set additional employment conditions, such as completion of academic degree or specific scholarship outcomes. This annual evaluation to determine tenure eligibility usually occurs over a probation period of five to seven years, requires a signed acceptance by the faculty member, and increasingly includes a statement that the ultimate tenure decision will include consideration of the needs of the institution in light of enrollment, resource, and program trends. Therefore, appointment renewals and positive tenure recommendations are not automatic.

In contrast to students and staff, faculty is generally viewed as more autonomous and subject to fewer detailed personnel regulations on the length of the workday, vacation periods, and overtime pay. However, even the realm of daily work for faculty is undergoing a critical examination by external funding and legislative entities, who are challenging the accountability, relevancy, and productivity of higher education (Greenberg, 1993). If faculty members bargain collectively, the current union contract defines additional personnel regulations and procedures for the director to follow. The economic security and academic freedom of tenure, which historically has been a significant feature of faculty employment, is undergoing critical administrative and judicial review in response to increasing accountability demands by external funding and legislative entities (See for example, Hebel, 1999; and Wilson, 1999).

## Program Accreditation Standards

Accreditation standards are key guidelines that shape the selection, assignment, and development of faculty resources. Historically, CSWE program accrediting standards have represented a significant influence on human resource management in the social work program. therefore, an overview of this influence is provided. Additional information and accreditation-related content is presented in Chapter 7.

It is important that a program director understand and apply the intent of CSWE accreditation standards on human resources, communicate these standards to the various program constituencies, and help central administrative officials understand and support these accreditation requirements. The 1994 evaluation standards, for example, define minimum academic and social work practice credentials for faculty within specialized curriculum and administrative areas, prescribe the minimum number of faculty assigned full-time to the social work program, and detail human resource administrative requirements. As noted in Chapter 7, an important administrative practice is a careful reading of the exact language of the current accrediting standards in order to promote human resource quality.

# Managing Personnel Conflicts

Resolving personnel-based conflicts and formal grievances is an essential, time-consuming and stressful responsibility for the program director. It ranks among the most frequently cited reasons for leaving the position (Swaine & Flax, 1992). An earlier study of position role conflict by (Carroll, 1974; and Macy, 1990) determined that those faculty salary and promotion decisions, followed by academic tenure and faculty hiring decisions, were the most conflictive. Conflict in a program evolves from formal work relationships between members, faculty and students, faculty and staff personnel, and between the director and program personnel. The program director should not view conflict as a mark of personal failure; it exists naturally in the environment. However, the effective resolution of grievances among social work education personnel is extremely important. The effectiveness of the program depends upon an extraordinarily high level of faculty cooperation in order to coordinate instructional efforts, provide an integrated, non-redundant curriculum, and maintain focus on program outcomes agreed upon by all faculty.

Administrative decisions that can result in formal faculty and staff grievances include personnel issues such as tenure, promotion, salary recommendations, workload, performance evaluations, and work assignments. A growing number of personnel conflicts finding their way into the courts are related to discriminatory treatment and sexual harassment. One result of federal statutory protections and the growing prospect of legal review are that administrative decisions must become more fully documented, open, centralized, formalized, and systematic. Administrators must work to clearly define policies and procedures that were previously inconsistent, vague, or unfairly applied (Chait, 1995).

Clearly, the program director has a crisis management plan that includes a liability inventory (problems or situations that have potential to create a crisis), working relationships with administrative officials who can assist with resolving crisis situations, and knowledge of the institutional resources that can provide legal and personnel consultation. Personnel conflicts are confronted in a timely manner, and the director is familiar with both program-based and institution-based grievance procedures as documented in the operational manuals. Since its creation in 1915, the American Association of University Professors (AAUP) has provided leadership in promoting faculty welfare and interests. Many institutions incorporate AAUP procedures in their faculty grievance management structures.

The program director should focus on creating a climate in which conflicts are less likely to occur. Administrative practices such as sound course planning, program management, and systematic faculty evaluation can help create such a climate. An open climate of trust, respect, and opportunity to communicate informally can work to prevent conflict by having an "open door" access policy. Other ways of creating a positive climate include identifying meaningful work activities (such as making new, challenging, or more appropriate teaching assignments) and negotiating attractive incentives within the institutional reward system (such as securing additional travel funds and research time).

Conflict, which can be both a motivating and a destructive force in working relationships, is a natural dimension of any program's work climate. Effective management with the overall aim of promoting harmony among personnel is a goal for the director. Effective conflict management has no one formula for success. A director uses a blending of competencies such as interpersonal skills including respect, trust, bargaining, negotiating and influencing; sensitivity to group process and relationships; clear sense of program goals and purpose; ethical clarity and commitment; organizational astuteness; knowledge of self and colleagues; and willingness to shoulder leader responsibilities and risks. Tucker (1984) has identified administrative guidelines for addressing conflict situations in an academic program setting. An adapted list of these have been placed into four categories of administrative guidelines and are presented in Figure 6.3.

# Academic Program-Based Human Resource Administration Arenas

The human resources of the academic program, as previously noted, are the foundation of the entire educational enterprise. Quality personnel translate into quality programming. Faculty and staff personnel whose overall performance is consistently substandard not only limit a program in terms of

# FIGURE 6.3

## Administrative Guidelines for Conflict Management

Professional - Working Relationships

- Keep in touch with the feelings, attitudes, and personal crises of faculty members. Through frequent meetings, the director can discover latent conflict situations before they emerge.
- Be sensitive to faculty members with personal problems but do not necessarily get involved.

Communication

- Use techniques of active listening to raise morale and to understand the perceptions of faculty members who might be engaged in conflict.
- As soon as possible, clarify misconceptions that might cause conflict.
- Communicate clearly with the faculty about any unprecedented action that might cause conflict.

Governance - Administrative Oversight

- Be aware of the current and growing tensions in the program and the host institution.
- Structure the program's formal decision procedures in such a manner that conflicts can be discussed, aired, and dealt with through normal governance procedures.
- Do not take sides in a conflict that does not concern the welfare of the program.
- Find out whether disputants perceive the stakes as high or low. If they are perceived as high, try to reduce them.
- Be prepared to make discreet inquiries about reported potential and actual conflict.
- When appropriate, use faculty committees to establish policies and procedures that govern situations in which conflicts have occurred and might occur in the future.
- Do not violate laws or institutional regulations when dealing with conflict.

Mediation - Problem Solving

- Intervene only if the operation of the personnel is impaired.
- In cases of conflict, determine what conflicting values are held by the parties.
- Do not intervene in conflicts unless you have reason to believe that intervention can help the situation.
- Find out whether parties believe the conflict is amenable to solution. Try to persuade them that solutions are possible.
- Try to change any conflict to an opportunity to problem solving.
- Be prepared to be called as a witness to or observer of a conflict. Keep records of action and involvement in conflicts.

that individual's work assignments, but also tend to (1) damage the moral level of all personnel; (2) reduce program productivity; (3) lessen the quality of program governance and (4) foster personnel tensions and conflicts. Consequently, the performance of the academic program director in this program domain directly builds and shapes overall program quality. Critical basic processes with some examples of some administrative practices that are necessary for building and maintaining productive personnel are illustrated in Figure 6.4, which can be used as an organizing framework for examining the program domain. The administrative processes related to these interrelated human resource dimensions will be described.

## FIGURE 6.4

### Human Resource Administration Leadership Dimensions*

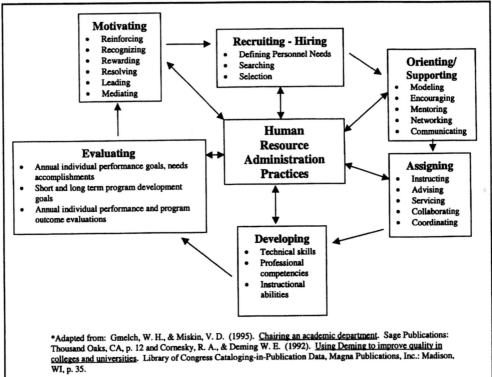

*Adapted from: Gmelch, W. H., & Miskin, V. D. (1995). Chairing an academic department. Sage Publications: Thousand Oaks, CA, p. 12 and Cornesky, R. A., & Deming W. E. (1992). Using Deming to improve quality in colleges and universities. Library of Congress Cataloging-in-Publication Data, Magna Publications, Inc.: Madison, WI, p. 35.

# Recruitment and Selection Procedures

A useful starting point in examining human resource administration is to place administrative tasks inherent in this program domain within the context of the entire academic enterprise. The overriding importance of the program personnel to the quality, stability, and future of the program necessitates a director to view the recruitment of new employees as an integral part of the program's systematic evaluations and long-range development plans. Even when primary personnel recruitment responsibilities are delegated to a search committee and various human resources offices located throughout the host institution must be involved in the recruitment process, direct administrative oversight of the search process is imperative and the day-to-day contact with every program employee rests with the director.

Even though the personnel procurement process can differ to a degree in order to match the administrative structure, policies, procedures, and traditions of the host institution, the director ensures that the basic steps of personnel recruitment, selection, and hiring, occurs to fill a faculty or staff vacancy. These steps, which are administratively coordinated by a program director and completed in collaboration with faculty colleagues and institutional-based officials, described as applied to the process of filling a faculty position vacancy, which tends to be a more complex procedure compared to hiring secretarial and technical staff personnel.

To promote program development when filling a position vacancy, the director might include in the position vacancy description the outcomes of Strengths, Weaknesses, Opportunities, Threats (SWOT) analysis (Stoner and Fry, 1987). From a SWOT or similar type of program assessment process, both minimum and preferred qualifications can be identified in order to (1) define the position within continuing faculty resource needs, (2) identify professional specialization's needed to address current and future curriculum trends of the program, (3) define performance and academic competencies needed when creating descriptions of position vacancies, and (4) evaluate each viable applicant objectively as a resource for both current and future program developmental needs. Following this appraisal step, the next step in filling a position vacancy or adding program personnel is to develop a documented rationale to obtain formal approval from the central administration of the host institution of the position vacancy using an approved draft position description to advertise, select, and recommend applicants.

## Position Vacancy Description

The position vacancy description should include two major categories of information. The first category of information includes:

- A summary of the overall position teaching, research, and professional service responsibilities.

- Stature of the academic program and selected distinguishing characteristics.

- Location of the host institution and unique opportunities.

Figure 6.5 provides in the form of a faculty position vacancy listing the second category of information that should be included in a position vacancy announcement in order to provide an accurate comprehensive description for review by applicants.

## FIGURE 6.5

### Faculty Position Vacancy Listing Example

Information Categories:

1. Description and name of your academic program, department and institution, including the following:
   - Mission statement
   - Particular clientele served
   - Degrees and/or certificates granted

2. Academic rank of the opening and position status (tenure-track, full-time, contract, etc.)

3. Descriptions of teaching, research, and service responsibilities, academic/curriculum specialties, and other faculty duties.

4. Minimum qualifications, specification of academic degree, professional/academic experience required, etc.

5. Preferred qualifications such as advanced academic specialties, research competencies, and instructional methods.

6. Special characteristics or expertise desired such as areas of specialization, or the ability to work in a team environment.

7. Starting date of applicant screening.

8. Starting date of employment.

9. Statement of special considerations, e.g. encouraging disabled persons, veterans, minorities, and women to apply.

10. How to apply, including name, address and telephone number of contact person and application requirements such as placement file and current letters of recommendation, sample of a single authored writing sample, World Wide Web address, etc.

Program-based planning and evaluation data, therefore, represent a major source of information for the development of qualifications to determine if the program needs a full-time faculty addition or has, for example, greater need for contracting with several part-time specialty-oriented instructors. An officially approved position vacancy description is also needed to objectively evaluate and select candidates, and to assess the fit between program needs and the professional competencies of finalists (Klein, Weisman & Smith, 1996).

## Faculty Search and Selection

A second step in the faculty recruitment process is the need to organize a program-based task group of faculty and other appropriate program stakeholders to complete the selection and recommendation process is a second step in the faculty recruitment process.

In order to involve a cross-section of program constituencies, provide an accurate representation of the program and the institution to applicants, efficiently complete a labor-intensive process and, ultimately, identify the most desirable applicants, a committee structure is used for faculty personnel search and selection. Faculty personnel committees may be created on an *ad hoc* basis, or in large programs may exist as a standing entity. Because the institution's governing board must officially make faculty appointments, faculty personnel decisions are essentially recommendations that make their way through the administrative structures of the institution's personnel decision hierarchy until a final contract is issued to the recommended applicant.

Throughout the process, the director seeks to promote the complementary between and among program factors as the program's goals, culture, and mission, and long-term program advancement priorities; short and long range personnel needs; interests, strengths and gaps in the current faculty resources; planned faculty retirements, shifts in institutional priorities; professional and accreditation trends; alternative full-time and part-time staffing patterns; and faculty performance evaluation resources. Annual performance evaluations, for example, can help a director maintain a sense of where each faculty and staff member is in their career paths, who might be leaving for other employment, health and personal issues, retirement planning, and other personal, professional, and career factors that will influence continuing employment. As a result, program vacancies can be filled in a planful manner with evolutionary type processes that reflect personnel trends, along with human resource needs to accommodate program changes, goals and evolving mission. The ability to express the mission, goals, and long-term development plans of the program is also an important dimension of presenting a favorable image of the program to high-demand candidates and being able to accent the positive aspects of the program, institution, and geographic location.

Because baccalaureate social work program requires diverse faculty, a variety of formal and informal techniques are used to make position openings known to a broad range of qualified people. Distributing the position vacancy announcement is an important process to help assure that the recruitment net is cast as widely as possible to get the best pool of candidates. Information networks within the professional and academic social work community should supplement the formal position announcements that the host institution routinely list in publications such as the *Chronicle of Higher Education*.

Examples of information distribution methods and aggressive faculty search approaches would include the following:

- List position vacancies on the institution's homepage and link the description of the program to that site to enable readers to gain an overview of both the college and university as well as the program context for the vacancy.

- Target mailing of position vacancies to potential sources of candidates such as social work doctoral programs.

- Mail personal letters to colleagues asking for recommendations of possible candidates.

- Focus listing of position vacancies in publications that are routinely read by social work practitioners and educators such as the NASW News, Social Work Education Reporter published by CSWE and the BPD UPDATE Newsletter.

- Post Position vacancies on selected listserves such as the one provided by the Association of Baccalaureate Program Directors.

- Individualized mailing to follow-up any inquires that includes such information as fact sheets that identify program and institutional characteristics, strengths and development plans and a community profile provided by the local chamber of commerce.

- Publish listing in sources identified by the institution's affirmative action office in order to promote a broader diversity of applicants.

- Regional and national conferences are an excellent source for completing a variety of recruitment efforts such as talking with possible candidates and making informal contacts designed to solicit recommendations.

## Candidate Screening and Selection

Candidate screening and selection are steps used to review the applicant pool. After advertising the position vacancy and collecting applications, the screening process begins. The screening and selection process consists of a basic process, although unique faculty search and selection procedures that conform to institutional-specific search policies, procedures, collective bargaining agreement stipulations, and affirmative action requirements are addressed.

The director's administrative oversight responsibilities related to the screening and interviewing phase involves orienting committee members by providing selection information used for decision making throughout the process (initial informal contact, first-level selection, final offer, etc.) with focus on such factors as: time frame of the screening and campus interviewing effort; institutional policies and procedures; state and federal affirmative action guidelines; labor contract agreements and legal requirements governing the interviewing; and information gathering procedures are used in the candidate assessment process.

## FIGURE 6.6

### Administrative Oversight of Personnel Recruitment And Selection Process

Administrative oversight of the search committee's recruitment and selection phase requires the program director to be certain the following tasks are completed:

1. Orient members of the search committee to such factors as program personnel needs, program evaluative reports identifying strengths and weaknesses, human resource policies and procedures of the institution, and the institution's affirmative action/equality opportunity requirements.

2. Monitor the policies, procedures and traditions of the institution in order to hire the most suitable faculty members.

3. Apply the officially approved position vacancy description to create a pool of applicants, complete formal evaluation and each qualified applicant, and select the top two or three candidates for campus-based interviews.

4. Adhere to all legal and contractual guidelines for personnel hiring.

Committee members individually evaluate each application by using a checksheet, which identifies all of the minimum and preferred qualifications identified in the official position vacancy description. From this process, candidates who meet all qualifications are then selected and the committee completes professional references either by mail or telephone. The goal is to identify two or three candidates who would be invited to complete a campus visit that would include a series of interviews with program and institutional officials, complete a teaching presentation, and be given opportunity to meet with program stakeholders.

## Campus-Based Candidate Interviewing

Because of the importance of the campus visit, which provides both candidates and the selection committee members opportunity to complete their respective assessments, careful planning, scheduling, and staffing of this process is essential (Perlman and McCann, 1997). Some important campus interview planning considerations are listed in Figure 6.7.

## FIGURE 6.7

### Campus Interviewing Considerations

- **Design** the visit to provide opportunities for individual and group interviews with representatives of every program constituency and institutional officers.

- **Plan** for the completion of teaching or formal presentations.

- **Arrange** institutional and community tours by a knowledgeable committee member.

- **Establish** staff assignments for the scheduling details such as transporting candidates, meals, preparation of printed visitation agenda, housing arrangements, etc.

- **Complete** a mailing prior to the visit including orientation materials that describe the program, curriculum, institution, community, etc.

- **Ascertain** special needs and interests of candidates prior to visit so that accommodations can be completed.

- **Structure** closure of the visit or exit interview to clarify information, answer questions to inform candidates of next steps, get a sense of the candidate's receptiveness to the opportunity, ascertain candidates decision process and make plans for a follow-up contact.

- **Complete** necessary arrangements or obtain prior administrative approval to extend a salary offer and employment related factors such as fringe benefits and academic rank

If an employment agreement with the first priority candidate cannot be reached, an offer can be extended to the next candidate in order of priority. After a finalist accepts the offer, the director remains the key contact for the new faculty member, forwarding personnel data to the institution and assisting the new faculty member with relocating and getting started in the new position.

Staff hiring is similar to faculty hiring, but is governed more directly by the human resource systems of the host institution. These bureaucratic systems require specific position descriptions, salary levels, and technical competencies. Professional staff such as secretaries, budget officers, administrative coordinators, and technicians is significant in helping set the tone of an academic program. For example, because of the scope and volume of information management that occurs at the social work program level, program secretaries often function as administrative assistants to program directors. They supervise part-time student workers and answer student inquiries. Therefore, faculty participation in the selection of professional support personnel is advisable.

# Personnel Orientation — Support Development

The baccalaureate social work orientation process needs to address the differing needs of the two major groups of individuals who enter social work education. Faculty members who come to educational programs from professional practice after having a taste of education by serving perhaps as a field practicum instructor or as a part-time adjunct instructor brings essentiallya practice orientation to classroom instruction (Webb, 1984). Even though some dimensions of this orientation may be helpful in the instructional role, a structured orientation process may be completed to add specialized knowledge and skills needed for effective teaching. Information such as comparative learning models, varied instructional strategies, course planning and organization, and alternative academic evaluation approaches are examples of specific types of information that a practitioner may need upon entering an educational role.

Faculty members who enter baccalaureate education directly from a research oriented doctoral degree program may also need similar information as that of the practice oriented instructor plus the need to acquire an understanding of specific nature of undergraduate education and practice as compared to an advance research oriented degree program. Role orientation issues such as learning to provide academic advising, teaching content related to beginning or baccalaureate professional competencies and functioning as a member of an instructional team within a prescribed curriculum structure may be common needs of faculty with newly acquired doctoral degrees.

Fully, some have performed social work instruction in such roles as field practicum or served as adjunct faculty in order to assess interest in full time teaching. These faculty may have a rich practice framework but have limited knowledge regarding instructional methods. Practice knowledge and skills cannot be directly transferred to the role of a social work educator; therefore, new faculty may need mentoring to acquire educator competencies. Knowledge about various learning models, skill in applying varied instructional approaches, course planning and organization, academic evaluation methods and curriculum are examples of information needs.

Six cultural spheres or dimensions of a social work program help to define the kind of orientation needed by social work faculty members. Each of these are identified below:

1. **Academic Discipline**: Social work in higher education is a distinct academic enterprise. This cultural dimension, which shapes the fit of the social work program within the academic community, includes characteristics such as its integrated curriculum that includes experiential, affective, and cognitive oriented learning expectations; specialized program outcomes, governance and autonomy structures; and a structured field practicum operation.

   A dimension of a quality accredited program is that curriculum content is carefully selected and structured in order to achieve defined program outcomes. Educational outcomes for each require course and curriculum sub-units or sequences such as human behavior and the social environment are defined. Figure 8.1 provides an illustration of a curriculum structure and sequences within the context of program mission, goals and rationale.

   A quality social work curriculum is structured vertically from introductory to advanced content between the required curriculum content sequences, as well as to insure that specified content flows across the knowledge, values, skills and purposes of the social work profession. The delivery of a unified curriculum in turn requires a structured instruction plan that provides the integration of cognitive, affective and experiences learning opportunities to move students across the learning continuum. This continuum begins with the initial acquisition of theoretical information and moves toward the performance phase where empirically based or anchored application of professional knowledge is demonstrated. A structured, unified outcome oriented in social work curriculum thereby requires faculty to teach prescribed "program-based content" as opposed to an "instructor preference content".

The combined professional and academic degree program characteristics are a part of its culture. Program features such as admission and retention standards, professional and academic advising and university based academic, psychological and specialized services used by social work students should be covered in orientation.

2. **Professional Discipline**: This cultural dimension is anchored in CSWE program accrediting standards, and includes influences from the NASW and various professional licensing entities, as well as the competing human service professions. Examples of information needed by new faculty include the organization and leadership of the state, regional, and local NASW operations; structure and organization of the state-based social work education associations; and specifications of the state social work licensing requirements.

3. **Program Standards**: This cultural dimension includes influences from accreditation standards and professional competencies required of entry-level practitioners. Examples are admission screening requirements, student rights, academic advising, and curriculum content and structure.

4. **Institutional Environment**: This cultural dimension includes influences from the history, mission, formal rituals, symbols, and leaders of the college or university. The institutional environment influence factors such as funding, the personnel reward system and program priorities. Examples of specific information in this sphere include governance structures and processes, faculty personal, psychological, social, and professional support resources, and reward and advancement operations.

5. **National System of Higher Education**: The rich historical development of the academy shapes the basic attitudes toward matters such as the function of higher education in American society, the development of knowledge, and the governance of these institutions. Access to periodicals such as the *Chronicle of Higher Education* keeps the program director informed of the scope, trends, and special issues facing higher education. These periodicals should be made available to new faculty.

6. **Instructional Orientation**: The delivery of a structured outcome oriented social work curriculum that compels students to demonstrate mastery of defined professional competencies, as previously noted, requires each faculty member to perform within the context of an instructional team as opposed to teaching as an autonomously oriented academic specialist. An individual and collective understanding by faculty members of the total curriculum content, sequence, and structure, along with the outcomes of each required course, is useful in advancing curriculum and institutional development. This understanding and instructional orientation is complemented by each faculty member's adherence to collectively defined course objectives. This type of collaboratively oriented instructional posture as a faculty member represents a highly coordinated and cooperative instructional orientation that requires deliberate efforts by a director to build and maintain in order to deliver a high quality social work curriculum.

# Mentoring of Social Work Faculty Members

Although institutional orientation can acquaint the new employee with facilities, benefit programs, support services, and general employment practices, a mentoring program for new faculty and professional personnel is recommended for socializing individuals into the academic, professional, and social milieu of the social work program. The effectiveness of a well-structured mentoring program in an academic setting is widely documented (Merriam, 1983; Cain, 1977). The feedback from a mentor provides an effective supplement to the annual performance evaluation. The mentor provides information, role modeling, guidance, and support. A faculty mentor can serve as an "institutional door opener" to help the new employee begin networking. He or she can introduce teaching and research resources such as audio-visual materials, course preparation tips, teaching practices, and norms in the program (Merriam, 1983). Faculty mentor relationships normally exist for one academic year, and then are replaced by peer or college-based consultation and collaboration activities in which all faculty members participate.

Mentoring faculty members works most powerfully when it is a formal structured process in which the director matches and assigns designated faculty members or, in small programs, engage the entire social work faculty in coaching, supporting, and orienting a new colleague. Furthermore, the director provides faculty development support by consistently demonstrating genuine concern for a faculty member's professional development and career progress, securing financial support to enable participation in professional development opportunities, facilitating membership in interests, professional, and interdisciplinary support/task groups, creating work assignments that build on professional strengths, interests, and challenges, and addressing institutional barriers for career advancement (York, Henley and Gamble, 1988; Gmelch and Miskin, 1995).

# Work Assignments

Completing annual faculty teaching, student services, scholarship, professional service, and program-based administrative assignments is a complex process that requires a director to systematically consider a range of program and human resource factors as well as maximizing the effectiveness of faculty resources. These include short-term program development and operational priorities, strengths, interests, and expertise of faculty members, program outcome evaluation data, and evolving student needs. Managing the course scheduling and making faculty work assignments, therefore, is a key administrative responsibility of an academic program director and represents a complex administrative responsibility that can raise issues for students, individual faculty members, and the program operations.

The program director is typically responsible for assigning faculty to teaching, student services, administrative, research, and professional service activities. In doing so, he/she attempts to match the personal strengths, interests, and professional development needs of faculty members with the needs and priorities of the program. This complex process requires careful planning, communication, and negotiation.

The degree to which the program director makes, supervises, and evaluates work assignments varies among institutions. Some institutions hold the director fully responsible for the effective use of human resources. At other institutions, faculty members determine their own teaching, research, and professional assignments, whereas the director coordinates resources such as classroom space, educational materials, and secretarial support. If the program operates under a collective bargaining agreement, faculty workload assignment procedures are explicitly defined; if the program is small, informal discussions might suffice to determine course offerings that effectively accommodate student needs and interests. The trend, however, is toward increased accountability for the director and required adherence to all institutional policies and procedures.

Work assignments for faculty as noted previously involves long-term planning and the systematic use of evaluation data in order to strategically enhance program quality. Therefore, a program director completing workload assignments may consider the following factors:

- Institutional faculty workload policies and procedures related to teaching, research, and professional service.

- Position descriptions and contractual agreements that were used to recruit and hire each faculty member, which identifies basic work assignments and performance expectations.

- Historical patterns of course offerings, which are adjusted incrementally to accommodate such factors as shifting student enrollment, faculty interests, and curriculum modifications.

- The interests, expertise, and preferences of individual faculty members within the context of career and professional development plans.

- Institutional and external sources of grant and financial support opportunities that can be accessed to promote faculty development.

An annual master course plan is a method for a director to identify course offerings and assign faculty two or three years into the future. The master course plan lets students know when specific courses will be offered, so they can plan for completing their degree requirements. The master course plan also gives the director an opportunity to discuss evolving professional interests with each faculty member and allot research time to faculty members without jeopardizing the courses students need. Making long-range assignments enhances the work environment and reduces stress for new faculty members. The program director writes load reports listing the course assignments completed each academic term, formal reports describing the outcome of assigned research, and an annual program report describing the significant accomplishments, needs, and priorities of the program.

A significant workload assignment consideration by a program director may be the tenure eligibility requirements of the college or university and the tenure status of each faculty member. The relationship between workload assignments, professional development and academic tenure are examined later in this chapter. A common requirement of faculty members, especially in larger sized social work programs, is the need for faculty to successfully demonstrate instructional, service and scholarship competencies during the pre-tenure phase of appointment (Sansone, Bedics and Rappe, 2000). Therefore, a key administrative guideline is that institutional-based tenure and academic promotion requirements are inextricably linked to the types of teaching, service and research assignments that faculty members must complete in order to develop credible tenure and academic promotion outcome evaluation documentation.

# Development of Faculty

Instructional team building, which is of fundamental importance to overall program quality, requires the director to promote the technical skills, professional competencies, and instructional abilities of each faculty member and for the faculty as a whole. The socialization of an academic scholar into the role of a social work faculty team member requires a deliberate effort (Webb, 1984). Planned opportunities for faculty members to observe the performance of colleagues, collaborate in assigned projects, report professional development workshops, and demonstrate successful instructional approaches are examples of modeling oriented development strategies.

The program director should continually strive to introduce professional development practices to improve the program and revitalize personnel. Other administrative approaches designed to foster professional growth include

- Have a monthly "show-and-tell" gathering in which faculty members can explain and discuss innovative teaching techniques and research activities.

- Schedule courses in a more flexible way to provide "release time" for faculty scholarship and professional activities. For example, combine two sections of the same course, or schedule class meetings one or two nights per week.

- Modeling is an example of a viable approach that an academic program administrator can use to systematically orchestrate faculty orientation and professional development as well as promoting higher performance norms within the program.

- Develop new teaching assignments. Try team teaching, or encourage teachers to develop new curriculum content for their courses or design new elective course offerings, which focus on an evolving practice or professional focus.

- Host informal luncheons and receptions to recognize faculty accomplishments. Creating a social service research and program consultation entity within an accredited social work program is another means to revitalize the program and its personnel. A program-based research and consultation center can provide structured opportunities for faculty, including:

- Develop a in-service training of staff employed, for example, in public child welfare or private organizations that provide family violence services.

- Participate in program development, research, and evaluation services, such as community needs studies and pilot program evaluations.

- Offer contractual technical services to human service organizations, such as questionnaire construction, coding, data entry and data analysis.

- Encourage and support the development of both formal and informal information and support networks among faculty with colleagues in allied disciplines and community-based practitioners.

Focus by the director on strengthening the essential partnership between social work practice and education required for an effective field instruction program is a continuing need. The creation of a faculty-staffed research and service center, for example, can help a program fulfill its public service mission, increase its external resources (for example, by hiring part-time instructors or supplementing faculty travel), and in general improve a program's work environment, faculty morale, and overall vitality.

A number of researchers identify the increasing emphasis at both the baccalaureate and graduate social work educational levels as being placed on scholarly productivity in order for programs to become more firmly anchored into the host institution and for faculty to succeed in the academy (Bloom & Klein, 1995; Green & Bentley, 1994; Green & Secret, 1996; Hull, 1991; Johnson & Hull, 1995; and Ligon, Thyer & Dixon, 1995). Therefore, program directors facilitate the development of faculty scholarship by providing support, opportunities, and assistance in this realm of faculty position responsibilities. The following is a list of strategies identified by Hull (1991); and Creswell & Brown (1992) that directors reported as being useful to encourage the publication aspects of the faculty scholarship role:

Along with trends in higher education toward increased accountability, efficiency, and productivity, there is a growing plea for a more balanced relationship between teaching and scholarship. Boyer (1990) notes that college and university emphasis on research has been so overwhelming that faculty are rewarded for publications over all else. Social work knowledge can be created and disseminated in a variety of ways beyond the use of standard refereed

**FIGURE 6.8**

**Administrative Strategies for Promoting Faculty Scholarships**

1. Provide advice and encouragement on the importance of publishing as a condition for tenure.

2. Reduce workload through lower teaching loads, modified schedules, release time and sabbaticals.

3. Provide funding for conference travel when faculty is presenting a paper.

4. Provide support for production costs such as typing, supplies, postage, computer searches, work-study students and consultants.

5. Keep faculty informed of writing opportunities such as calls for journal or conference papers.

6. Provide study or research grants to faculty.

7. Recognize publicly productive faculty to administration, students and peers.

8. Advocate, collaborate, guide and provide mentoring resources for faculty.

9. Encourage faculty to collaborate on research with other faculty including one's self.

10. Assist faculty to explore possible funding sources to support research.

11. Offer to critique papers for colleagues.

12. Model scholarship through one's own efforts.

13. Create opportunities through one's own contacts as director.

publications, which historically have been the restricted basis for academic promotion, tenure, and monetary reward decisions. Contemporary colleges and universities are reviewing the teaching, scholarship, professional, and citizenship responsibilities inherent in the role of a faculty member. This review is being promoted by external pressures for higher education institutions to become accountable to the public that provides financial support, the need to clarify the ambiguous weighting of teaching, research, and service in the traditional institutional reward systems, and an effort to increase the relevancy of academic work to meeting the needs of contemporary society.

A faculty performance and work assignment framework has been designed by Boyer in an effort to expand the parameters used in evaluating academic contributions. The Boyer Model, as noted in Chapter 2, recognizes four types of scholarship (Boyer, 1990, pp. 15-25). These types include

1. **Teaching.** The scholarship of teaching requires a faculty member to engage and encourage students to become active learners and critical thinkers and to also communicate their pedagogy to academic peers.

2. **Discovery.** The scholarship of discovery requires a faculty member to test ideas with academic peers and to communicate ideas in both traditional ways (such as refereed journals) and in other professional formats that are currently evolving (such as video productions and teleconferencing).

3. **Integration.** This type of scholarship involves giving meaning to the products of discovery scholarship by applying them to larger intellectual patterns or perspectives. This process, for example, could include using media to convey knowledge to non-specialists.

4. **Application.** This type of scholarship involves applying knowledge to problems outside the institution. The faculty member develops a proactive outreach effort to establish collaborative linkages between the academy and the contemporary needs of society.

Boyer concludes, "We need scholars who not only skillfully explore the frontiers of knowledge, but also integrate ideas, connect thought to action, and inspire students." (p. 77)

As a faculty evaluation and development process, the application of the Boyer Model within a program is based on the belief that teaching, scholarship, and professional service are interrelated and complementary faculty responsibilities; therefore, they are inherently reinforcing to each other. The integration of scholarship, teaching, and service responsibilities of social work faculty is an implicit dimension of CSWE faculty resource accrediting standards and is a growing dimension of quality social work educational programming. The interview can also be the basis for achieving academic tenure as new faculty complete the 5-7 year pre-tenure phase of employment. Excellence in teaching, service, and research are the three traditional areas of performance; this summative development process that a director can foster is examined in the evaluation section of this chapter.

Because social work education has a rich tradition of integrating the practice and academic communities to prepare students, it is well positioned to more fully apply the scholarship model that Boyer advocates. The program director can work toward expanding the definition of academic scholarship by enlarging the definition of scholarship outcomes within the program and developing coalitions with other applied disciplines such as nursing, journalism, and telecommunications to create more appropriate criteria for tenure, merit, and promotion evaluations. Applied disciplines need to consider significant professional tasks and use a broader basis for promotion and tenure. Evaluation criteria for social work faculty reflects social work's traditional commitment to contemporary social needs as well as a concern for effective teaching.

# Performance Evaluation

Faculty evaluation, when based on clearly specified performance standards and coupled with reasonable work assignments and ongoing professional development, has significant potential for strengthening the program over time. The program director's responsibility for performance evaluations is ordinarily defined in the personnel or operations manual of the institution and is another major component of human resource administration responsibilities of a program director. Again, this may or may not be a position responsibility that a director completes as defined by the program administrator or governance standard.

Performance evaluations are a significant basis for decisions on retention, tenure, promotion, and salary increases. A strong argument can be made that facilitating the growth of faculty and staff through a systematic development and evaluation plan is one of the director's most important responsibilities. The scope and complexities of faculty performance evaluation processes represent the single focus of a number of academic program administration publications (Seldin, 1985; Arreola, 1995; Braskamp & Ory, 1994; and Boice, 1992). Therefore, an overview of performance evaluation is provided here with the invitation for the reader to study this position responsibility in depth by reviewing the sources cited. Because of the significance of the academic tenure processes in higher education, this process will be examined.

A formal personnel assessment process can help achieve personal, professional, and program goals and balance the faculty responsibilities of teaching, professional service, and scholarship (Seagren, Creswell, & Wheeler, 1993). The benefits of a personnel assessment process is identified in Figure 6.9.

## FIGURE 6.9

**Personnel Assessment Benefits**

- Defines specific work expectations and priorities.

- Helps personnel define and pursue long and short-term performance goals and maintain focus on outcomes.

- Establishes a written record of performance accomplishments, which can be used in making informed personnel decisions.

- Promotes continuing communication between the program director and program personnel, with a focus on performance feedback and planning.

- Integrates assessment into other administrative responsibilities such as resource development, accountability, utilization, and allocation.

- Strengthens an individual's sense of appreciation and promotes collegiality.

- Enhances the sense of professional development and program-based support.

- Promotes retention of faculty and fosters a positive program atmosphere for all personnel.

- Enhances ongoing self-development responsibility within a work environment that values academic freedom, personal respect, and professional integrity.

- Promotes program renewal to accommodate shifts in student demographics, curriculum content, and professional standards.

A personnel evaluation consists of two separate but overlapping components: a *summative* process, in which the director makes decisions related to position advancement, and *normative* process, which focuses on professional development. The formative process continues throughout the academic year as the program director and the faculty member work together to achieve goals. The summative evaluation marks the end of one cycle and the beginning of the next. This annual cycle of collaborative planning, followed by a formal evaluation, moves the program toward defined goals while it moves faculty and staff toward professional potential.

Whereas the summative evaluation focuses on past accomplishments, the formative process is forward-looking. It requires commitments from the individual and the program to shared goals. Each faculty or professional staff member submits a plan identifying performance development goals and activities for the coming year. Faculty goals might be in the areas of teaching, administrative service and program development, research, scholarship and publication, or professional service. After receiving the director's approval, the plan becomes an outline for the self-assessment reports that are completed the following year by each employee and the program director. The final outcome of the process is a rating of "satisfactory" or "unsatisfactory" in each of the four basic faculty performance areas including research, scholarship, publications, and administrative service. Additional position-related performance competencies can be added to the generic responsibilities such as technical competencies and resource development abilities.

Points associated with the rating can be used to determine, for example, the faculty member's percentage of annual merit pay increase. Institutional level promotion, tenure, and budgetary decisions are usually made prior to the end of each fiscal year to coordinate with annual budgeting and auditing cycles. Therefore, the summative evaluation of faculty at the program level usually occurs during the fall semester of the academic year. It is based on a tenure, promotion, and performance evaluation process specific to the program. Developing criteria for evaluation is a serious issue. A list of administrative considerations that a director should recognize when conducting faculty-centered evaluations are identified in Figure 6.10.

A professional portfolio is an increasingly popular answer to identify the types and scope of performance outcome documentation. Faculty members can use a portfolio to document their work in a variety of ways, including

- Publications

- Field instruction documents

- Letters of recognition

- Course descriptions

- Student course evaluations

- Peer evaluations

- Videocassettes

- Computer-assisted teaching materials / software

The teaching portfolio has been called "a factual description of a professor's major strengths and teaching achievements... which collectively suggest the scope and quality of a professor's teaching performance" (Seldin, 1991, p. 3). The portfolio is being used increasingly in professional programs such as social work to document faculty performance beyond the traditional "publish-or-perish" criteria. It encourages a more realistic balance among scholarship, teaching, and professional service responsibilities.

The portfolio approach offers distinct benefits to social work program personnel. It helps faculty members report outcomes of teaching, especially alternative methods such as experiential, field-based, simulation, and computer-assisted instruction. It expands the definition of scholarship to include such items as writing program manuals (such as field/practicum, student services monographs) and designing new, innovative courses. It also underscores the value of high quality professional and academic advising services.

## FIGURE 6.10

### Faculty Performance Evaluation Guidelines

- Faculty and staff evaluation is an imprecise process; multiple sources (e.g. students and colleagues) of performance data should be applied.

- Effective human resource evaluation is not a once-a-year formal activity, but it should be an individual process of periodic formal and informal communication between each employee and the director that routinely provides timely feedback that notes positive performance accomplishment, as well as needed improvements or concerns.

- Criteria for evaluating performance and agreement on specific evidence that will be examined must be clearly defined.

- Performance in work that involves "people processing activities" is difficult to measure because it is not possible to separate the influences of the work system or the collective effort from the influences of individual efforts.

- Performance evaluations must be focused on goals that are clear, behaviorally specific, realistic, manageable and foster self-appraisal, goal setting, and program commitment.

- There must be agreement about what should be evaluated within a position description; clearly defined performance objectives for the next evaluation period and specific indicators of performance success.

- Numerous sources of quantitative and qualitative assessment data should be used. Possible sources include student evaluations, peer reviews, and self-reports.

- Evaluation reports should be formal, written systematic procedures based on documented performance outcomes with examples, report strengths, limitations, and needed improvements that identify suggestions for improvement; and be completed in the context of program development.

- Evaluation, although systematic, must be individualized and based on standardized performance norms to foster personal and professional commitment.

- Motivation, evaluation, and communication development are inextricably related human resource administrative responsibilities that promote performance effectiveness of personnel and program operations.

# The Tenure Review Process

The cornerstone of faculty development is academic tenure and represents a key program-based administrative responsibility of a program director. Academic tenure, in general means that after a faculty member has successfully completed a five to seven year probationary period of employment, there is assurance of continued, permanent employment unless there are unforeseen circumstances such as financial exigencies or the academic program is closed. The awarding of academic tenure essentially guarantees "life-long" employment of a faculty member; therefore, a program director develops a thorough understanding of the faculty tenure procedures of the college or university in order to either directly administer or provide oversight of this significant personnel development and continuing employment process.

Tenure and promotion in academic rank are related, therefore these two decision procedures may be separate or combined within the college or university, therefore administrative procedures at the program-level should be designed accordingly. Since the tenure and promotion review and recommendation process begin with a peer review process at the academic program level, the social work program or the organizational unit which houses the program may also have an approved, written tenure document that is tailored to the teaching, research and service responsibilities of social work discipline. This program based document should be in strict compliance with all of the tenure policies, procedures and standards of the institution since the evaluation process continues through the administrative hierarchy of the institution with the final tenure or promotion decision made by the governing board of the institution. Tenure and academic promotion standards are anchored in the institutional academic governance structure and reflect the overall mission of the institution (Sansone, Bedics, and Rappe, 2000).

A comprehensive examination of the growing complexity of the tenure process is beyond the scope of this publication. For a new program director, the importance of adhering to the institutional policies, procedures and standards cannot be overstated nor can the significance of understanding the faculty handbook because it is this institutional document that has been increasing defined by the courts in tenure matters as the official document governing the tenure process. An analysis of court cases, employment law and higher education by Ward Mullaney & March Timberlake (1994) reveal the significance of handbook information in deciding tenure disputes. Based on a summary of their analysis and an examination of tenure by Brand (1999), Wilson & Reamer (1992), Figure

6.11 provides selected examples of fundamental administrative guidelines that a program director understands.

## FIGURE 6.11

### Tenure Policies and Procedures - Administrative Guidelines

- Tenure, created to protect academic freedom of faculty members, has evolved to become an employment contract between the faculty member and the institution, therefore the specific duties, rights and responsibilities of all parties should be specifically defined in writing and distributed accordingly.

- Explicit written information describing institutional-wide tenure reviews and appeal procedures, performance standards, academic credentials (i.e. doctorate degree), standards of collegiality should be published in the institution's personnel/faculty handbook; this regulatory information constitutes an employment contract.

- Faculty members should be informed of tenure policies and procedures at the time of their initial appointment, receive formal annual evaluative feedback, and be given access to opportunities, guidance and resources needed to successfully complete the pre-tenure, probationary period of employment.

- Documentation required for tenure review is a concise, coherent evidentiary written record of teaching, research and professional service performance, should contain both quantitative and qualitative data from multiple sources including self reports, and should present sufficient evidence to substantiate tenure eligibility without the need for further interpretation.

- Tenure application materials and documentation should clearly demonstrate compliance with both the academic requirements of the institution and the disciplinary standards of the social work profession.

- Peer review is a fundamental feature of tenure evaluation which begins with evaluation by faculty colleagues that can be supplemented by external reviews completed by prestigious faculty within the discipline.

- The official basis for interpretation, clarification and definitions of institutional policies and procedures governing the tenure process when disputes arise is the information published in the institution's personnel/faculty handbook.

- The official time frame for earning tenure, options and required justification and administrative approval to shorten or lengthen this time should be explicated, published and distributed to all parties.

- Institutional personnel policies and procedures should be in place to safeguard tenure decisions against personnel actions that are arbitrary, capricious or violate constitution rights of faculty members.

- Pre-tenure faculty candidates have the right to be informed of annual evaluation outcomes, and in tenure disputed instances, have the right to deny or rebut allegations of unsatisfactory performance.

- Dismissal from a tenure appointment is in actuality a severing of an official employment contract; therefore, all legal federal employment protections must be applied in these instances.

Because of the significance of tenure in relationship to faculty development and evaluation, the director focuses on assuring that the processes strictly conforms to all institutional policies, standards, procedures that govern the tenure process. Assurance that academic administrator's role in the tenure review process according to Ward Mullaney and March Timberlake (1990) who have identified a list of academic due process safeguards. These include:

- Composition of the review committees follow the procedural rules of the handbook and university common law practices;

- Tenure decisions are based on substantive reasons supported by evidence and in accord with handbook criteria and the mission and needs of school and university;

- Candidates are properly notified about the decision and the reasoning behind it;

- Candidates are allowed to respond to any charges contained in the reasonsing;

- Faculty are protected from premature legal intrusion into faculty process;

- Any grievances are properly processed.

# Motivating Personnel

A review of the personnel administration dimensions illustrated in Figure 6.4 begins with the hiring of high quality personnel. The major motivational efforts of the director is focused on creating an individualized professional development program. It is important to remember that faculty and professional staff, who are the two major categories of program employees, have very different personnel characteristics and work orientations. Faculty are a very specialized program resource. Organizations that are human service oriented in their overall purpose cannot routinely apply a clearly designed, specialized technology because of the complex, variable needs of clientele. Reliance by the organization is, therefore, placed on the specialized expertise and professionalism of the employees. Social work faculty, therefore, possess a demonstrated repertoire of professionally sanctioned competencies, provide documented evidence of professional qualifications, and participate in institutionally sponsored or financed professional development offerings to ensure that the general purposes of the college or university are being addressed, and that the overall goals of the academic program are being achieved. Common characteristics of employees who are specialized professionals identified by Baldridge and Deal (1977) include the following. Faculty:

- Demand autonomy in their work. Having acquired considerable skill and expertise in a field, professionals demand freedom from direct supervision.

- Have divided loyalties. Professionals have loyalties to peers at the national levels, which may sometimes interfere with loyalty to their local employer.

- Have strong tensions that may exist between professional value and the bureaucratic expectations of the employing organization. Conflict between professional specialties and the employing organization are common.

- Demand peer-oriented evaluation of work performance. A believe that only professional colleagues can accurately judge performance, which is accompanied by a belief that administrative superiors in the organizational hierarchy cannot accurately evaluate professional specialties.

Faculty members, therefore, are essentially self-motivated; therefore, opportunities for significant work assignments and professional development is essential.

Another important reality to keep in mind in personnel management is the continual change processes that impact a social work program that requires consistent and planned personnel development. The programmatic adaptations of the college or university to better accommodate shifts in students academic interests, the need for curriculum modifications to incorporate the revisions of the Curriculum Policy Statement as it undergoes the mandated eight year review cycles and the refinement of educational outcome adjustments to incorporate practice innovations that evolve from research and field-based developments are examples of the sources for change that program personnel must accommodate. Leadership focused on both program and personnel development are needed to accommodate continual program changes.

Figure 6.4 is designed to also illustrate the interrelationships of the six personnel administrative processes that combine to motivate individuals and the aggregate performance of all program personnel. A thorough examination of the complex process of motivating faculty and staff as the two major groups of program employees is beyond the scope of this publication. Figure 6 provides examples of questions that a program director may ask when reviewing the personnel practices associated with each of the six administrative processes.

## FIGURE 6.12

### Personnel Motivation - Development Administrative Considerations

Personnel Recruitment - Selection - Hiring
- How is the need for personnel identified, expertise defined, and is there systematic use of program outcomes to prioritize needs?
- How are the opportunities for professional development, innovation involvement and advancement communicated during the personnel search process?

Orientation - Support of Personnel
- How effective is the faculty-mentoring program working to help personnel gain timely promotion and career advancements?
- Which personnel are not participating in information and electronic networks with colleagues and how do these individuals gain collegial stimulation, peer-based learning, professional support, and academic collaboration?
- What are the methods the program uses to publicly announce and celebrate professional accomplishment faculty and staff members?
- Are professional achievements directly linked to the salary and career advancement structure of the institution?
- Are there stable resources for professional development including academic leaves, travel funds, and campus workshops/in-service training opportunities?

Assignments
- How effective are the efforts to routinely change continuous teaching and position assignments to add variety and challenge to work responsibilities?
- What are the varied types of the opportunities for assigned time for scholarship each academic year, periodic sabbaticals for full-time advancement studies and grant development to help develop individual and program resources?
- What is the general morale of the personnel, what are the major stresses and what support opportunities exist to promote job enjoyment?

Performance Evaluation - Goal Definition
- Is there a program-based formal annual performance review to evaluate professional outcomes, formulate performance goals and resources available for implementation?
- What are the efforts to promote congruence between individual personnel and program goals?
- What are the sources and frequency of feedback provided to personnel?

Personnel Development/Training Resource Provision
- What are the means used to schedule annual in-service development programs focused on interests and needs identified by personnel and by program outcome data?
- Are there stable sources of funding for faculty and staff to attend professional development/enrichment workshops, conferences and other types of programs to address defined professional and program development priorities?

As noted previously, personnel administration is a very complex process that represents the major role challenges for program directors. A review of the resources cited throughout this publication, routine attendance at conferences and workshops, regular review of the literature, periodic discussion of the state-of-the-program by all personnel and regular consultation from an administrative superior are examples of practices which may be helpful to promote one's personnel management effectiveness.

# Managing Unsatisfactory Personnel Performance

Unsatisfactory personal performance and conflict occurs in every academic program, no matter how exemplary is the operation, capable are the personnel, adequate are the resources, or effective is the director or values stature of the academic enterprise within the college or university. As noted in the generic position description in Chapter 1, and in the previous listing in this chapter of human resource related administrative tasks, the director is responsible for addressing unsatisfactory personnel performance. This represents a very complex and extensive process within the context of human resource administration.

The following are examples of some administrative approaches a director considers when faced with addressing unsatisfactory performance of a program employee, presented for application within the context of resources, opportunities, controls, and decision procedures of the host institution.

- **<u>Personnel Policies and Procedures of the Host Institution</u>**

  A thorough review and understanding of the institution's personnel policies for staff, faculty, technicians, and student employees is essential, as is the specific provision of the union contract if the campus is organized collectively. Specific regulations regarding such diverse personnel matters as academic tenure, official performance requirements for secretarial staff, and employment probation for student employees are examples of detailed personnel information needed by a director in order to address unsatisfactory work performance.

- **<u>Consultation and Collaboration Processes</u>**

  Effectively addressing unsatisfactory performance on an individual, case-by-case basis requires a dimension of the creative problem solving approach within the regulatory context of the personnel policies and procedures of the institution as well as other contingency regulations such as contractual obligation, affirmation action considerations, tenure provisions, and so forth. Therefore, it behooves a director to confer with an administrative superior for advice and administrative guidance as well as conferring with such specialized officials such as affirmative action officers, institutional legal counsel, and union representatives.

- ## Systematic Formal and Informal Performance Evaluation Processes

Unsatisfactory performance is identified within a holistic performance appraisal process that includes systematic annual evaluation and professional development procedures of the program. Problematic performance can more readily be identified early, is part of a written annual appraisal that also identified both strengths and limitations, has defined performance target goals within a specified time frame, and has clear definitions of indicators of success for each of the performance objectives. Consistent and objective measures and standards are key ingredients of the evaluation process.

- ## Goal Oriented Performance Feedback Procedures

Motivation oriented administrative approaches as previously described includes frequent formal and informal recognition, feedback, rewards, and reinforcement of desired behaviors as a dimension of the performance norm of the program. Consequently, personnel receive frequent feedback from a variety of sources that supplement the self-evaluation reports and formative evaluations done annually.

- ## Explicit Job Expectations and Performance Standards

A thorough understanding of job expectations supplemented by an individualized operationalized definition by the director for each employee is helpful. In addition, each employee systematically completes documented self evaluation of performance within their position description and in consultation with the program director to establish specific and realistic performance and development goals that are updated annually during a formal performance evaluation process. Promotion and tenure requirements are be defined within each faculty's interests, strengths and job description, along with resource provision (e.g. release time, mentoring, grant support, teaching development workshops, etc.) in order to be successful. Technical staff needs in-service training on a regular basis in order to maintain information technology competencies.

Effective program administration requires directors to be continually alert to conflict among the many program stakeholders. Like specific administrative tasks found in the other four program domains, this is a very complex phenomenon. Continual study, completion of organizational conflict workshops, and conflict management skill development to enhance this facet of administration is helpful. Remaining alert to inherently conflictual situations such as performance evaluations or admission decisions, fostering effective communication and decisions within the program, and routinely consulting with one's administrative superior are other examples of recommended routine administrative practices.

## Summary

Program personnel consume the lion's share of the annual program operating budget, represent a valuable resource that has the inherent potential for promoting program quality, and is an essential ingredient in every program domain, operation, and initiative. Therefore, it is imperative that a director provides effective human resource administration that includes a range of tasks inherent in such essential responsibilities as recruitment, orientation, utilization, development, evaluation, and motivation.

A contextually oriented human resource administrative approach requires the director to acquire an understanding of the host institution's personnel policies and procedures as well as external professional, legal, and credentialing standards that affect human resources. It is useful to develop working relationships with administrative and technical officials within the institution who can assist with personnel development, evaluation, and decision making. Applying an institutional-wide, ecologically oriented, administrative framework can help the director prioritize the administrative tasks associated with human resources and identify administrative practices those that overlap with position responsibilities in the other domains (academic affairs, governance, student affairs and financial resources). An institutional oriented perspective also enables a director to distinguish the major officials, resources, and development opportunities located within the host college or institution that can be mobilized to assist with day-to-day personnel administration and development.

The diverse tasks and leadership requirements in the human resource domain require a periodic review of administrative responsibilities. A review can help the director evaluate priorities and identify information needs. The Self-Evaluation Inventory found in Appendix E is designed to assist the program director in evaluating the level of relative importance, direct involvement, and amount of time delegated to each task inherent in human resource administration.

# References

Arreola, R. A. (1995). Developing a comprehensive faculty evaluation system. Bolton, MA: Anker Publishing Co.

Baldridge, J. V., & Deal, T. E. (1977). Governing academic organizations. Princeton, New Jersey's Carnegie Foundation for the Advancement of Teaching. McCutchan Publishing Co.

Bloom, M., & Klein, W. C. (1995). Publication and citations: A study of faculty at leading schools of social work. Journal of Social Work Education, 31, 377-387.

Boice, R. (1992). The new faculty member. San Francisco: Jossey-Bass.

Boyer, E. L. (1990). Scholarship reconsidered: Priorities of the professorate. Princeton, NJ: The Carnegie Foundation for the Advancement of Teaching.

Braskamp, L. A., & Ory, J. C. (1994). Assessing faculty work. San Francisco: Jossey-Bass.

Cain, R. A. (1977). Critical incidents and critical requirements of mentoring: Implications for in-service training. Unpublished doctoral dissertation, Columbia University Teachers College.

Carroll, A. (1974). Role conflict in academic organization: An exploratory examination of the department chairman's experience. Education Administration Quarterly, 710, 61.

Chait, Richard P. (1995, Spring). The future of academic tenure. The Department Chair 5(4), 1-20.

Council on Social Work Education. (1994). Handbook of accreditation standards and procedures. Alexandria, VA: Author.

Creswell, J. W., & Brown, M. L. (1992, Winter,). How chairpersons enhance faculty research careers. The Department Chair 2(3), 19-20.

Flax, N. & Swaine, R. L. (1995). Academic affairs. In Macy, H. J., Sommer, V. L., Flax, N. & Swaine, R. L. (1995). Directing the baccalaureate social work program: an ecological perspective. Jefferson City, Missouri : Association of Baccalaureate Social Work Program Directors.

Gibbs, P. (1995, Winter). Accreditation of BSW programs. Journal of Social Work Education 31(1), 4-16.

Gmelch, W. H., & Miskin, V. D. (1995). Chairing an academic department. Thousand Oaks, CA: Sage Publications.

Green, R. G., & Bentley, K. J. (1994). Attitudes, experiences, and career productivity of successful social work scholars. Social Work, 39, 405-412.

Green, R. G., & Secret, M. (1996). The publications of social work scholars in social work and non-social work journals. Journal of Social Work Research 20(1), 31-41.

Greenberg, M. (1993, October 20). Accounting for faculty members' time. The Chronicle of Higher Education, XL(9), A68.

Hebel, S. (1999, October 29). A new governor's approach rankles colleges in Colorado. The Chronicle of Higher Education, XLVI(10), A44.

Hull, G. H. (1991). Supporting BSW faculty scholarship. ARETE, 16(2), 19-27.

Johnson, H. W., & Hull, G. H., Jr. (1995). Publication productivity of BSW faculty. Journal of Social Work Education, 31, 358-368.

Klein, W. C., Weisman, D. & Smith, T. E. (1996). The use of adjunct faculty: An exploratory study of eight social work programs. Journal of Social Work Education, 32(2), 253-263.

Ligon, J., Thyer, B. A., & Dixon, D. (1995). Academic affiliations of those published in social work journals: A productivity analysis, 1989-1993.

Macy, H. J. (1990). Role analysis study of chairpersons in academic departments offering accredited baccalaureate social work degree programs. Unpublished doctoral dissertation, Ball State University, Muncie, Indiana.

Merriam, S. (1983). Mentors and proteges: A critical review of the literature. Adult Education Quarterly, 33(3), 161-173.

Perlman, B., & McCann, L. I. (1997, Summer). Departmental planning: The first step in recruiting. (From Baron Perlman and Lee I. McCann's book entitled, Recruiting Good College Faculty, Anker, 1996). The Department Chair, 8(1), 2-3.

Sansone, F., Bedics, B., & Rappe, P. (2000, Spring). BSW faculty workload and scholarship expectations for tenure. The Journal of Baccaluareate Social Work, 5(2), 27-46.

Seagren, A. T., Creswell, J. W., & Wheeler, D. W. (1993). The department chair: New roles, responsibilities and challenges (ASHE-ERIC Higher Education, Report No. 1). Washington, DC: George Washington University School of Education and Human Development.

Seldin, P. (1991). The teaching portfolio. Bolton, MA: Anker Publishing Company, Inc.

Seldin, P. (1985). Evaluating faculty performance. San Francisco: Joseey-Bass, 1985.

Stoner, C. R., & Fry, F. L. (1987). Strategic planning in the small business. Cincinnati, OH: Southwestern.

Swaine, R. L., & Flax, N. (1992). BSW program directors: Characteristics and role experiences. ARE TE, 17(2), 16-28.

Tucker, A. (1984). Chairing the academic department. Macmillan Publishing Company.

York, R. O., Henley, H. C., & Gamble, D. N. (1988). The power of positive mentors: variables associated with women's interest in social work. Journal of Social Work Education, 24(3), 242-250.

Ward Mullaney, J., and March Timerlake, E. (1994). University tenure and the legal system: Procedures, conflicts, and resolutions. Journal of Social Work Education, 30(2), 172-184.

Webb, N. B. (1984). From social work practice to teaching the practice of social work. Journal of Education for Social Work, 20(3), 51-57.

Wilson, R. (1999, October 22). How a university created 95 faculty slots and scaled back its use of part-timers. The Chronicle of Higher Education, XLVI(9), A20.

# Chapter 7

# Accreditation and the Direction of Baccalaureate Social Work Education Programs

"Accreditation is a system for recognizing education institutions and professional programs affiliated with those institutions as having a level of performance, integrity, and quality that entitles them to the confidence of the educational community and the public they serve." (CSWE, 1994)

The purpose of this chapter is to examine how program directors, in doing the work introduced in Chapter 1 and expanded on in subsequent chapters, can also effectively address accreditation standards and incorporate preparation for accreditation reviews into the ongoing life of the program (1). Please see (1) Notes at the end of this chapter.

Accreditation is one of the areas of work new directors need to learn and incorporate as they move from a teaching faculty focus to the larger arena that is program administration and direction. The director is viewed by all other stakeholders as the "point person" regarding accreditation: the responsibility for accreditation outcomes is focused here. That said, the wise director strives to provide leadership to the process of referencing accreditation standards and

---

*Note: While the 1994 Evaluative Standards and Handbook are cited in this chapter and elsewhere in this book, newly revised standards should not change the applicability of the book's messages. This is because, while specific wording of standards or the exact number of standards may change over time, the social work education issues with which the standards treat do not much change. Readers should have little problem finding the appropriate standards for a cited issue from among the set scheduled to appear in 2001-2002.*

facilitates faculty efforts to understand standards and to work effectively along the general lines the standards reflect. Faculty can also "lead;" indeed their leadership in areas of their expertise and responsibility is very much a needed component. No one model of effective program leadership regarding accreditation exists, though many offer possibilities. It is clear that the director cannot be the only actor or activist.

Becoming and remaining accredited has become quite important to social work education programs. Anxiety regarding accreditation is common, and for several reasons. It is possible for a program to "fail" - to be denied accreditation, or have accreditation withdrawn. The self-study process is both long and involved, and a great deal of what is often seen as "extra" work and costs are borne by faculty members and program administrators - efforts and costs often viewed as apart from, and competing with, the "normal" business of social work education. A college administrator might make it known that getting or retaining accreditation is a must for the director, adding anxiety and stress, and causing the director to obsess about this demand. Accreditation is done by a body outside the educational institution, presents the demands of social work practice for educator responses, and thus may seem foreign to the program. Institutional administrators might, for their own reasons, have negative perceptions of the demands accrediting bodies make on their resources, or on limiting their own administrative autonomy. Social work educators are perhaps especially prone to the feeling that an accreditation review is necessarily a questioning of their ability, dedication, and expertise. All these factors, and others, suggest the possibility of an adversarial relationship between programs and accreditors, in which whatever has to be done by the program is done grudgingly, to be gotten over with as quickly as possible, and then back to "business as usual."

# Principles Underlying Effective Thinking About Accreditation

Experienced directors, having been through one or more accreditation reviews, know more about the process and its potentials and might have successfully guided a program through accreditation review one or more times. Still, their mindset may be as described previously. This chapter suggests that a very different mindset is needed - most importantly on the part of program directors — in order for a program to be most effective with accreditation. This mindset merges efforts to promote program quality with efforts to gain or maintain program accreditation. The critical term is *program quality*. Following are the

principles that comprise this effectiveness mindset, and that will be developed
as the chapter progresses:

- Becoming and remaining accredited, important as they are to students
  and the program, are not and cannot become the central focus for
  program directors. Rather, developing and maintaining a quality
  program is and remains the central focus.

- The purpose of the accreditation standards is in helping define quality
  social work education. However, the dynamics of changing
  professional norms, practice innovations, evolving educational
  technology, and an expanding knowledge base are more rapid than
  changes in accreditation standards. Thus definitions of "quality" have
  to evolve importantly out of these sources, and the relevance of social
  work education programs to them will remain a live issue (Munson,
  1994). The Commission on Accreditation has to be concerned to
  keep accreditation standards responsive to these dynamics and their
  changing demands for program relevance.

- A quality program is not at all likely to experience adverse
  accreditation decisions. Success with program quality leads to
  accreditation and its continuation.

- The more continuing contact and fusion there is between accreditation
  standards and the program, the more likely positive outcomes will
  be achieved, and the less onerous the actual accreditation activities
  are for the program.

- The accreditation process can be used by the program to meet goals
  it defines: the whole process is more for the program's gains than for
  the accrediting body/entity or other concerned people/stakeholder.

Accreditation-related activities can usefully be viewed in terms of the
three levels of administrative responsibility discussed in Chapter 1. Most
traditional thinking about accreditation assigns it to the "unanticipated tasks"
category, rather than to either routine tasks or to program advancement. The
argument here is that (1) very little need be unanticipated, (2) much work on the
program that eventually relates to self-study writing or site team reviews can be
built into the routine work of the director and others in the program, and (3) a
cycle of accreditation review can be innately tied to major program advancements
on a wide range of fronts.

# What Is Accreditation?

Educational accreditation has developed in the United States as a means for educational institutions, or specialized educational programs within those institutions, to be professionally reviewed relative to a set of minimum standards established and advanced by social work educators for the field as a whole. This is essentially peer review, free of direct government control, and is within the voluntary, private sector. Submission to accreditation standards is voluntary for educational institutions and programs. The Council on Higher Education Accreditation (CHEA) is the current national organization that oversees six regional accrediting bodies (for entire institutions) and a large number of specialized accrediting bodies, including the Council on Social Work Education (CSWE). CHEA accredits CSWE to conduct accreditation responsibilities for social work education programs in the United States (plus Puerto Rico, Guam, and other territories). Canadian programs are accredited by that country's national association. CHEA sets standards by which it accredits its member accrediting bodies. One measure of its impact is its continuing emphasis on outcomes-oriented education and accreditation. Accrediting standards of its member bodies, including CSWE, are likely to move significantly toward stressing educational program documentation of attainment of student and program objectives. The emphasis on program inputs in earlier accreditation standards will increasingly be offset by standards focused on outcomes.

CHEA's accreditation concerns, in turn, are heavily influenced by larger issues in the United States educational community and the wider society. The contextual factors cited by Hafner and Obligner (1998) suggest how pervasive the influence of these factors on the entire accreditation enterprise might be: Reduced public funding of education leading to increased competition and cost-cutting; more non-traditional students requiring new educational delivery mechanisms; increased use of electronic information technology in education leading to changes in the nature of teaching; pressures for innovative governance structures and approaches; and increased accountability for program effectiveness and consumer satisfaction and confidence all act as contexts for an educational program's accreditation.

Accreditation involves programs documenting their compliance with curriculum and other standards. For individual programs, these standards set targets, act as reminders, and are challenges. The CSWE eight-year accreditation cycle sets a recurring time frame within which the program's purposes can be rethought; in which views of the future's demands on and for social work practice are focused. Accreditation standards reflect the thinking of the larger professions of social work and social work education about what comprises a quality social work education, in general terms. Although this is not the only source for defining the substance of a quality social work education program, it is a key source, representing the larger profession and, therefore, the overall quality of practice.

# Why Accreditation Exists

Why accreditation at all? Will it continue to exist? The definition offered at the outset of the chapter suggests why accreditation is needed and will likely exist in much of its current form for the foreseeable future. Accreditation does provide useful societal responsibilities and thus is likely to continue in some form on a permanent basis. It offers assurances to prospective students that a program has been reviewed by an outside, expert body and found to have met standards the profession sets for itself. The general public - including potential consumers of services — can expect that graduates of an accredited program will have been taught in a manner consistent with curriculum standards, and evaluated for attainment of knowledge, skills, and professional values. Accreditation also helps ensure that the educational institution's finite resources are being used well and consistently with institutional mission and purposes. One specific type of "public actor," state social work licensing boards, has accepted CSWE accreditation as their assurance that students are ready to sit for licensing exams, and all but one state limits their examination to graduates of CSWE-accredited programs (AASWB, 1999). Thus, accreditation provides assurance to the public from an outside, competent body, of educational program quality and capacities to be found in graduates. Program applicants, students, graduates, future employers, and service consumers can gain some assurance of the education and learning that have (or will have) occurred. At specific points in time, accreditation tasks do require special faculty efforts and do occupy a great deal of a director's attention. For programs attempting to become accredited, it is roughly a four-year process of pre-candidacy, candidacy, and then initial accreditation review, requiring on-site visits by commissioners from the Commission on Accreditation (COA), program and materials development, and creation of reports to COA. For programs going through reaffirmation (reaccreditation) review (the first reaffirmation is four years after an initial accreditation because of the great deal of new program development underway, and every eight years thereafter), the self-study process will likely add work on some new self-examinations (program purposes, main themes for goals and curriculum), creation of the self-study document, and completion of the site visit itself.

# Background for Understanding Social Work Education Accreditation

## The Council on Social Work Education

The primary purpose of the Council on Social Work Education(CSWE) is to be the specialized accrediting body for social work education at baccalaureate and master's levels in the United States. CSWE does not accredit social work doctoral programs, nor does, directly, any other independent body. They are looked at, to some degree, as a part of the educational institution's accreditation. The Council has other responsibilities beyond accreditation — publications, conferences and meetings, collaborating with allied national organizations and interest groups in advancing the quality of social work education and practice, and promoting the policy interests of social work education programs — that employ the talents of a staff of nearly 30 and the annual contributions of many hundreds of volunteer social work educators on the Board, on commissions, and on specialized committees and task forces. The Council's Board of Directors must approve accreditation standards before they can go into effect.

## The Commissions on Educational Policy and on Accreditation

These two permanent commissions of CSWE are mandated to carry out the Council's education program standards development and accrediting responsibilities. The 14-member Commission on Educational Policy (COEP) is charged with creating a new Curriculum Policy Statement (CPS) every seven to eight years. The CPS is the profession's basic statement of curricular content to be included by programs at both baccalaureate and master's levels. The CPS traditionally has been both a statement of social work education philosophy and of curriculum content, based on the inputs of and review by the social work education community. After the CPS is approved by the CSWE Board, it is sent to the Commission on Accreditation (COA) for incorporation with Evaluative Standards. The curriculum component of the COA's Evaluative Standards is required to be consistent with the Curriculum Policy Statement.

The 25-member Commission on Accreditation (COA) is quasi-autonomous within CSWE; its members are appointed to 3-year terms by the CSWE Board president, and the Board must approve new accreditation standards and changes in existing standards. However, only COA can propose Evaluative Standards, and only it renders accreditation decisions on programs, with no Board oversight. COA is charged with developing candidacy, eligibility (relating to the institution), and evaluative (relating to the social work program) standards. These standards are designed to embrace all aspects of a social work education program, starting with program mission and goals; then moving through areas of program governance, structure, and resources; nondiscrimination; faculty; student development; curriculum; alternative programs; and innovative programs. Evaluative Standards also go through extensive review and comment by the social work education community, with final CSWE Board approval. Evaluative Standards revision follows the cycle set by COEP for a new Curriculum Policy Statement, to ensure that these two components of the accreditation standards remain linked and mutually consistent.

Beyond standards development, the Commission on Accreditation sits as the permanent body to make decisions on program accreditation. COA is staffed by the Division of Standards and Accreditation within the Council. Its professional and clerical staffs aim at promoting program understanding of accreditation standards and procedures, and at technical consultation on program development related to meeting expectations of the standards. Commissioners of COA make pre-candidacy visits to programs wanting to become accredited, and annual visits to programs during the candidacy period. They are involved in specialized training sessions for programs along with staff. The approach of COA and its staff to programs is designed to be professional, collegial, and supportive of the development and maintenance of program quality.

Historically, these two commissions have worked apart from one another, with the Commission on Accreditation accepting the CPS from the Commission on Educational Policy and then working with programs to help them incorporate the CPS and other Evaluative Standards into their curricula and program design and functioning. Recent efforts at more closely connecting the work of both commissions are bearing fruit. The next set of revised accreditation standards is to appear as a single document, more integrally relating these two documents than is the case with the current two separate documents that programs must now address.

## The Handbook

Details of the COA's rationale, composition, and procedures can be gleaned from a close reading of CSWE's *Handbook of Accreditation Standards and Procedures*. The *Handbook* is published as a revised edition each time accreditation standards undergo revision. It has been developed as a one-stop compendium of "all you need to know" about accreditation. It contains all standards, procedures, forms, and guides to parts of the overall accreditation process, in over 220 pages. The current *Handbook* is dated 1994, when the last major revision was completed; the next edition will likely be dated 2001 or 2002, and will contain another full revision of the Curriculum Policy Statement (now called Educational Policy Statement) and Evaluative Standards.

It is designed to be used in step-wise fashion, moving from pre-candidacy through to re-accreditation reviews, so that a new program can begin with candidacy content, and then move through the *Handbook* to initial accreditation and then reaccreditation (called "reaffirmation"). The only materials currently outside the *Handbook* are guidelines that the Commission has developed to explain a new procedure or accreditation policy; one current example being the "Guidelines for Distance Education Proposals in Social Work." The next *Handbook* should incorporate any types of guidelines such as these.

A detailed familiarity with all parts of the *Handbook* is important grounding for program directors in relating to accreditation (see the fourth of the "characteristic duties and responsibilities" in the director's position description in Chapter 1). This familiarity keeps a director and faculty in touch with how accreditation is being presented (the whats and whys), reminds them of deadlines, and what needs to be communicated in a materials submission to the Commission. Certain sections are particularly important for the director and faculty working to promote program quality who want to use the *Handbook* in support. Sections on evaluative standards, the Curriculum or Educational Policy Statement, the self-study guides, and the forms are apt to be most useful. All of these provide content on the issues and inputs that make up social work education, and directors and faculty can use them to learn how to apply the vocabulary of accreditation.

## Sources of Information or Help with Accreditation

There are a number of sources of information and intelligence about accreditation. Some sources are more basic and have continuing value, whereas others can be perused periodically for information of value. The *Handbook of Accreditation Standards and Procedures* from CSWE, discussed previously, is basic. Have at least one copy for the program. Every faculty member should be familiar with its contents and have copies of the accreditation standards with which to review and stay current. A director might want to assign presentations and follow-up discussion of sections in faculty meetings as one means to get this content into use. Ideally Staff should be very familiar with standards, particularly those affecting their work areas. Students can be oriented to the standards, have their own copies of curriculum and other standards, and have full access to the *Handbook*.

All programs entering into reviews by COA have an educational specialist assigned to them. Experienced social work educators who are familiar with the standards and work of COA, educational specialists, consult with programs on their accreditation efforts. Their purposes are to help programs understand the standards and COA procedures, including problem-solving around program development to meet accreditation standards. These specialists work within the Division of Standards and Accreditation (DOSA) of CSWE. Each of four educational specialists works more or less actively with over 100 programs at any given point in time, and thus has the ability to pass on ideas tried elsewhere or warn away from poor practices. The educational specialist should be a director's first "port of call" when an issue relating to standards arises. An ongoing dialogue with these professional staff people should be considered as a basic help-seeking tactic for program directors. Educational specialists' inputs are limited to technical consultation about the standards and developing the program relative to standards content, but this covers a wide range of content. They are paid to give authoritative responses to questions regarding accreditation and to be expert in interpreting the standards and how COA works. These staff work mostly at the CSWE office (located in Virginia) but also provide consultations at social work education conferences (CSWE's Annual Program Meeting, the annual BPD Conference, and at state-level meetings to which they are invited). Programs that are between accreditation reviews can continue to consult with the educational specialist assigned to them.

Other social work program directors also can be approached for consultative information regarding accreditation, but a *caveat* is in order. Unless these directors (or other faculty) have served on the Commission on Accreditation, they are not likely to have a deep and accurate understanding of either the standards or how and why accreditation proceeds. They can talk about their own program-based experience, but that is only one case study and it might have different institutional, regional, and administrative contexts. These directors can share their accreditation materials, including their self-study report, but these materials may be poor models for another program with distinct goals and contextual factors. So the best advice is to talk to a number of other directors - at BPD meetings, at state-level social work education meetings, at CSWE's Annual Program Meeting, or call them on the phone, or go visit their programs. Gather their experiences and perceptions, which is their best advice for succeeding with accreditation reviews. Get several viewpoints to ensure that you are not gaining all your knowledge from what turns out to be a fairly unique case. Remember that you are talking with them not as accreditation experts, but as experienced social work educators who have their own experience with accreditation.

To stay current a director routinely reads professional papers and journals that discuss program quality issues, and relate accreditation to the evolving issues presented in these types of publications. One finds that there is little systematic research on accreditation, so opinions, case studies, and even "war stories" on accreditation experiences are much in evidence. Be cautious about them for they might present a skewed view of accreditation and how and why the COA operates. The substance of accreditation decisions is held confidential between COA and its staff and the institution being reviewed, and thus is not available to researchers. CSWE staff has not been able to do related research beyond the basic descriptive summaries of COA actions now provided in The Reporter. With a new information system coming online at CSWE, this situation will change by late 2000, with fuller descriptive and trend analyses becoming available.

Social work consultants exist to provide the program director with a wide array of possible services for a fee. Consultants offer services that DOSA educational specialists cannot provide, such as recommending particular textbooks or reviewing drafts of a self-study report. Consultants can be used at any time, not just during an accreditation review process, although the typical extensiveness of an accreditation review may particularly lend itself to calling in a consultant. It is important for a director to know why a program needs a consultant's help in order to be able to judge whether a particular candidate will be able to provide the product that a specific program wants (CSWE does not "vet" social work education consultants, and anyone can "hang up a shingle" if they want). CSWE will share a list of commissioners who have rotated off the COA within the past few years. These ex-commissioners know social work as a profession and as an academic specialty, as well as the accreditation standards, and this comprehensive perspective and understanding can be a very useful resource. But there are many others, too, experts in curriculum or some area of it, whom a director might consult on developing a course or sequence. There are field practicum experts. There are very experienced social work educators who might help talk an administration through the process of developing a new field program. A program might hire someone to work the faculty through its thinking on program purposes, or to read a draft of the program's self-study report and provide feedback, or to role-play the site visit so that a new or nervous faculty can experience the process and realize how they can be effective in it.

Wahlberg (1992) recommends two consultant visits as useful for most programs: the first about half-way through an accreditation cycle, pretty much as a surprise to the faculty so that "normal" conditions prevail, for feedback on how the program's usual operations look. The second is the dry-run of the site visit. One good idea is to have a consultant line item in every year's budget, with the ability to spend or roll over that money to the next year depending on needs the program defines for consultant use and continuous development. One or more of these paid specialists may move a program's understanding or capacity ahead in quantum leaps. Typically, their use is found to be well worth the money.

# Most Productive Ways of Viewing Accreditation

## Knowledge About Accreditation Standards

A part of understanding accreditation well and then using that knowledge as a program director comes from being able to separate accreditation myths from facts. A number of myths have sprung up and stayed alive, and these need to be examined critically for their utility.

**Myth 1: The accreditation standards forbid many activities.** Some social work educators blame the standards from stopping them from taking a useful initiative. A close reading of the standards will reveal that they do not forbid any activity. Instead, they are written in positive terms, stating outcomes and functioning that have over time become defined as minimal and standard within the field of social work education. The line between university or program policy and the accreditation standards is often blurred in student, faculty, and others' minds, occasioning many calls to DOSA staff for clarification. The academic program, for instance, sets specific requirements for field placements, within the general guidelines of the standards. It is these specific "do's" and "don't" that often upset students the most, and program staff sometimes confuse the general mandate of the accreditation standards with detailed policy or procedures defined by the program. These are often more prescriptive than the accreditation standards. Rarely do the standards dictate specific program policies. It should be understood that if the standards do not explicitly address a given aspect of program operation, there exists no objection to program initiative in this area. If the standards do not address something, the program is free to determine whether and how it will proceed on that point.

**Myth 2: The standards must be followed doggedly.** The standards are, for the most part, written in fairly general terms rather than detailed. Remember that standards have evolved over almost five decades, and must be applied to the specific circumstances of approximately 600 social work education programs. Great explicitness (such as one way of computing student or faculty full-time equivalents) must give way to a more general requirement (that programs have adequate faculty resources given student body size and demands, and document this adequacy - which they do partly by computing their faculty-to-student ratio using formulae and approaches typical of their institution). The standards were never designed to lock programs into a prescriptive model in which meek compliance was expected, and standards will not be so designed.

**Myth 3: Accreditation standards stifle creativity.** Several issues are at work here. First, both the evaluative standards and the Curriculum or Educational Policy Statement have tended to grow in substance, scope, and detail over their several revisions. Rarely has content been deleted, until the work on the current Educational Policy Statement. This trend reflects, importantly, the increasing complexity of social work practice and the practice contexts it encounters (think of the new demands created by managed health care, for instance). There has also been something of a tendency on the part of both the accreditation and the educational policy commissions to provide more detail to more fully explain an area or standards - details that might have been left to programs to create in the past. The increasing demand of more educational content creates pressures on programs to find ways to respond, to the extent they have limits in the numbers of courses and credit hours they can require. No easy answers exist. A given course can be crammed only so full of content before both teaching and learning become compromised. Using cognate courses in the liberal arts curriculum can help here, but as these typically are not under control of social work faculty, course content might not be wholly useful to social work majors.

In writing accreditation standards there is always a dynamic between crafting sufficient content so programs are helped to create quality programs, versus crafting too much content that is then viewed as impinging on individual program creativity. New program directors and faculty typically are overjoyed at a good deal of detail in the standards to the extent they are still learning what constitutes good practice in social work education. Experienced directors and faculty, in contrast, are more likely to think that their creativity is being limited by narrow demands for program conformity. The different perceptions might exceed the reality here. All baccalaureate programs, it is true, are required by accreditation standards to prepare students for practice at a beginning professional level. How this is defined explicitly is left up to the individual program, however. Also, specialized content can be offered after the professional foundation and content used by entry-level practitioners has been delivered.

Program goals can best evolve out of a combination of possible sources: (1) those arising in the institution, (2) those resident in the service region, (3) those reflecting student needs and interests, (4) those reflecting faculty interests, and (5) those defined by social work practice and educational sources (e.g. the Curriculum Policy Statement and the NASW Code of Ethics). Figure 2.1 in Chapter 2, and the discussion related to it, play out these possible sources.

Thus a great deal of leeway exists for themes or emphases created by and for the individual program to drive that program and its uniqueness. Were a program to adopt a rural practice focus or theme, this would likely derive from regional needs and the university mission, along with practice needs and realities, and not from anything in the accreditation standards. Empowerment or strength themes, or a particular way of looking at equity or diversity, might be adopted by a program out of a combination of institutional mission and collective faculty values. These defining themes are part of how the program can distinguish itself from others and play out a distinctive program orientation in its curriculum and operations.

Evaluative Standard 8 on program innovation was created to counter the perspective that programs cannot be innovative and be accredited. However, few programs take advantage of this possibility to define a truly new approach to educating for social work practice. There are natural limitations at work here: students need a social work education that they can use career-long and that the agencies hiring them can embrace; accountability to students can limit the creativeness involved. An innovative program has to exist alongside the standard program at least until the innovation has been well proved and can become the "standard" program; this "pilot-type" initiative means extra resources, time and efforts for faculty and staff, who might already be overwhelmed with wide-ranging time demands.

**Myth 4: Most programs have problems with standards, with getting accredited or staying accredited.** Most programs, in fact, fare very well in their accreditation reviews. There is little direct information on large numbers of COA decisions, but that which exists (Wilson, 1996; Mabrey, 1998; Gibbs, 1995) shows the large majority of programs receives positive COA decisions. The accreditation process is designed to provide a great deal of information and consultation at the outset, so programs begin from a strong base and then can build on that base with commissioner and staff consultations. Thus, most programs are granted candidacy (a 94% success rate in Wilson's study), and are granted site visit authorization (84% success), or granted initial accreditation (91% success). Over 72% of programs were successfully reaccredited, the remainder being placed on conditional status or, in a few severe cases (eight programs over seven years in Wilson's study), had their accreditation withdrawn. Some 95% of programs placed on conditional or withdrawn were able to work their way back to being fully accredited (see Triche, 1995 for one case example). Throughout the process of a program's becoming accredited, a great deal of program and materials development occurs, and faculty and staff are often doing a great deal of learning as a result. The high levels of successful results cited previously are tangible testimony to the hard word, dedication, and ability brought by most programs to the program development and accreditation processes.

**Myth 5: All programs are asked by COA to write interim reports.** This is more fact that myth. Nearly all programs granted initial accreditation are asked for an interim report, due in nine months, on specific aspects of the program's curriculum or other operations. This result might be expected, given that these new programs are still undergoing a good deal of development and refinement. Yet a majority of all programs that are reaccredited are also asked for interim reports by COA. Specific areas of concern are identified: these may reflect an area of program weakness seen by COA, or an area for which the program is working but has not accomplished the desired result yet. Most programs succeed in satisfying COA with their first interim report, but some programs show lingering problems that COA attempts to address through two or three interim reports over that many years. Programs that don't give evidence of resolving areas of concern might be in jeopardy of being moved to conditional status, so hard work on resolving issues is definitely needed.

**Myth 6. The Commission on Accreditation has secret agendas as to what it is looking for and it does not share them with programs.** Commission procedures have been crafted carefully to avoid even the appearance of unshared bases for evaluating programs. First, only the formal written documents provided by programs, written commissioner visit or site team visit reports the program has seen and written a response to are used by the Commission in a review of that program. The Commission applies only the written standards to a program, and, for any issue identified, must by its procedures cite one or more accreditation standards as the basis for raising the concern. Commission letters to programs attempt to explain the rationale for a COA decision, and DOSA staff are available to explain and discuss further a given decision because they were present while it was being made. The perception of a communication gap appears often to exist when the general language of a standard is open to some interpretation and programs think COA has a particular interpretation that it is not sharing with programs, although this is not the case. The fact that the *Handbook* currently lacks a glossary of terms can also contribute to possible confusion if there are different meanings ascribed to some terms used by social work educators. The term "infusion" of values and ethics content that is required in the Curriculum Policy Statement is an example. "Infusion," as operationally defined by the COA, suggests that values and ethics content should appear in all courses and be apparent throughout a course. Certainly, "infusion" could be taken to mean that this content should be addressed in course objectives, apparent in course texts and the course outline, and included in required readings and in the course bibliography. One or more assignments might incorporate work with values and ethics. A response like this would likely be seen as a strong approach to "infusing" this content in courses. Exactly how and the extent to which "infusing" is done is up to the program, driven more by program mission, goals and objectives, and program values rather than by the Curriculum Policy Statement's requirement that the content be systematically built into the curriculum.

Contrast the understanding of "infused" content with the language in the CPS for the curriculum areas of diversity, promotion of social and economic justice, and populations-at-risk content. Each of these areas, according to the Commission on Educational Policy's thinking and language, are to be "included" or "incorporated" in the curriculum. COA understands these as more general terms than "infusion," open to quite divergent approaches by programs, again consistent with program purposes and curriculum focuses. The program might create one or more specifically-designed courses in the curriculum to carry major responsibility for any of these areas, or might use some pattern of course modules or experiences to create the desired "incorporation." Approaches outside the classroom - speakers series, symposia, etc. - could also be used. However, a program wanting to stress any or all of these areas of content could also opt to infuse them throughout the curriculum, as well.

Having said this, there are very few terms anywhere in the accreditation standards that carry such differing connotations for program efforts. Most terminology is quite face-apparent and straightforward, and can be used that way by programs. One other realization about how standards get created might help here. A given standard is drafted and then revised by groups of commissioners on the COA, and then is further revised through reviews by the social work education community. The resulting standard is often less clear than when it was first identified, with add-on thoughts or components clouding what might once have been a single quite clear idea. One possible means to cutting through confusing standards verbiage is this: Every standard can be visualized as being based on one or more principles of sound social work education. Although the specific language of a standard may be perplexing, these underlying principles are typically clear and widely shared. If programs think on the underlying principles, they may gain a better understanding of why the standard exists in the first place, and what it is trying to accomplish.

A concern, for example, with adequate secretarial supports in the standard dealing with program resources is sometimes interpreted by programs and institutions as a requirement that all programs must have a social work secretary. Not so. The principle this standard enunciates is that these complex professional programs with their field components and strong ties to social work practice typically require more and more expert secretarial services than do most academic disciplines. As academic degree programs designed to prepare students for entry into an applied or practice-oriented profession, they are far more complex than liberal arts majors because of the use of the field practicum; numerous interactions with social work practitioners via advisory boards, field instruction, and liaison work; and faculty service to the profession. Student advising is far more complex and intensive in such programs. All these factors create a more holistic student-centered orientation and the resulting need for communications and information to flow among program and field personnel. Having a well-trained secretary available to do critical parts of this work (e.g., meeting arrangement, technical materials preparation) has proved, over time, to be a hallmark of an efficient and effective program, freeing faculty up for the roles for which they were hired. This principle, once grasped, is easier to understand and argue for than the seeming arbitrariness of "equivalent of one full-time secretary." The adequacy of secretarial supports to meet program needs does have to be demonstrated, whatever the level of provision. Such thinking about program resources is not foreign to anyone familiar with social work education, and the arguments to the institution's administration for this kind of program resourcing flows easily from this understanding.

**Myth 7: Each Commission on Accreditation interprets standards differently, so it's critical to know what the Commission really wants to know as your program is being reviewed.** With three-year terms for commissioners, roughly a third of COA commissioners rotates off after every June COA meeting, to be replaced by new commissioners. To limit the variability in perspectives and resulting decisions and interpretations that might result from this situation, structured procedures are applied to systematically foster continuity and objectivity. New commissioners are invited to attend the Commission meeting before their term begins to observe the work of preceding commissioners. As their terms begin, new commissioners are oriented and trained to commissioner work, with models of previous work used for training. DOSA educational specialists work with the commissioners assigned to a work group to ensure that new members are clear on procedures, protocol, and the nature of work products expected. Socialization to the work ethic of the Commission occurs for new commissioners as they write their review briefs (or reports) and then find how other commissioners have reviewed the same program. Similar training occurs as commissioners (who are all experienced site visitors) prepare for their commissioner site visits to programs in the candidacy stage. DOSA staff, who experience less turn over than do volunteer commissioners, serve as the "historical memory" of the Commission, noting any trends in decisions away from previous patterns and bringing these to the attention of the Commission. Because the standards remain intact and all COA decisions must reference those standards, there is far less drift than might be expected in this human setting and the intensive work demands it entails.

**Myth 8: Some standards are more important than others.** No
standard was written to be ignored. Thus any standard is available to be cited,
perhaps in combination with others, to reference a Commission concern with a
program. Every standard should be addressed. It is also true that some standards
are cited by COA as problems with programs far more frequently than others. It
would be erroneous to conclude, however, that this is because these often-cited
areas are the ones the Commission "really" cares about. There are other, more
compelling reasons why a standard might be the focus of COA concern with
many programs. One of these is a change in expectations for how social work
educators do a part of their work, and the difficulty programs have in coming to
terms with new expectations. A good current example of this phenomenon is
the standard requiring systematic program evaluation of the degree to which
program objectives are being achieved (Evaluative Standards 1.4 and 1.5 in the
1994 edition). This focus on evaluating and documenting actual outcomes relative
to pre-defined program objectives replaces an earlier model of evaluation that
rarely looked at whether program objectives were achieved. Instead, the former
model tracked student progress, students' reactions to instructors, alumni reports
of how they felt looking back at their education, results of state social work
licensing exams for program graduates, and perhaps feedback from employers
on how graduates were faring as social workers. Although each of these is
worthy of inspection, none of these types measures anything directly pertaining
to a program objective. Program faculty struggle with this "disconnect" as they
try to maintain traditional measures of program inputs and quality control, their
need to hear how students feel about themselves and their learning, and their
need to know if graduates are passing licensing exams. The shift to requiring a
systematic program outcome model of evaluation also incorporates more formal
and structured means of documenting that learning did occur, and that planned
program impacts elsewhere in the community or institution did, in fact, occur.

Securing resources for a program is presented in this book as a basic,
indispensable way to build (buy, bring in) quality and be able to approach or
exceed the levels of resources envisioned in accreditation standards. Reviews of
areas of concern and non-compliance in baccalaureate programs (see Wilson,
1996; Mabrey, 1998) reveal that deficient program resources are a fundamental
problem that manifests itself in most parts of the program. Programs with limited
numbers of faculty who struggle to keep up with the demands of large numbers
of students likely will show the strain in almost predictable ways. These faculty
might be more limited in their ability to pursue scholarship or professional
development, for example. They may be less able to stay on top of program
monitoring and evaluation. They might not be able to afford the new technologies
that make library collections much more powerful and accessible. They may

not make rich use of technologies in the classroom (e.g., videotaping or video-based teleconferencing) or as adjuncts to teaching (online teaching and learning utilities). They might begin to falter in the number and intensity of field liaison contacts. They might have less time to develop and maintain strong student organizations and strong field and program advisory groups.

This litany of associated woes should underscore, for the reader, the importance of the content in Chapter 3 on Financial and Physical Resources. If program directors can understand that their base budget from the institution will likely never be enough to meet all current needs adequately plus underwrite program growth as well, they will know that attaining quality and protecting it means that other funding sources and in-kind resource supports have to be secured. Federal grant funding (e.g. Title IV-E and others) provides a margin of funds to both secure the purposes of the grant and to enhance the program itself (but beware of being pulled too far in a direction the program and its mission and goals don't point to). Some programs have used the program's advisory board as a serious fund-raising entity, providing tens of thousands of dollars in added funds, perhaps for dedicated purposes for which base funding has limited impact (e.g. student scholarships, visiting scholars, specialized telecommunication equipment, travel or study tours, etc.) (Joyner, 1998). Some visionary educators talk about social work programs becoming associated with profit-making entities that have service implications and whose profits go to the program (a non-profit entity itself) (Evens, 1998). It is this type of energy and creativity that marks excellence in the director, the faculty, and in the program, and fosters positive reactions from the Commission on Accreditation: here is a program not just passively accepting the budget it is given and making do with that, but one that knows it needs more and takes the initiative to secure more funds: initiative, responsibility, and creativity (invent, beg, borrow, and steal the ideas).

**Myth 9: Interpretive guidelines are the same thing as standards.** The 1994 revision to the evaluative standards continued the practice of including Interpretive Guidelines along with many evaluative standards. These were intended as clarifications of the standards, as suggested responses to a standard, or as examples, but not as additional standards content. Programs should not write their self-study reports to the Interpretive Guidelines. Future standards might or might not include Interpretive Guidelines. Recognizing the dynamic, evolving nature of social work education, however, the Commission on Accreditation will need to address means to relate the accreditation standards to new conditions and demands - to keep the standards current and meaningful and useful for program use.

The Interpretive Guidelines in the 1994 standards employ conditional tense ("should") in place of requirement language ("must") in the standards themselves, which is another important difference in the two types of content. Interpretive Guidelines typically have been added to earlier standards in response to requests from the social work education community for more clarity or examples related to a perplexing standard. Most numbers, for example, exist not in the standards but in the interpretive guidelines, in response to program questions for example about how much of a given resource is needed. Thus, the equivalent of one full-time secretary for a baccalaureate program is *recommended* in the interpretive guideline to Evaluative Standard. Although only a recommendation and not a requirement, reflecting the experience of many social work educators, this is often erroneously interpreted by program directors or administrators as a clear requirement. However, this is not so. The standard requires adequate secretarial resources to meet program needs. If a program can document that all its secretarial resource needs are being met with less than 1.0 secretarial FTE, there is program compliance with the standard. (Note: that the Evaluative Standards being revised for 2001-2002 do not include Interpretive Guidelines).

## How to Test or Dispel These and Other Myths for Yourself

In forming their own understanding, effective program directors and faculty will ultimately rely on themselves to test the truth value of these and other views of accreditation. There are some straightforward ways to do this. First comes knowing the standards well and referring back to them to see exactly what they say and don't say. Program stakeholders commonly think or assume the standards say something when, in fact, they don't. Although the standards broadly embrace social work education, they do not deal at the detailed level at which most issues are raised (e.g. exactly what student entrance requirements and procedures will be developed by a program). Most things are left to the innovation and discretion of program faculty and their institutional contexts.

A further part of the mindset promoted in this chapter is based on the fact that, like the U.S. Constitution, if something is not in there, you can make up your own mind about it. And most of what occurs in running a baccalaureate social work program is not explicitly referenced in standards. If standards do not "dictate" how to run a social work education program, the program director and faculty have to become more self-reliant in creating program policy, structure, content, and procedures. If the standards clearly do not tell you how much of a particular type of curriculum content is needed, for example, the program faculty will have to determine this themselves, as described in the discussion of the director's role in Chapter 1. The argument here is that programs and their directors always take the initiative; asking not "what am I allowed to do?" but "what do I know I have to do (self-reliant, expert)?" The questions and challenges are noted in the standards, but the "answers" come from social work educators defining quality out of their own knowledge of the field and the discipline and out of the wide range of inputs they take in as part of their own learning of this enterprise. Even this book, chock full of sound thinking, experience, and advice that it is, should not be the focus of program director reliance. This need to become informed, to be self-reliantly critical, is clearly a subset of the wider need directors and faculty have to keep learning about their jobs and the contexts for them. Some general educational and practice sources exist to provide useful and often authoritative information: the *Chronicle of Higher Education, NASW News*, the *Journal of Social Work Education*, the *Journal of Education in Social Work*, the BPD listserve, and the CSWE Web site. Directors and faculty who come to social work education out of practice typically have little theoretical background in curriculum design and educational/pedagogical theory. Newly-minted doctoral graduates might also lack good backgrounds in the whys and hows of creating curriculum or comparative instructional methods anchored in advanced learning theories needed in an academic program that prepares students for professional practice positions. Many CSWE publications address this area. Colleagues in an education department of the host institution can suggest sources from their expertise and perspective. Several texts exist (cited in this book) that directors and faculty can rely on to move their understanding of these complex issues into an ability to critique and act in their own social work education programs.

## Knowledge of the Site Visiting and Accreditation Review Processes

The site team visit can be intimidating and nerve-wracking for many programs. Understanding what and why it is and how it can be useful to the program are useful components to an effective mindset toward accreditation. A two-person team spends three days meeting with relevant groups inside and outside the program to view the program's reality as they can see it against the written self-study and other program materials with which they have already become familiar. They are social work educators chosen for their ability to do a peer review of the program. They are an extension of the Commission on Accreditation (sometimes called its "eyes and ears") but are not sitting commissioners. They look not for standards compliance but for areas of program strength and weakness. They are not trying to "trip up" a program but to understand it in a pervasive and formal way. They communicate that

understanding back to the program and to COA in a written report, and the
program - always given the last word in a COA review - provides a written
response to the report for COA consideration along with the report and the self-
study.

Site visits, and the rest of the accreditation process, are often thought of
as something of and for the Commission on Accreditation. Part of a more
successful realistic mindset is to view each component of the process, including
the site visit, as a learning challenge for the program and an opportunity to test
the program and grow accordingly. It's clear to most programs that the work of
self-studying that occurs roughly over a two-year period produces a great deal
of knowledge about the program. If all this knowledge is poured into the self-
study and then sent off to COA never to be thought of again in the program,
what a colossal waste of time and talent! Site visit teams look at a program at
one point in time, and yet curriculum, resources, practice theory and the
professional competencies needed (and other program elements) are constantly
evolving. The self-study process can incorporate this fact through use of such
strategies as a "sequence development plan" that shows how a given area of
curriculum has evolved to where it is when "visited," and to where it is likely to
evolve and why (3). Please see Note (3) at the end of this chapter.

Regarding the site visit specifically, much can be done before, during,
and after the visit to capture program gains. Write down what the program, and
each individual faculty member, wants to get out of the site visit: specific questions
to be answered, perspectives to be tested or learned, ideas to be tested, and
materials to be critiqued. A debriefing session completed after the site visit can
examine how well the program met its objectives. Both short-term and long-
term program issues or needs could be built into this "agenda." Look at the visit
as an *opportunity*, not as a form of torture. The program director can go over
these program purposes with the site visit team chair so that their existence is
known. Even if meeting these purposes is not among the site visit team's
objectives, the existence of program purposes for the visit will probably allow
some informal attention to them, and program faculty can still target these
purposes, no matter how or whether a site visit team reacts to knowing of them.

A director meets with each of the stakeholder groups (faculty, field
instructors, students, administrators, and advisory board) before the site visit so
they become familiar with the site visit process. Address their questions and
concerns and identify their roles in contributing to program development (past,
current, plus projected). Focus their parts of the "program story" to be told to
the site visit team; perhaps dry-run a session to get them comfortable by role-
playing. Also identify the things they want to learn during the site visit, and how
to get them included in the process.

Zastrow (1999) notes that the site visit process is an opportunity for the program to articulate resource needs to the administrative officials of the host institution, and that the program is best open and honest about these needs with the site visit team. A site visit team focus on these resource needs in their report might have a strong impact on future resource decisions made by the institution's administration. Honesty and openness are excellent policies for a site visit, as for other parts of the process.

There is a potential problem here, however. Many college presidents and other administrators view the purpose of accrediting bodies as important to push the institution to fund a program at higher levels, and may have a hard time seeing past this view to hear the important educational inputs being made. Part of the self-reliant mindset being presented here is that program directors not rely on the accreditation process to win arguments around resources or other issues with administration that the program cannot win for itself. "Because the accreditation standards require it" is not a strong statement of rationale for an educator, whose arguments should be couched in pedagogy and best practice for teaching, learning, and program advancement. Accreditation standards do not prescribe many specific resources, so they are unreliable allies. Certainly, many accreditation reviews do focus critically on resources, and additional resources might result after a site visit. Ideally, though, the self-study process has identified and documented needs, and these needs are being addressed going into the site visit, and not afterward. This posture demonstrates a program director's self-reliance and administrative competence and is an important component of program leadership strategy.

When the Commission on Accreditation reviews a program, it uses the written record described earlier to make considered judgments about compliance with standards. At least two commissioners read all materials and write independent "briefs" documenting their review, recommendations, and citations and rationales for their recommendations. There are four staffed work groups of commissioners that divide the 80 or so programs on each of three annual COA agendas (over three or four days in February, June, and October) among themselves. The entire workgroup receives the two written briefs and then hears oral arguments from their authors. A group recommendation results from these presentations and the discussion following them.

Positive actions can be recommended, with or without an interim report focused on future work by the program. Adverse judgments include (1) denial of candidacy, (2) denial of site visit authorization, (3) denial of initial accreditation, (4) placement on conditional accredited status, (5)withdrawal of accreditation, or (6) receipt of an interim report.

Two levels of adverse judgment are reflected in the terms "concern" and "noncompliance." *Areas of noncompliance* with standards are serious negative factors whose existence is viewed as threatening the quality or integrity of the program. Any standard, theoretically, could be the focus for a finding of noncompliance - seriously inadequate numbers of faculty, or a non-functioning program evaluation system are possible examples. A finding of one or more areas of noncompliance must be made to justify all the adverse decisions mentioned previously, except for receipt of an interim report, which is occasioned by a finding of one or more areas of concern. *Areas of concern* are areas in which partial compliance with standards is found, and the program is judged by the COA to be less endangered by the existence of these problems than would be the case for a finding of noncompliance (examples might be an incomplete program evaluation system or lack of some content specified for a curriculum by the Curriculum Policy Statement). The program is required to address both types of issues; however, noncompliance areas can lead to withdrawal of accredited status, whereas concerns cannot.

Determining into which of these categories an issue is placed is a judgment call by commissioners, resulting from often extended discussion of the issue in a specific program review. The impact of the issue on that program is the focus, or how one problem interacts with others in the program, not some normative judgment going beyond that program. That is why one program with an issue of faculty adequacy, for example, might receive a "concern" whereas another is found to be in "noncompliance" with the same standard. In the latter case, the issue of faculty adequacy is more grievous to program health, and/or is related to other resource issues that compound it. It doesn't help a program to know what other programs experienced in their Commission review because the COA makes only case-specific analyses and judgments. The resulting COA letter is tailored closely to each individual program and, as described in Chapter 2, how that program is uniquely configured to both constant and dynamic environmental contexts.

This approach of the Commission is rich in individualizing an analysis and suggestions for future work. It also raises the specter of inconsistency across programs. COA spends a fair amount of time in its three meetings a year looking at its decisions across programs, asking if each can be justified, and talking through differences to learn how consistency in decisions can be reinforced. The fact that at least two commissioners do independent reviews of a program, and write up "briefs" (reports) with recommended actions, acts as an internal quality check on consistency; differences between these two readers can lead to extensive discussion to work through to a reasonable conclusion on the program.

The DOSA staff member also reads the program's materials and forms an opinion that can be solicited by the Commission work group as a further check against too-quick, poorly-informed, ill-considered decisions.

## Skills in Communicating About the Program

An important area of skill is the ability to communicate clearly and incisively about the program - what it is, why it is, what it intends to accomplish - to diverse populations. Students are one important such population group, as they seek to understand the whys and wherefores of their educational programs, and to be engaged in governance of that program. Field practicum personnel and practitioners are another such group, as is the program's advisory board. Institutional administrators and faculty in other disciplines are also an ongoing audience that needs to learn about the program. All these "audiences" have ongoing "needs to know" with which the director learns how to communicate. The Commission on Accreditation is another - albeit periodic - audience to which the program must be communicated.

A difficulty with the distance between the Commission and a program is that often a written report from the program is the only "evidence" presented. In some cases, good programs are hurt by the poor reports they write. What to do and not to do in writing self-studies, progress reports, interim reports, and responses to site visit reports can be very useful here. A review of a draft self-study report by a paid consultant is a cost-effective way of evaluating the clarity and quality of the report.

## Do and Don't

*Don't* begin a discussion with a claim that the program is in compliance with a standard, and then go on to greater or lesser length to say something about the issue. Only the Commission is empowered to make a formal judgment about a program's compliance with standards, so you waste paper by stating what you probably obviously believe. Instead, key emphasis should be on demonstrating, explaining, etc. Let the Commission use your "evidence" to come to the conclusion that that evidence itself suggests.

*Do* be sure to respond to *all* standards, and to *all* parts of a standard or issue or information request. Before the review brief form became widely used, or in cases in which it is not followed as the outline for discussion, programs surprisingly often simply did not provide self-study discussion of a standard. With nothing to go on, the Commission would be very tempted to assume noncompliance, or at least a program weakness worthy of concern. Sometimes a Commission letter will cite an area of concern or noncompliance, citing two or more elements, or asking for more than one piece or type of information. If the program responds but does not address each component of the concern, a continuing concern is the most likely result. Read letters very carefully for each aspect of a concern, and provide full discussion on each part.

*Don't* write an interim report that is shorter than the Commission letter requesting it. Appearing to take the process lightly by responding very briefly on a complex issue that the Commission letter treats at length is quite likely to draw a negative response. The issue is raised seriously, not frivolously, by COA; and program directors would best engage it similarly.

*Do* think about the ideas and educational principles that underlie a standard. The way a standard is stated may make less sense to you than the underlying content. A focus on a specific amount of workload for administrative work allows fixation of that number rather than on the underlying issue of adequacy of workload for administrative work - which may be demonstrated to be more than 25% of a workload. The interpretive guidelines were added to standards, over time, to hopefully explain a standard more fully, or explicate it. Often these guidelines help; sometimes they do not.

## "Telling the Program's Story"

Seasoned directors are defined by many things, as Chapters 1 demonstrates. One of these is the ability to speak or write at length, thoughtfully, concretely, and in detail, about their programs. This ability is formed from knowledge and experience gained over time, serious study of the business of social work education and practice, and thinking about their work as social work educators and the issues arising in it. It can get expressed in many ways, serving the social work program most positively: in campus-wide meetings of educational program leaders; in faculty meetings of social work; in forums with field instructors and social work practitioners; in meetings with students; in the generation of materials defining and describing the program. Such directors focus, too, on enabling faculty to gain understanding, skills, and experience along these same kinds of lines - a form of "building the program's capacity."

There are, for instance, many ways to present a course syllabus. In "telling the story" of a social work course, the seasoned director would logically promote very detailed and extensive syllabi, with (1) a clear statement of course purpose and how that course integrates with others (so that students can track how their learning has been designed to grow within, across, and between individual courses and field); (2) course objectives (tied to sequence- and program-level learning objectives, and reflecting both what is being put into the course and what resulting student learning should be); (3) discussion of text(s) and other major sources; (4) a detailed course outline with subject headings sufficiently developed to give a clear sense of content coverage and purpose, required and recommended readings; (5) assignments in sufficient detail to clarify what knowledge and skills are being developed and/or tested; and (6) bibliography of further readings and other sources for a deeper understanding of the content area and to support research assignments.

Syllabi developed with this kind of fullness are highly empowering for students, who can use them to gain a deep understanding of what they will be learning, how, when, and why. Commissioners reviewing a program's syllabi can see how its more abstract statements of purpose "hit the road" in detail and in action with students, and can test the congruence in thinking between statements of program philosophy and actual curriculum implementation.

Most directors and faculty become adept at telling *what* a program does, and this content often comprises most of a self-study. Often conspicuously lacking in self-studies or other reports, and oddly so for social workers, is the content on process: *how* a program operates. The "how" content lets a reviewer learn how a program has tackled its work, the ways it has had to think and problem-solve to get to the bottom-line "what." The personality and climate of a program are made much clearer with this type of content, and types of expertise that might not be evidence only in "bottom-line" discussions are made manifest.

Content on another word - *why* - also often seems conspicuously absent, this time both in the accreditation standards and in programs' discussions of themselves. This chapter has argued that the "why" of a standard can be found in the ideas or principles underlying the written standard: the standard exists because a principle of quality social work education is being reinforced and enforced. Perhaps the lack of a manifest "why" in standards leads programs to give scant attention in their self-study to why they do what they do; but this is the most important content in telling one's story.

Content on program purposes - mission, goals, objectives - may be one of the few places that the typical self-study examines why this focus or that. Community needs are often cited as the justification. But what justifies a particular configuration of faculty knowledge and skills across a body of faculty? Or what justifies a particular approach to group student advising, or a particular pattern of field liaison work? Why this program evaluation instrument and not that one? The opportunities for a program to share its decisional processes, documenting where there are strong educational rationales as opposed to mandates from above, or limited options based on resource realities, or even for no particular reason than something in which the faculty might want to re-think that part of their program.

One of the strengths of the self-study part of accreditation is to raise not only the "what," but also all the other possible questions as well, and require a fairly well-formed answer. Our lives are seldom so formally and systematically examined. This is one opportunity to do this kind of examination and benefit the program and future students as a result.

# Dealing with Accreditation in the Context of Program Directing

## Between Accreditation Reviews

After either gaining initial accreditation or being reaccredited, it is natural to assume that a letdown in accreditation-related activities would occur in most programs. One hears stories of directors who pull out a previous self-study document, dust it off, write a few updates to it, and send it along as the self-study for the next eight years. Quite an extreme picture, surely, and one fraught with peril, given how accreditation standards and related expectations change over time, and given that the whole purpose of self-study is important to capture the future of the program, and not just its past or even its current reality. To counter this problem-filled pattern of six years off and then two years of furious activity, Wahlberg has argued (1992) for a planned and staged program of activities during the six years before the next self-study process begins. His discussion is a useful example of melding "regular" program operations with work that keeps the program focused on quality and on standards maintenance.

After the site visit, to avoid a complete letdown after the intensity of the visiting process, Wahlberg recommends (1) celebrate, with all appropriate players; and (2) have a debriefing session, on the site visit, on the COA letter and work needed, and on the process of self-study. What was learned (by each of the different constituency actors) about what to do and not do next time? What did the program learn about itself, coming from site team and from itself? If the program was asked to submit an interim report in a year, it is advised not to wait until two weeks before the report is due to pull out the COA letter and cobble together a response. Wahlberg advocates designing the response to a COA letter shortly after its receipt because work toward a good response might take months to complete (such as design and use of a new program evaluation tool). Next he recommends planning for use of the next eight years, and this planning could be an agenda item for as much as 18 months (analyze all suggestions, observations, and ideas; plan change strategies; develop time frames; establish a committee or a number of task groups; put these on a wall chart, on everyone's computer).

The number of categories of possible changes in Wahlberg's article is impressive: curriculum development or redevelopment, re-evaluation, planning; student follow-up studies; committee structure (community advisory committee, admissions committee, coordinating committee, grievance committee, field placement committee); field studies; new and continuing instructor training, new placements development, student evaluation revision; plans to rewrite the field manual, student handbook, advising guide, program fact sheet, brochure, work sheets, and program of study; development of relationships with other programs on campus; development of relationships with other campuses, community colleges, junior colleges, and MSW programs; re-evaluating of all syllabi (BPD and APM syllabi exchanges); faculty orientation, development, and scholarship; program component development (e.g., minority student recruitment & retention, program evaluation/data series development).

He urges that programs distinguish ongoing program work (including program outcomes evaluation) from special projects (e.g. new courses, special programs, grant work, mission or goals changes, agency-based projects, alternative programs, and importation of new technologies); and plan for both to work together harmoniously. "On-going" suggests continual effort, results, data and reports generated, and the ability to self-examine at some pre-set intervals.

The key point to all this is that much of the work of "self studying" will have been accomplished or be well underway before the formal two-years of self-study start. In essence, self-studying will be built into on-going faculty and other meetings, individual faculty assignments, student projects, advisory board and field instructor meetings. The pressurized work most programs experience during the final two-year period will be leveled out over a much longer period, and self-studying will have been somewhat integrated with the regular semester-to-semester functioning of a program.

## Concrete Ideas for "Normalizing" Accreditation Activities, or Lessening the "Divide" Between Running a Program and Doing Accreditation Activities

Consistent with Wahlberg's view, but going beyond it, is a thesis of this chapter that accreditation is best dealt with by "normalizing" knowledge of it and activities related to it within the routines of a social work education program. This is the opposite of thinking of accreditation, and the standards it uses, as something foreign, external to the program, and something of a time-limited process with which the program and institution have to contend only every several years. What is being suggested instead is, first and foremost, a mindset change for many educators. The quality concerns in the standards are intrinsic to the quality of the program and its leadership, and how the program functions normally. Thus, a set of guidelines of concrete ways that this divide can be bridged are the focus of the final section of this chapter.

- Every faculty member (and administrators responsible for the program, including those to whom the program director reports, along with advisory board members, field instructors, and students) needs to have a copy of the evaluative standards and Curriculum Policy Statement. Both can be downloaded from the CSWE Web site (**http:/ /www.cswe.org**) at no cost. Making this information widely available will enable program actors to bring it into play in meetings, orientations, retreats, or for classroom assignments.

- At least once a year, a substantial meeting is needed to go over the accreditation standards, discuss their intents and impacts on the program, and program status relative to standards. There should be no other agenda item, to ensure adequate attention to "thinking like a commissioner." Exercises in which a program component is critiqued, or a past self-study dissected, will help faculty use standards in thinking about their syllabi, their teaching, the relationship of program mission and goals to ongoing activities, and integration of curriculum components. Use of formal program evaluation data during this meeting will underscore that which can be measured as opposed to "softer" data about program functioning. Although both are valuable for informing ongoing program decisions, facility in using formal data will normalize this skill across the faculty (and model research-based practice for students, as well).

- Have all faculty engage in working with the accreditation standards as much as possible - through receiving site visitor training, being a site visitor, and attending BPD and APM workshops on standards and accreditation issues. Create both individual and program impacts for these engagements: beyond an individual faculty member gaining personal experience and knowledge in this area, expect a report back to the entire program on what was learned and on insights that might help the program relate to standards in the future.

- Employ one or more consultants, or "visiting" or exchange ("guest") faculty from other social work programs or from academic programs within the host institution, to come on campus for periodic sessions on curriculum, field, program assessment, or other issues of program quality. A great deal of faculty learning can result from having an expert work on and in your program - both about the specifics of your program, and also larger issues and perspectives on the field that a specialized academic program or practice professional expertise brings. Succeeding in gaining an annual budget allotment for "program development" (in addition to individual faculty development, which is great for faculty but often does not benefit the program directly) means that this type of focused analysis of program elements will be both feasible and expected - inside and outside the program. The availability of retired, seasoned social work educators or practitioners is often overlooked as a program development resource, as is the growing availability of information technology that the program can use to access specialized consultation or assistance in a very cost effective manner (Walz, Craft, Blum, 1991). Having field instructors, advisory board members, and other social work practitioners involved in some of these sessions can promote their wider awareness of how local issues exist or differ elsewhere, and how answers to local questions can germinate elsewhere.

- Get faculty used to writing formal reports on the program: descriptions of components, procedural statements, curriculum committee linking parts of the curriculum, elaborating definition of practice, job descriptions, and formal assessments of outcomes. To the extent these become usual, periodic, on-going events and products, their incorporation into a self-study is easier, and more sure because faculty "do that for a living." Involve all faculty in writing up parts of the self-study, or curriculum and other documents done between accreditation reviews that are tied to standards. Faculty will be more apt to understand general expectations for their teaching, and why these exist.

- Do job descriptions for all administrators, faculty, and staff. Do one for the program's advisory board, as well. Although social work educators are well aware of the complexity of their jobs, they often lack effective ways of communicating this to their administrators, social work program colleagues, or to faculty outside their program. A job description is a widely-understood means to capture the scope

and depth of your job, and quickly relates to workloads and eventually
to resources needed to meet those workloads including personnel
searches. Role conflicts and overlaps can also be identified, as will
be expectations of one another because these documents are shared
among program actors.

- Do annual faculty productivity plans so that scholarly work,
  embracing all the possible arenas for such activity included in the
  evaluative standard discussing it, can be clear for each faculty member.
  This is an enabling document, for it helps chart how a faculty member,
  no matter what his/her current level or type of scholarship, can build
  on that base. Both individual and program needs can be considered
  here, with implications possible for program evaluation and
  curriculum development

- Consider creating committee productivity plans for each of the faculty
  or faculty-student committees of the program. These plans can factor
  in work identified in the accreditation standards --e.g., evaluation of
  program objectives attainment, monitoring of program quality,
  curriculum analyses, bringing new knowledge into the program, and
  anticipating impacts on the program from outside actors or factors.
  As these plans help focus the work of committees, and set year-to-
  year deadlines for accomplishing a part of the overall work, the
  "products" that result can be captured for self-study use.

- Look to institutional resources to augment staffing and to pay for
  program evaluation activities. The technology of educational program
  assessment will continue to grow in importance to higher education
  institutions. Skill development of social work faculty might be
  justified partly in terms of later benefits to the university community.
  There are several cases in which social work faculty have been asked
  to take leadership roles in campus-wide efforts because of their
  experience in this field through responsiveness to accreditation
  standards. This type of wider focus and benefit that is argued in
  Chapter 2 as necessary for the program director might, in at least this
  area, apply also to other social work faculty.

## Summary

The program evaluation and administration mindset of this chapter is
that accreditation is viewed as an asset to the social work education enterprise.

Many concrete examples of this mindset or perspective exist. Social work syllabi are likely among the most fully developed in any program in the institution. Campus-wide curriculum development efforts may value the skills needed to create such syllabi, and the values that underlie social work efforts to empower students. Similarly, social work field practicum programs are typically the most fully thought through and realized of any educational program with an experience component. As this type of program grows in appeal to students for its "real-world" testing abilities, social work educators are well positioned to train others in what produces quality experiences. The accreditation standards underscore the importance of maintaining strong links with the practice community, and field and advisory boards are the usual on-going mechanisms to this end. As partnerships between educational institutions and their communities become more common, social work educators again are among the more experienced educators in building bridges (joint actions, projects, etc.) between the educational institution and the community.

From this "quality enhancement" perspective of program accreditation, formal periodic program review results in an increased self-consciousness of the stakeholders about the effectiveness of current educational practices being applied. Such review allows these practices to be modified to improve the quality of the academic enterprise. As a result of the director applying a "quality enhancement" lens on the accreditation process, dynamic program advancement is fostered in such ways as

- Providing ongoing opportunities for collegial dialog focused on improving the relationship between faculty intentions, instructional methods, student performance, and program outcomes.

- Applying instructional methods that encourage students to shape, reflect, build on, and apply the knowledge that they are gaining.

- Providing structured learning opportunities for students to develop critical and comparative perspectives about the strengths and limitations of the conceptual and professional lenses through which they have learned to view social problems, professional issues, and practice theories.

- Preparing students to leave the academy sufficiently confident and professionally competent to function effectively within the contemporary realities of evolving practice.

- Providing an educational milieu that ensures the availability of opportunities for students to experience the intellectual excitement of discovery, interaction, critical discourse, and professional challenges that faculty experience.

- Explicitly connecting social work with liberal learning and other disciplines and professional specializations to help students synthesize and bring what is learned in one context to others and to join collaboratively in advancing the knowledge base of the profession.

In conclusion, this chapter has examined the ways that program directors, leading their faculties, might most usefully think about and act regarding program accreditation. Accreditation certainly requires program attention, but it need not be highly unpredictable or even unnerving. These thoughts are dedicated to promoting that as a reality for social work education programs.

# Notes

(1) This discussion often uses the term "program" to talk collectively about the work done by faculty, admininstrators, and staff. This is done consciously to reflect the view of the Commission on accreditation and its accreditation standards that programs are accredited, and an accreditation review looks at each component element as a part of a total program (e.g., evaluation is of attainment of program objectives, not of individual faculty work or progress of individual students - important as these are, they are not usually part of the program's objectives). Individual course syllabi are looked at in the context of program purposes. "Thinking and acting as a program" is reinforced, rather than individual actions or stances.

(2) Recommended sources for learning more about curriculum design and development are:

(3) This example is shared by Dr. Harry Macy out of his faculty's work at Ball State University's Social Work Program. This is but one example of strategic program development utilized in this program. (Personal communication, 1999). The reader should also turn back to the discussion of strategic management in Chapter 2 of this book.

# References

American Association of Social Work Boards. (1999). Social work laws and board regulations, author. (www.aaswb.org).

Council on Social Work Education. (1994). Handbook of accreditation standards and procedures, (Fourth Edition). Policy Statements on the Role and Value of Accreditation, adopted by the Council on Postsecondary Accreditation, April 15, 1982; page 3.

Council on Social Work Education. (1994). Handbook of accreditation standards and procedures, (Fourth Edition). Council on Social Work Education, Alexandria, VA.

Evens, W. (1998). "Resources: BPD new director training." Presentation at the Annual Program Meeting of CSWE, Orlando, FL, March 1998.

Gibbs, P. (1995, Winter). Accreditation of BSW programs. Journal of Social Work Education, 31(1), 4-16.

Hafner, K.A., & Oblinger, D.G. (1998). The future compatible campus: Planning, designing, and implementing information technology in the academy. Bolton, MA: Anker Publishing Co, Inc.

Joyner, M. (1998). "Resources: BPD new director training." Presentation at the Annual Program Meeting of CSWE. Orlando, FL, March 1998.

Mabrey, T. (1998, Winter). Accreditation decisions in social work education: Looking for patterns, 1985-92. Journal of Social Work Education, 34(1), 21-30.

Munson, C. (1994, Winter). Characteristics of excellence in social work education. Journal of Social Work Education, 30(1), 42-53.

Triche, C. (1995). "Rising like a phoenix: A program survives withdrawal of accreditation." Paper presented at the 13th annual BPD Conference, San Francisco, CA, October 1995.

Wahlberg, J. (1992). "Between accreditation reviews - Changing our vision: Affirming our past, shaping our future." Paper presented at the tenth annual BPD Conference, San Antonio, TX, September 1992.

Walz, T. J., Craft, & Blum, N. (1991, Winter). Social work faculty in retirement: A national study. Journal of Social Work Education, 27(1), 60-72.

Wilson, S. (1996). An analysis of Commission on Accreditation decisions in social work education: 1988-1995." Paper presented at the 14th annual BPD Conference, Portland, OR, October 1996.

Zastrow, C. (1999). Personal communication, June 6, 1999.

# Bibliography

Dinerman, M., & Walden, T. (1989). Social work accreditation: The view from below. Journal of Teaching in Social Work, 3(2), 17-33.

Drumm, R., Suppes, M. A., Kersting, R., & Medlin, N. (1998). "Small social work programs: Strengths and challenges in autonomy and resources." Paper presented at the 16th Annual Baccalaureate Program Directors Conference, Albuquerque, NM, October 1998.

Gibbs, P. (n.d.) "Attitudes about and analysis of accreditation in social work education." Paper submitted for publication.

Gibbs, P. (1996). "Searching for accreditation's alternative paradigm." Paper presented at the 14th Annual BPD Conference, Portland, OR, October 1996.

Heintzelman, K. (1997). "Assessing the impact of the revised curriculum policy statement." Paper presented at the 15th Annual BPD Conference, Philadelphia, PA, October 1997.

Johnson, H.W., & Hull, G. (1990, Fall). The rest of the story: Baccalaureate social work program no longer accredited. Journal of Social Work Education. 26(3), 244-253.

Woehrle, K., & Ennis, F. (1997). "Computer assisted curriculum development for accreditation." Paper presented at the 15h Annual BPD Conference, Philadelphia, PA, October 1997.

Wolk, J., & Wertheimer, M.. (1999, Winter). Generalist practice vs. case management: An accreditation contradiction. Journal of Social Work Education, 35(1), 101-113.

Young, K.E., & Associates. (1983), Understanding accreditation. San Francisco: Jossey-Bass.

The author would like to acknowledge the generous sharing of ideas for this chapter by Betty Guhman, Emelicia Mizio, Miriam Raskin, Jack Sellers, Mary Ann Suppes, and Charles Zastrow.

# Chapter 8

# Academic Program Administration: An Overview

The seven previous chapters have focused on administrative tasks related to program operations or domains. These chapters have been designed to focus readers on taking swift and decisive action to address program demands, and many readers will find no need to go beyond them. Others, however, may wish to delve more deeply into the theories, concepts, and literature that underlie academic program administration. This chapter provides further discussion of an ecologically-oriented administrative leadership framework; considers significant institutional, professional, and environmental factors that form the administrative context of the director's job; discusses a more assertive leadership framework than heretofore presented; and connects the reader to recommended sources in the literature for further explorations.

## Ecologically Oriented Administrative Framework

A useful administrative framework for a program director is what we term an "ecological-systems perspective," to be used to identify program supports, development opportunities and barriers to improved effectiveness. We suggest that directors "take on" this perspective, much as they might put on a pair of eyeglasses. The perspective changes perception in two ways — the way one views a situation and the way one sees oneself in a situation. One can apply a new perspective, or framework, to understand or examine organizational behaviors, processes, and policies to understand the position of undergraduate social work program director.

Systems-oriented thinking is probably familiar to those who read and teach social work, but a few points of discussion may help to clarify the philosophy of this approach as applied to academic program administration. A linear cause-effect process of breaking problems into as many separate parts as possible and examining each part as a means of explaining the whole, useful as it may be in the scientific laboratory, does not work well in human resource administration. Systems thinking goes beyond arbitrary divisions of knowledge and disciplinary boundaries. It is a way of thinking about any kind of action, situation, or problem. A systems perspective is the opposite of the mechanical view of the world, with its simple cause-effect relationship or linear causality. Nonlinear causality denotes relational, unanticipated changes, human systems, and processes that are anchored in a mutual causality view of interactions between and among individuals within a relationship system; each participant's emotionality, the system's overall emotion field, and the interaction with other co-mingled systems and subsystems.

The systems perspective recognizes the constant change and flux in human systems, the wholeness of activities, the interdependence of people and their environments, and the required focus on the functional relationships between entities that comprise a defined social system. An administrative emphasis is placed on process, the nature and quality of the interactions, and the relative effectiveness of functional relationships, as well as the internalizing of a nonlinear perspective or management orientation that guides administrative actions, decisions, and interactions. A systems-oriented perspective holds that failure to recognize connections and patterned interactions will result in wasted efforts and fosters repetitive or less effective actions.

Many authors have recognized the need for a conceptual shift from viewing the world as a hierarchy of systems to viewing it as an interconnected web of life (Capra, 1982; Belenky, Clinchy, Goldberger, & Tarule, 1997), and of the importance of viewing the ecological interrelationships between people and their environments. Various labels have been applied to an ecosystem approach, including the "life model" of social work practice (Germain & Gitterman, 1980), "systems thinking" (Berger & Federico, 1982), a "systems approach" (Anderson & Carter, 1974; Longres, 1990), "ecological perspective" (Germain, 1979, 1991), "the social systems model" (Chess & Norlin, 1991), "holistic management" (DeGreene, 1990) and "nonlinear" change dynamics (Warren, Franklin, & Streeter, 1998). Although emphasizing different concepts and incorporating threads from various theories, all of these perspectives reflect the basic assumptions derived from the work of Ludwig von Bertalanffy (1968), a biologist who first proposed the General Systems Theory. Scholars representing numerous disciplines within the social sciences such as anthropology, economics, psychology, political science, and sociology have adapted his theory to describe the internal processes of human systems and phenomena associated with an ecosystem's complexities.

Sommer (1995) recommends the use of the "new" science of "fractals" to demonstrate the importance of a holistic administrative perspective. Fractals are computer-generated models drawn by the interaction of equations; equations that change as they are fed back upon themselves. They produce forms and shapes of such intricacy that they can never be successfully measured. Fractals require qualitative measurement, focusing the attention of the observer on the shapes and patterns of the whole rather than the parts. They teach the futility of reductionist thinking and of breaking down the whole into never-ending discrete parts.

"Fractal-type organizations," according to Wheatley (1992), "have learned to trust in natural organizing phenomena, they trust in the power of guiding principles or values, knowing that they are strong enough influences of behavior to shape every employee into a desired representative of the organization" (p. 132). Because much of the labor of the individual academic is performed alone or only in the company of students, academic environments provide more opportunity to enhance these "fractal-type" conditions. Program directors who are able to clearly express the mission, purpose, values, and direction of the program - along with work expectations that support autonomy - can set the stage for natural organizing to occur (Sommer, 1995).

Translating a holistically administrative orientation to work organizations, one can learn a lot about the way an organization solves problems (Wheatley, 1992). Is the whole examined? Do people step back from the problem in order to observe the shape and form it takes from the many variables involved? Are people encouraged to look for themes, patterns, interactions, and linkages rather than isolated causes? An observer can determine the organization's values and methods of doing business by simply observing any member of the system, from custodian to administrator (Wheatley, 1992, p. 132).

Suppose, for example, a director has two faculty members within her program who repeatedly argue over the philosophy of education. Two individuals are mutually and simultaneously influencing each other's behavior so that the behavior in each is the product of the interaction between the two (Sweet, 1998). If she attempts to break down each difference into as many pieces as possible in order to understand each aspect of their disagreement, she may enter an endless cycle of argumentation that reaches few conclusions and wastes valuable administrative time. If she takes a holistic view of their arguments, or the way in which the two professors interact, she might discover that the real issue between them is one of status or political power. Taking a systems approach (Sommer, 1995) - viewing the individuals as inseparable, co-determined entities with reciprocal, adaptive interactions - might lead her to a new understanding of the problem and to a solution much faster.

# Ecologically Oriented Administrative Concepts: Contingency Oriented Decision Making

## Environment Scanning - Goodness-of-Fit

Due to the infinite number and variations of functional relationships found within the five operational domains of an academic program, among the program's stakeholders and between a program and its institutional and external environments, there is no one "ideal" way of administering a CSWE accredited social work program. An ecological-systems perspective provides a useful administrative framework for a program director to understand and balance influences, communication, relationships, controls, and feedback from various internal and external environments of the academic enterprise. Economic, social, legal, and political trends outside the institution and constituencies both inside and external to the institution help to shape the character of the academic program. The director views the program as an open system which recognizes the dynamic interrelationships and interactions between the environments of the program and its stakeholders in terms of input-transformation-output of allocated resources, educational processes, program operations, and governance procedures (Weiner, 1982).

Three interrelated administrative practices that apply an ecological-systems perspective include contingency-oriented management, environmental scanning and assessing the goodness-of-fit dynamics of a program. These three practices can be used together as they play off one another.

### 1. Contingency-Oriented Management

A contingency-oriented leadership management process almost naturally evolves from an ecological administrative perspective which focuses on the interrelationships of such factors within an accredited program as the organizational structure, institutional contexts, program domain tasks performed by faculty, stakeholder interests and the external regulatory environmental influences. According to Carlisle (1973), a contingency approach to administration:

... supports the notion that there is no one best way to lead people, organize groups, arrange tasks, or manage an enterprise. Also, there is no one best system for planning, controlling, budgeting, coordinating, or integrating the operations of an organization. A manager's effectiveness and the techniques [used] are entirely functions of a properly integrated situation. The interpretation consists of assessing the primary factors in the situation and selecting and applying the techniques and methods that are appropriate to the situation as determined by the particular factors. (p. 73).

The interpretation or assessment process identified by Carlisle is followed by the decision making step that is anchored in the theoretical concept that the effectiveness of organizational decision making is enhanced when there is opportunity for the involvement and participation of personnel in addressing specific situations or problems faced by the organization. Therefore, a key administrative task inherent of contingency management is the need to foster the development of a decision and collaborative process that is designed to involve the most appropriate personnel in addressing organizational problems, completing work tasks and participating in the planning process.

Further elaboration of contingency-oriented management is provided by Bensimon, Neumann, and Birnbaum (1989, p. 15) who state:

Contingency theories attempt to indicate how the leaders' behavior is shaped and thus constrained by situational factors and unfolding events, including pressures to conform to others' expectations, institutional regulations and routines, orders by superiors, nature of the task, perception of the external environment, feedback about organizational effectiveness, environmental complexity and stability, organizational structure, interdependence of subunits, complexity of tasks, and subordinates' orientation toward goals. Some observers suggest that leaders' behavior may be shaped by their level in the hierarchy (leaders at lower levels have less discretion), the nature of the functions of the organizational unit (production leaders can be more directive than research leaders), characteristics of the task and the technology (leaders of low-complexity tasks can be more authoritarian), size of the organizational unit (leaders of larger units engage in less support behavior), lateral interdependence (leaders of interdependent groups are less responsive to their subordinates), subordinates' competence (effective leaders emphasize performance with weaker subordinates), and presence of a crisis (leaders are expected to act more decisively in crises) (see, e.g., Bass, 1985; Fiedler, 1967, 1971, 1987; Hersey & Blanchard, 1977; Mintzberg, 1973; Sayles, 1979; Yukl, 1971, 1981).

## 2. **Environmental Scanning**

A contingency-oriented administrative approach relies on the use of an administrative assessment process called *environmental scanning*. Environmental scanning, the second ecological-systems administrative practice perspective, is the assessment of the level of complementarity between the program and its institutional-based and external regulatory, resource and development entities (Sommer & Macy, 1995). It calls for a program director to be attuned to the environment of the program as well as the program itself. Maintaining a systems perspective will facilitate this focus or perspective.

In environmental scanning, the program director looks at all micro, mezzo and macro-sized systems located in the environment to: (a) define the "nested" or embedded environmental systems that affect the social work program; (b) identify the major entities that influence the academic and professional service responsibilities of the program and study how they interact; and (c) promote compatibility between these entities and the program.

The director's planning, leading, organizing, staffing, coordinating, motivating, budgeting, reporting, and evaluating processes need to consider external and internal influences and to focus on the interrelationships, differences, and commonalties of the subsystems in the program's environment. Interpersonal relationships and information flow, both inside and outside the organization, strongly influence the quality and quantity of environmental scanning that can be done. This scanning process also helps the director to examine the environment in terms of existing program tensions, obstacles, and opportunities.

An ecological systems administrative perspective which anchors the scanning or assessment process is illustrated in Figure 8.1 which uses a series of circles to provide a representation of the various environments of a social work program.

The micro system—the program director—is in the center, nested inside larger and larger circles representing other systems to which the director is connected. Each system has its own component parts, its own facilitating and restraining forces, and its own processes of functioning and adapting. Each system — from micro to macro — is at once a whole system and a part of many other systems, a *holon*. Each stands in interaction with its larger environment. Appendix F identifies examples of significant organizations, interest groups, trends, and a range of entities found within each of the circles or nested environments illustrated in Figure 8.1. The examples identified within each layer of the external systems, (see Appendix F) moving from the program's most micro to most macro systems are factors considered when completing the assessment or scanning process.

## FIGURE 8.1

### Nested Systems

In the ecological perspective, the director is the micro-system nested inside increasingly larger systems.

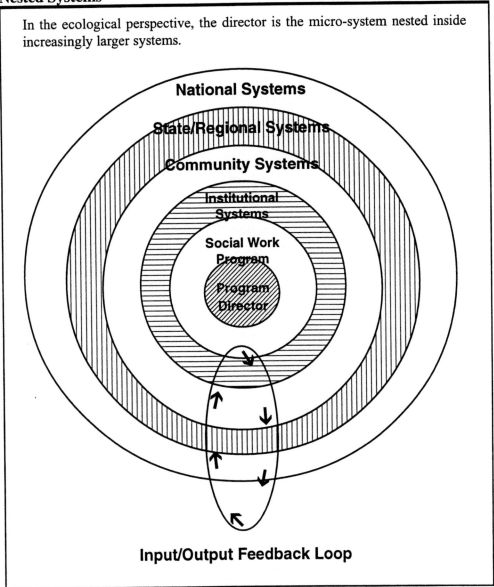

**National Systems**

**State/Regional Systems**

**Community Systems**

**Institutional Systems**

**Social Work Program**

**Program Director**

**Input/Output Feedback Loop**

National economic, social, legal, and political trends depicted in the outermost layer of Appendix F, influence the broad mission and priorities of higher education. Hafner and Oblinger, (1998), among others, discuss influences impacting higher education institutions that house social work programs.

Monitoring higher education and social work trends is helpful to the director when setting program development priorities. Knowing that the number of traditional students will dramatically decline during the next decade, for example, the director can lead faculty efforts to accommodate the needs of part-time students. Increased emphasis on student recruitment, development of more flexible field instruction options, scheduling of required courses to be offered at night, and increasing the number of paid field practicum options are examples of increasing the access to the social work programs.

As colleges and universities incrementally shift priorities to accommodate such internal and external environmental influences, there are corresponding transformation pressures placed on academic programs to improve governance, relevancy, access, effectiveness, efficiency, outcomes, and marketability. Such influences, in turn, may affect the administrative priorities of a social work program in its attempts to better fit or meet the needs of state or regional needs.

Through their research and policy initiatives national constituencies and human service coalitions also influence the general priorities of social work education and practice, although their influence is less direct than that exercised by accrediting and licensing entities. National organizations and coalitions such as the American Public Welfare Association and the National Institute on Social Work Research would be included here.

To stay informed, a social work program director routinely reads publications that examine the international, national, and institutional trends that influence higher education. Weekly news publications such as *The Chronicle of Higher Education,* academic administrative newsletters such as *Academic Leader -The Newsletter For Academic Deans and Department Chairs,* and publications of the Council on Social Work Education such as the annual report, *Statistics On Social Work Education In The United States* are examples of useful academic administratively-oriented readings. The CSWE accreditation standards are required reading as a key source of external, quality oriented guidelines that can influence program planning and development options.

At the state and regional level, examples of environmental influences include economic and employment conditions, relationship with the state-level National Association of Social Workers (NASW) chapters, licensing or regulation of social work profession, and the amount of educational resources available and competition for those resources. It is important to be aware of the thrust of the governmental systems within the social environment of the program as it varies over time. For instance, a state government may declare child abuse to be a high priority and make educational grants or stipends available to workers within the child welfare agencies. It is important, therefore, for a director to be linked effectively to information sources to keep abreast of legislative and executive issues and have access to and a working relationship with legislative advocacy and information networks as well as key legislative and executive officials in order to make timely program-based responses to both opportunities and threats.

At the community level, the program director might consider a variety of influences and factors. These include the social service and professional practice network, public perceptions of the program and institution, social work and institutional alumnae/alumni network, the connectedness of the program and institution to the community, and the existence of competing social work programs. Program directors may find themselves in a key position to address the education and training needs of the social work community. Or, they may find that a significant number of their alumnae/alumni who are interested in obtaining masters degrees, thereby signaling the need for development of a new degree offering.

External program constituencies such as regional human service coalitions, area legislative officials, state-level public welfare, health, and community development officials, and social work practitioners are potential sources of assistance. These stakeholders can help the program, for example, in creating continuing education programming, obtaining grants for applied research, staff development, and completing the CSWE accreditation process. Practitioners may also serve as field instructors, adjunct faculty, and alumnae/alumni representatives for the program.

To provide long-range program planning and leadership, a director keeps up with social work professional issues such as employment patterns, NASW practice standards, human service legal regulations, and social welfare legislative and funding changes (Gibelman, 1999). These issues, over time, help shape professional practice priorities, contemporary knowledge needed by entry-level practitioners, and specific practice competencies required by emerging social service delivery systems. In order to remain informed of contemporary professional developments, a program director can maintain a diverse formal and informal information network comprised of NASW-sponsored newsletters, legislative alerts prepared by various advocacy and special interest groups, access key electronic bulletin boards such as the one for baccalaureate social work program directors (bpd@listserver), and routinely attend local and state-level legislative and human service coalition meetings. In addition, a program director can attend such annual conferences as those sponsored by the Association of Baccalaureate Social Work Program Directors, the National Association of Social Workers (NASW), the Council on Social Work Education (CSWE - www.cswe.org), and key state and regional social work educational conferences in order to stay informed about social work education, accreditation, and practice.

Maintaining an information network requires a major commitment of time and effort, but it is invaluable to the program director in long-range planning and being pro-active in administrative approaches. Therefore, it is viewed as an essential administrative function that is understood, supported, and affirmed by the central administration of the institution.

An indirect result of efforts to maintain compliance with the CSWE accrediting standards is that a baccalaureate social work education program actually extends the institution's focus on serving students in a total fashion. Programs, in essence, focus on the entire individual in a holistic manner, and serve students who have disparate needs that require a range of personalized support and developmental services to complement the provision of a rigorous academic professionally oriented degree program (Black, Jeffreys & Hartley, 1993; Cobb & Jordan, 1989; Cole & Lewis, 1993; Gibbs, 1994; and Koerin & Miller, 1995).

## 3. Goodness-of-Fit

The third administrative practice that applies an ecological systems perspective to program administration is a *goodness-of-fit* assessment to examine how systems interact. Goodness-of-fit is a concept used by some systems theorists to describe how well the system matches with its environment. Germain and Gitterman (1980) described this phenomenon as it is related to individuals:

Thus, adaptation represents a joint achievement of individual and environment in reaching a goodness-of-fit between adaptive skills and qualities, the progressive forces in this person, and growth-supporting properties and structure of the environment. (p. 80)

Figure 8.2 illustrates the various distinct components that can comprise a baccalaureate social work program from an ecological perspective.

An ongoing assessment of the relative compatibility between the program components illustrated in Figure 8.2 is an important factor in defining a program planning and administrative priorities which can promote effective management (Wheeler & Gibbons, 1992; Johnson, 1990; and Halter & Gullerud, 1995). Examining the exchanges between systems will identify tension points, undefined areas, obstacles, and untapped opportunities (Flax & Swaine, 1996). At each point of interaction, one might ask the question: "How is each system perceived by the other system?" Similarly, at each decision point it is valuable to ask the question, "What is in the perceived interest of other systems at this point of decision-making?" Feedback, both positive and negative, is crucial in this assessment process.

# FIGURE 8.2

## The Baccalaureate of Social Work Program Components and Interrelationships

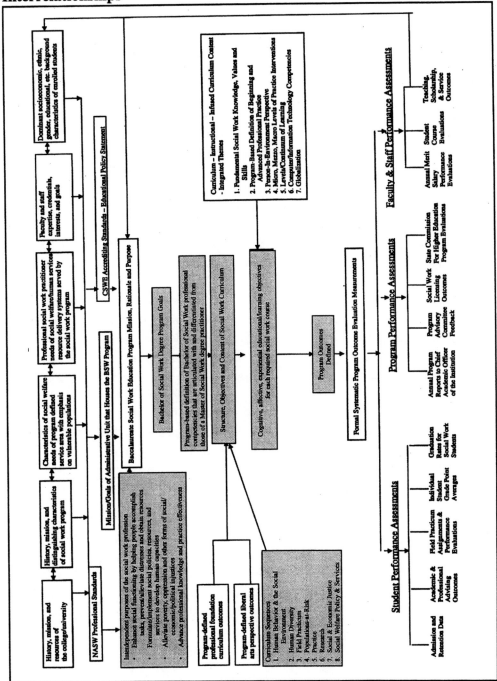

If, for example, the objectives of the social work program are "out of sync" with the mission of its institution, an inhibiting rather than a facilitative environment may exist. This "mismatch" produces some interesting organizational dynamics. The program director may appear deliberately "anti-organization," as if self-destruction was the ultimate program priority, or the program may appear to purposely isolate itself from the mainstream of institutional life, as if "to hide from view" was a major administrative strategy. Such a lack of "fit" influences the director's position. The impact may be seen in the level of routine administrative conflict that exists between the director and other institutional decision makers, in the nature of program priorities, in the types of administrative strategies used to promote program interests within the institution, and in the level of antagonistic communication between the director and administrative superiors. In the most extreme cases, this mismatch can threaten the very survival of the social work program (Johnson and Hull, 1990).

Anderson (1962), in his review of the educational dimensions of preparing students for successful entry into professional career roles, identified fifteen specific problem areas, all of which are applicable in some degree to social work education programs. These problem areas are viewed as the basis from which a number of potential program institutional tensions or conflicts naturally occur which, in turn, are a source for the conflicting and unique administrative responsibilities inherent in baccalaureate social work degree programs. The fifteen specific problem areas identified by Anderson have been adapted to baccalaureate social work education and grouped according to six overlapping administrative tension areas identified below:

(1) Translating the dynamic and distinctive program objectives of a professional society into educational outcomes; developing these objectives into an accreditable academic curriculum; and continually reforming program objectives in order to maintain ongoing relevance within a dynamic human services profession.

(2) Maintaining the autonomy and resources needed to provide a value-based, professional degree-oriented education program within an institutional structure designed to promote standardized, cost-effective, outcome-oriented, educational outputs.

(3) Balancing the acquisition of specialized social work knowledge within a required liberal arts oriented curriculum and developing methods of integrating these two types of knowledge orientations within a standardized, CSWE accreditable curriculum.

(4) Maintaining working relationships with officials from both the university and the professional communities, whose goals and performance expectations for the program and students differ.

(5) Reconciling university admission and program standards with those required by a professional degree program while maintaining an appropriate number of high quality competent practitioners to meet the market demands of professional human service delivery systems.

(6) Developing and maintaining a program of sufficient quality so that graduates can compete favorably with students from other universities for positions in the social work profession, maintaining distinct academic boundaries between competing academic disciplines such as psychology, sociology and criminology, and implementing a curriculum that requires cognitive, affective, and experiential learning opportunities to enable selected students to demonstrate specified competencies that are commensurate with dynamic national professional practice and ethical standards (pp. 14-24).

These different tension areas collectively represent a formidable challenge to the faculty and the director to "fit" a baccalaureate social work program within its institutional "home" by striving to continually improve the complementarity of program and institutional purposes, functions and operations.

## Example of the Application of Contingency Management - Environmental Scanning - Goodness-of-Fit Administrative Practices

Program directors facilitate the development of a professionally-oriented educational milieu that fosters, in a holistic individualized fashion, the academic and professional performance by selected students who are required to demonstrate prescribed practice competencies in order to receive baccalaureate social work degrees. This holistic educational orientation, designed to serve students in an individualized oriented manner, cannot be routinized easily. The exact specifications for creating an effective teaching-learning process, for example, cannot be defined specifically or replicated exactly across the entire curriculum. As a result, the social work program operationalizes a very effective contingency-oriented student services network with a diverse range of academic, personal, financial, and social development entities located both within and external to the institution in order to supplement and support academic development of social work students.

The structural illustration of a baccalaureate social work program, provided in Figure 8.2, can be used to exemplify the application of environmental scanning and the goodness-of-fit assessments. The following example, which focuses on the student characteristics component of the structural illustration, illustrates how a director would apply an ecological systems administrative perspective and use a contingency-oriented program management approach to improve the complementarity between program-based and institutional-based student affairs operations.

## 1. Student Characteristics - Demographic Profile

The academic profile of students served by the institution and the complementarity of the academic background of students to the program's admission and retention standards influence the nature of academic and professional advising that students will need, along with the type and level of academic and professional support services needed to help social work students achieve program performance outcomes. If the majority of students enrolled in the institution and the social work program are, for example, first generation college students, have "average" SAT test scores, and have lived in an area with limited ethnic diversity, their advising and professional socialization needs will differ from academically "superior" students whose parents are college graduates and originate from an ethnically diverse locale. If the majority of students enrolled in the program have very little opportunity to socialize with persons of color when growing up, for example, the number and scope of experiential learning opportunities is a program emphasis and becomes an administrative priority for the director. Routine monitoring, by the director, of the demographic profile of students enrolling in the institution is completed by the program.

## 2. Social Welfare Delivery System - Practitioner Needs

The types and levels of professional BSW competencies needed by social service systems in the geographic region served by the institution, the compatibility of these needs to the program goals, curriculum content, and educational outcomes are systematically monitored to help maintain program relevancy. A program-sponsored advisory group of practitioners, for example, can assist a program to identify service trends and evolving practice methods, thereby goodness-of-fit is promoted. Mobilizing and supporting a program advisory group becomes an administrative priority along with systematic evaluation of employment patterns of graduates.

## 3. **Institutional Resources**

Environmental scanning is used to identify the institutional operations and officers who represent institutional-based resources such as academic evaluation or student recruitment. These operations are routinely assessed to promote the linkage to program needs and evaluative operations. Student performance and program outcome evaluation needs of the program help provide current evaluative data for use in program development and defining advancement goals. The evaluative requirements of regional accrediting organizations of colleges and universities are a source of institutional data and evaluation procedures that are incorporated into and used to supplement a program-based outcome evaluation process. The student recruitment system (see Figure 4.3) used by the institution represents potential means for adapting the program's recruitment priorities to the institutional-based procedures to increase the number, quality, and diversity of social work students. Social work faculty participation in the institution's recruitment efforts used include helping admissions staff with outreach presentations, meeting with visiting students, providing current social work career literature to recruiters, and establishing an alumni network to contact potential students. These types of initiatives promote the "fit" of the program within the institutional mission and priorities.

The "fit" of vertical relationships between the program goals, the program's definition of entry-level or beginning professional practice, and the program-defined outcomes in turn, directly shape the selection of curriculum structure and content as illustrated by the shaded program components found in Figure 8.2. Three program outcome examples are provided.

1. Demonstrate commitment to the purposes, values and ethics of the social work profession, and to social change through the provision of services to individuals, families, groups, communities, and organizations and participate in professional initiatives that promote economic and social justice.

2. Apply an ecological systems perspective in understanding human development and behavior, analyze interactions among individuals, and evaluate transactions between individuals and their environment.

3. Use program outcome measures, practice evaluation measures, and apply research findings to advance professional competencies and service effectiveness.

These three specific program outcome examples match or are consistent with the needs of social workers in the regional social welfare service systems, which, in turn, shape the program's mission and goals and the formal, program-based definition of baccalaureate degree professional practice. Conceptual knowledge, values and skills inherent in each of the outcomes are explicitly presented within the required basic curriculum sequence and in the primary curriculum cognate, and are taught using cognitive, affective, and experiential instructional methods. Student performance is systematically evaluated to ascertain that graduates indeed can demonstrate the acquisition of these three formal program outcomes. The program design structure, illustrated in Figure 8.2 therefore, attempts to illustrate the connectedness (vertical and horizontal) of all the major components of a program to each other and to create a dynamic, goal-oriented, systemic educational processes that is continually being delivered, documented, evaluated, and advanced.

At the institutional level, numerous variables affect the goodness-of-fit for the program director. These include the public or private sanction of the institution, undergraduate college or combined undergraduate social work educational program, the size and location of the institution; church-related or nonsectarian; relative research, teaching, professional service in reward systems emphasis; values regarding professional degree programs (Icard, Spearmon & Curry-Jackson, 1996); economic "health" of the institution; type of student recruited; administrative structures and processes (Shank, Piliavin & Mailick Seltzer, 1994); union or nonunion; and degree of shared vision and shared voice of the institution.

Given the fact that all systems are in a constant state of change, their relationships are also dynamic (Murdrick, Steiner & Pollard, 1992). Assessment of goodness-of-fit, therefore, is time-bounded. For instance, appreciation of the mission of social work education by college may exist only as long as a particular dean or president is in office. A change in administration personnel may suddenly change the perceived value of a social work program within the larger institution. Or, in economic hard times, priority shifts may be established within the institution that reduces the relative value of the social work education program by favoring response to human problems and needs in a much different way than would social work educators (Blostein, 1999; Reinardy & Halter, 1994).

Two other "tools" are offered in Appendix K to help the reader begin the environmental scanning and goodness-of-fit assessment processes: 1) a detailed listing and diagram of elements contained within each major system (macro, mezzo, and micro) and 2) a scanning checklist with initial questions about each system layer. This checklist provides a beginning step in the ongoing organizational scanning and assessment that is part of the ecological administrative framework analysis. The results of these processes can provide a more holistic view of the program's current status and direction as well as help determine areas needing additional attention and energy (e.g. contingencies) to help the program director, faculty members, and professional staff deal with obstacles, take advantage of opportunities, and develop the program's potential.

# Organizational Characteristics of Colleges and Universities

Colleges and universities are complex bureaucratic organizations. They have such classical features of a bureaucracy as a formal hierarchical decision structure, an official command-control-reward configuration, appointed officials with specific duties, formal regulations, and a central administrative authority that coordinates the educational enterprise. These institutions, however, also share some significant differences such as faculty-based curriculum control, and a peer-based academic tenure system. The complexities of academic program administration is exacerbated by the need for a program director to understand and competently apply both the bureaucratic, and the collegiate governance structures found in colleges or universities.

A summary overview of seven distinguishing characteristics of a college or university that directly influence academic program administration, planning, governance, and decision-making is provided to alert the director to the unique attributes of academic program administration. Each summary description also represents an invitation to explore the extensive theoretical field of higher education organizations and administrative research in order to gain a fuller understanding of the administrative process. The eight characteristics include:

- Chaotic organization structure

- Organizational culture

- Division of labor

- Position sanction

- Administrative role ambiguity

- Middle management administrative role dynamics

- Institutional structures

- Functional specialization of faculty and staff

## Chaotic Organizational Structure

No two organizations are exactly alike. Distinct variations in such fundamental characteristics as organizational mission and goals, nature of clientele served, application of specific technologies, characteristics of the personnel employed, decision and work structures, and relationships with external environments are common. Colleges and universities represent a unique type of bureaucratic organization that is identified by higher education researchers as an "organized anarchy" (Baldrige, 1971, Blau, 1973, Cohen and March, 1974).

In a university anarchy, each individual in the university is seen as making autonomous decisions. Teachers decide if, when, and what to teach. Students decide if, when, and what to learn. Legislators and donors decide if, when, and what to support. Neither coordination...nor control [is] practiced. Resources are allocated by whatever process emerges but without explicit accommodation and without explicit reference to some superordinate goal. The "decisions" of the system are a consequence produced by the system but intended by no one and decisively controlled by no one. (Cohen and March, 1974, pages 33-34)

Found within the "organized anarchy" structure of a colleges or universities, organizational features such as (1) ambiguous goals embedded in academic specializations, (2) reliance on self determined instruction methods, (3) specialized professional service, (4) discipline-specific oriented scholarship, (5) and academic governance dominated by autonomously oriented academic specialists. These features do not make a college or university a bad organization or even a disorganized one, but do make institutions of higher education difficult to accurately describe, understand, and lead.

As previously noted, there are growing demands faced by higher education institutions for increased financial and programmatic accountability, outcome oriented measures, improved productivity, greater cost effectiveness, and improved access and flexibility are among the major issues that directly conflict with the fundamental organizational and structure characteristics embodied in an "organized anarchy" structure. Any effective administrative model therefore, matches the distinctive characteristics of an organization. Contemporary pressures at the academic program levels require the development of innovative administrative practices that blend the respective strengths of historical higher education structures such as faculty determination of academic curriculum content with those found in innovative organization structures such as quality control based, team-oriented decision making.

## Organizational Culture

The nature of the organizational cultures found in colleges and universities is an important context for academic program administration. Organizational culture is a:

> ...pattern of basic assumptions that a given group has invented, discovered, or developed in learning to cope with its problems of external adaptation and internal integration, and that has worked well enough to be considered valid, and therefore, to be taught to new members as the correct way to perceive, think, and feel in relation to those problems. (Schein, 1995, p. 9)

Within a college or university, four distinct, co-existing cultures exist and are manifested in the different aspects of the academic institution, and thereby influence administrative operations of the baccalaureate program (Bergquist, 1992):

1. **The Collegial Culture**: This is the culture that finds meaning primarily in the disciplines represented by the faculty in the institution; that values faculty research and scholarship and the quasi-political governance processes of the faculty; that holds untested assumptions about the dominance of rationality in the institution; and that conceives of the institution's primary enterprise as the generation, interpretation, and dissemination of knowledge and the development of specific values and qualities of character among young men and women who are future leaders of our society.

2. **The Managerial Culture**: This is the culture that finds meaning primarily in the organization, implementation, and evaluation of work that is directed toward specified goals and purposes; that values financial responsibility and effective supervisory skills; that holds untested assumptions about the capacity of the institution to define and measure its goals and objectives clearly; and that conceives of the institution's primary enterprise as the inculcation of specific knowledge, skills and attitudes in students so that they might become successful and responsible citizens.

3. **The Developmental Culture**: This is the culture that finds meaning primarily in the creation of programs and activities furthering the personal and professional growth of all members of the collegiate

community; that values personal openness and service to others, as well as systematic institutional research and curricular planning; that holds untested assumptions about the inherent desire of all men and women to attain their own personal maturation, while helping others in the institution become more mature; and that conceives of the institution's primary enterprise as the encouragement of potential for cognitive, affective, and behavioral maturation among all students, faculty, administrators, and staff.

4. **The Negotiating Culture**: This is the culture that finds meaning primarily in the establishment of equitable and egalitarian policies and procedures for the distribution of resources and benefits in the institution; that values confrontation and fair bargaining among constituencies (primarily management and faculty or staff) with vested interests that are inherently oppositional; that holds untested assumptions about the ultimate role of power and the frequent need for outside mediation in a viable collegiate institution; and that conceives of the institution's primary enterprise as the establishment of new and more liberating social attitudes and structures.

Each of these four cultures combine to represent a complex system of shared beliefs and values that give meaning to institutional life as perceived by program constituencies, shape the perceptions of program personnel about how operations are completed, and influence the nature of the relationships among program stakeholders. Even though a specific institution may embrace one of the four cultures identified by Bergquist more strongly, the other three cultures are always present and interact with the dominant culture. He further states:

> The culture of academic organizations must thus be understood within the context of the educational purposes of collegiate institutions. The ceremonies, symbols, assumptions, and modes of leadership in college or university are always directed toward the institution's purposes and derive from its cultural base. (p. 210)

Program administration, in turn, is influenced by these interacting cultures that represent value-based or normative type parameters for such decision processes as specifically defining program goals, educational outcomes, and faculty performance criteria. Such common characteristics of higher education institutions as ambiguity of purpose, fluid nature of goals, and the absence of clear, measurable outcomes combine with the contrasting cultural dimensions to shape the nature of academic program administration.

## Division of Labor

Another organization feature of colleges and universities that shapes the administrative responsibilities of a program director and the nature of decision making at the academic program level is the division of labor among faculty and staff within these institutions. These contrasting faculty and staff administrative processes are closely related to the collegial and managerial cultural spheres previously identified. At the academic program level, two co-existing decision making structures are used routinely according to type of decision and work tasks. As noted in Chapter 6, a fundamental characteristic of faculty is academic autonomy that is based in expert knowledge, documented credentials, and peer-oriented performance evaluations. The teaching and research responsibilities, which are complex and dynamic, are thereby most accurately evaluated by professional collegiate specialists. Decisions related to such matters as faculty performance evaluations, academic tenure, and promotion are thereby made by formally selecting faculty according to such factors as rank and seniority. However, the individualistically oriented research and teaching goals and interests of faculty members may conflict with and should be reconciled with the common or general operational goals of the academic program.

In contrast to the academic decision model, administrative decisions related to the use of academic program resources including staff personnel could be centralized, routinized, and standardized in order to realize institutional efficiency and effectiveness. Within the institution's authority hierarchy, program directors as members of the institution's administration, are held accountable to formal bureaucratic standards that value such factors as cost effectiveness, formal communication, standardized work procedures, quantified productivity outcomes, written documentation, and formalized decision procedures.

The division of labor characteristic fosters differences in role perception held by faculty and administration. The academic model, for example, stresses collegial decision-making, unspecified division of labor, and integration of responsibilities. In contrast, the administrative model stresses clear lines of authority, specialization of responsibilities, and hierarchical decision-making structure. If the campus is organized collectively, union contracts exacerbate the administrative challenges of academic program directors by providing written protection of the faculty member's independence in the classroom, freedom of research initiatives, and the assurance of unencumbered time to develop the discipline (Brown, 1982). The director mediates these inherently conflictual decision models in the day-to-day management of the program, and in operationalizing the research, education, and public service goal mandates of the program.

## Position Sanction

The program director shares program administration with faculty in academic program operations (e.g. curriculum, tenure, etc.) where a "collegial" decision-making approach is warranted (Dressel, Johnson, & Marcus, 1969). Even though a program director has some authority over a faculty member's work by assigning and scheduling courses; for example, "the authority system cannot be considered a command system since faculty members retain considerable collegial power that is available for influencing administrative decisions" (Hill & French, 1967, p. 562). Therefore, the director's position is paradoxical. It is viewed by constituents as a leadership role; yet it is an administrative position that lacks commensurate formal authority. Political and special interest coalitions, as well as administrative superiors, can override significant administrative decisions made by the program director. The director views program stakeholders as a federation of interest groups of specialists who inherently represent potential authority and influence that can be mobilized and focused. Faculty colleagues, when viewed as an interest group of specialists, are seen as having authority based on their professional and academic expertise. Their research, teaching, professional service interests, and work goals tend to be specialized. In contrast, the program director focuses on broad program goals and augment limited formal authority with a combination of positional and personal influence in order to develop a consensus and effectively coordinate the specialized efforts of faculty colleagues (Tucker, 1984, Harper, Ramey & Zook, 1991).

Because of the lack of formal authority to impose a resolution, program directors, as noted earlier, use a situation-oriented or contingency model for decision making that relies on the extensive use of such leadership strategies as consensus-building, coalition-building, informing and education, and linking common interests among the competing program constituencies. This collaborative, decentralized approach requires effective professional or work relationships with program personnel that encourages participation by program personnel. The way the director leads or administers is an important means to foster the collective efforts of faculty and staff. Contingency management requires a special leadership style: "Rather than 'Do that and that,' the operating principle would be, 'Do whatever is necessary to achieve agreed-on-objectives, effectively and efficiently'" (McCorkle & Archibald, 1982, p. 111).

## Administrative Role Ambiguity

The dynamics of the position sanction exacerbates role ambiguity based on the uncertainty surrounding the program director's authority. This uncertainty is increased if there is no formal position description for the program director. In view of the significance that effective academic program administration has to helping promote the well being of the college or university and the significance of the daily decisions made at the academic program level within the institution, it is puzzling that only about one third of baccalaureate program directors reported having a written job description (Macy, 1990). In fact, ongoing research findings reveal that because the position responsibilities of academic program administrators are not defined specifically, faculty learn position-based competencies after assuming the role, and that institutions generally do not provide formal, systematic academic program administration training (Bennett, 1983; Tucker, 1984; Waltzer, 1975; Roach, 1976; Blau, 1994; and Gmelch and Miskin, 1993). Consequently, most faculty members enter the position uncertain of role responsibilities and parameters. As previously noted, adapting the appropriate generic position responsibilities (Figure 1.1) to the organizational structure of one's program is a useful orientation step for a new program director.

Another inherent source of role ambiguity is the need for a program director to simultaneously reconcile both institutional and faculty expectations, requests, needs, and influences while trying to maintain some level of professional identity, personal integrity, and prominence as an individual faculty member. The academic program, as a type of functional or organizational unit within the institution, represents a viable means to (1) coordinate the delivery of specialized curriculum content, (2) provide a suitable milieu for the development, preservation, and dissemination of distinct knowledge, (3) create an understandable management unit for faculty and students within a complex institutional hierarchy, and (4) deliver a professional degree program that requires a highly integrated campus and field-based educational design. Faculty members in a social work program are bound together by a common academic discipline orientation, share a common professional value system, and all are affected directly by the rise and fall of the discipline. At the academic program level, the institution's decision may be applied, adapted, and interpreted to program faculty at a level where the fundamental purpose of the college and university is operationalized.

Linking faculty and the institutional goals requires a mediating function inherent in the academic program director's role, which, in turn, produces a number of professional tensions among the competing role expectations of a program director. The director serves simultaneously as a manager of and a peer member within the faculty aggregation. The director works daily with the individuals who are subject to administrative directives made at the institutional and program levels and complete personnel evaluative oriented responsibilities and maintaining effective collegial working relationships. Consequently, role distortion and ambiguity is fostered for the faculty member who serves as a program director because "...persons who play roles in several different contexts may find their behavior in one context or situation affected by the susceptibility to, or their capacity for, the exercise of power in another." (Hobbs and Anderson, 1971, p. B-135).

The program director, therefore, is both a leader and manager of colleagues with whom much is shared for the sake of mutual interests, professional support and program development. Exercising authority within this type of collegial team is a difficult administrative challenge. Administrative practices - such as helping faculty perceive benefits by committing themselves to the philosophy and goals of the program; administering in a supportive, fair, and participatory manner; recognizing, unifying, rewarding, and developing competencies; and providing support, affirmation, and challenging assignments - are designed to facilitate the collective efforts of collegial personnel. Additional focus on motivating and facilitating the collective efforts of program personnel is provided in Chapter 7.

## Middle Management Dynamics

Because of their administrative position in the organizational hierarchy, academic program directors become the nexus of collegiality and institutional authority and are thereby routinely caught between the conflicting expectations of the dean, faculty, and students (Baldridge, 1971). This type of "middle management" position characteristic, introduced in Chapter 1, is subject to what Merton (1957) identified as "role set" phenomenon. This phenomenon is found within organization positions at the point where formal, competing organizational roles intersect. The director is at the locus or intersection of the program's vertical communication (between the program and higher levels of the organizational hierarchy) and horizontal communication (across administrative and program offices located in the same level in the hierarchy). In higher education institutions, administrative role conflict is common.

According to Blau and Scott (1982), the decision-making processes, as previously stated, involves both the formal chain-of-command administrative structures and the relative professional prestige and collegial stature of the involved personnel. Role overload is a common position frustration reported by baccalaureate social work program directors because of the disparate position assignments inherent in the part-time administrative assignments, being caught between competing, fragmentary role expectations held by program stakeholders served by the position; and experiencing role and time conflict between work, and personal responsibilities and between the teaching, research, and administrative functions of a faculty position (Macy, 1990; Swaine & Flax, 1992).

Effectively managing the dynamics of a middle management administrative position has been examined by Havassy (1990) who concluded that middle managers have:

- Capacity to simultaneously grasp the different and seemingly contradictory aspects of a situation at the nexus of multiple systems,...[to] see or create interconnectedness, [and] to develop a much richer understanding of a situation and its potentiality than would be possible by espousing one perspective at the expense of the others.

- Ability to effectively span the boundaries between various systems by maintaining loyalty to multiple groups...based on ability to see beyond temporary or issue-specific contradictions and conflicts.

- Ability to share in the view of each [competing interest] group without being limited to it and providing 'cross-system translation' [which] is expressing needs, expectations, and demands of one system in the terms and concepts of another system. (p. 105-106)

The efficacy of a director, as a middle manager, to apply such administrative competencies as conceptual, relational, organizing, negotiating, and communication abilities required to bridge among the various program-based interest groups and stakeholders directly influence the overall program quality and define the relative effectiveness of the program administrator.

## Institutional Structure Properties

Four major types of administrative structures house social work programs and help shape that nature of academic program administration (Flax and Swaine, 1996). These four structures include (1) an academic program under the administrative auspices of another academic discipline, (2) an academic program within a multi-disciplinary academic department, (3) an independent academic department offering only a baccalaureate social work degree, and (4) an academic program affiliated with a school of social work that offers both BSW and MSW degrees. The program director's primary responsibilities are basically the same in each of the four major types of administrative structures that house social work programs. However, the size of the institution and administrative auspices of social work program shapes management procedures. In social work programs that are housed in large public universities, the director is typically the chief executive officer of the administrative unit with broad formalized powers and direct responsibility for all financial, curriculum, and personnel matters. Directors of programs housed in small liberal arts colleges, in contrast, may have a different administrative environment in which informal communication, decision making, operational procedures, and administrative opportunities are common (Macy, 1990).

A summary overview of social work programs that employ two or three faculty is provided by Suppes, Drumm, and Kersting (1999) who identify strengths and challenges related to program size based on an analysis of the majority (65%) of the 100 program directors who completed a national survey mailed to a total of 167 social work programs. Major strengths are:

- Amount of individualized attention given to students
- Quality of advisement offered to students
- Responsiveness to individual student needs
- Amount of interaction in the classroom
- Knowledge of student's academic strengths and weaknesses
- Size of classes
- Relationships with practice community
- Amount of faculty liaison interaction with field instructors
- Amount of control over program development
- Relationships with social work colleagues
- Access to institutional administration
- Ability to initiate program changes

Time allotments for research/writing was the activity that the highest number of directors (48%) saw as a major challenge.

Among the conclusions and implications of the survey data, the authors identified the "…. broad areas of student development, curriculum development, autonomy, and resources…. strength areas within small programs and because of "…. the inability of statistical analysis to demonstrate any coherence in the challenge indexes, …. Program challenges in the study appeared to be unique and program specific" (Suppes, Drumm, & Kersting, 1999).

## Functional Specialization of Faculty and Staff

Organizations that are human service oriented in their overall purpose cannot routinely apply a clearly designed, specialized technology because of the complex, variable needs of clientele. Reliance by the organization is therefore placed on the specialized expertise and professionalism of the employees. Social work faculty, therefore, possess a demonstrated repertoire of professionally sanctioned competencies, provide documented evidence of professional qualifications, and consistently participate in institutionally sponsored or financed professional development offerings to ensure that the general purposes of the college or university are being addressed, and that the overall goals of the academic program are being achieved. Common characteristics of employees who are specialized professionals identified by Baldridge and Deal (1977) include the following:

- They demand autonomy in their work. Having acquired considerable skill, expertise in a field, credentials and a record of demonstrated performance effectiveness, professionals demand freedom from direct supervision.

- They have divided loyalties. Professionals have loyalties to peers at the national levels, which may sometimes interfere with loyalty to their local employer.

- Have strong tensions may exist between professional values and the bureaucratic expectations of the employing organization. Conflict between professional specialties and the employing organization are common.

- Demand peer-oriented evaluation of work performance. A belief that only professional colleagues can accurately judge performance, which is accompanied by a belief that administrative superiors in the organizational hierarchy cannot accurately evaluate professional specialties.

Consequently, faculty members employed by colleges and universities are a fragmented professional work force who organize as experts according to academic specialization and sub-specialties and characteristically identify more directly with the norms of an external professional society than with the employing institution. In addition, faculty members inconsistently participate in the institution's internal governance according to self interests, and because of the nature of advanced education socialization, tend to have a foremost commitment to expanding the knowledge base of an academic specialization through independent, privately-oriented research activities rather than accepting institutional goals. These characteristic faculty properties inherently conflict with the organizational standards for human resources within a traditional bureaucracy that values human resources as standardized, anonymous, controlled units of production. Therefore, the application of such classical management responsibilities as control, motivation, communication, evaluation, and rewards may be modified administratively by the program director to match the individual strengths, specialties, preferences, interests, and professional needs of faculty personnel. These modified administrative practices are a focus of the human resource domain examination presented in Chapter 7.

## Visionary Oriented Academic Program Leadership

Research and commentaries about the organizational characteristics of higher education institutions that conclude such unique organizational characteristics as goal ambiguity, mixed governance procedures, contrasting institutional cultures, and authority dispersion combine to require a specialized type of academic program administrative leadership. Academic program administration is shaped by the basis in which a faculty member is formally appointed by the institution to serve as a program director. Even though final formal appointment is completed by the chief administrative entity (e.g., Board of Trustees), three basic procedural methods are commonly used to appoint a faculty member as the program director. These methods, as noted in Chapter 4, include being (1) elected by the academic program faculty members for a defined term of appointment, (2) appointed with individual and/or collective input/support/approval of the program faculty, by the administrative superior of the position, or (3) appointed based on a formal rotational cycle among the faculty who serve in the position. Some variations of these three basic procedural methods, such as variations in length of terms, the composition of the committee composition, options related to successive reappointment, and stipulations that are part of a collective bargaining agreement, are done to fit the governance structure of a specific institution (Mobley, 1981).

Each of the different methods of appointment influences such position factors as the amount of faculty and administrative support the new director takes into the position and the amount of time available to provide program leadership, and to establish role performance expectations (e.g. maintenance versus change orientation) that the program stakeholders hold for a new appointee.

The distinguishing organizational features of higher education institutions, along with the official method used to fill the position of the program director, also shapes the leadership style and strategies that a director can apply to influence the operational structures, information processes, and prevailing attitudes or culture of a program (Bergquist, 1992). Modification of admission standards, curriculum content, governance procedures, and faculty performance standards are examples of structural changes. Process changes, in contrast, consist of such modifications as improving communication and information flow patterns among program stakeholders, improving conflict resolution procedures, and engaging new groups of stakeholders in the program-based decision processes. Efforts by the director to change prevailing attitudes of program stakeholders focus on how people feel about working in the existing structures and processes of the program or their level of commitment toward common purposes and how they view opportunities for professional growth and development.

A useful comparative typology for examining academic program leadership is a framework developed by Bolman and Deal, (1984), for examining organizations through four different vantage points or coherent perspectives, identified as "frames". These four frames include (1) a structural frame that emphasizes formal roles and relationships, (2) a human resource frame that focuses on the needs of people, (3) a political frame that considers the conflict over scarce resources, and (4) a symbolic frame that views organizations as cultures with shared values (Bensimon, Estela, Newmann, & Birnbaum, 1989, p. iv).

A program director becomes a kind of "visionary" type administrator who promotes program quality by applying a variety of technical, cognitive, interpersonal, and administrative approaches in a contingency-oriented, leadership style. The complexities and multiple contextual realities of academic organizations require administrators to develop the capacity to "....recognize the interactions between the bureaucratic, collegial, political, and symbolic [or cultural] processes present in all colleges and universities at all times, '....incorporate elements of several organizational perspectives..., [and] develop the flexibility to respond administratively according to differing interpretations of situational factors or contingencies." (Bensimon, Estela, Neumann, & Birnbaum, 1989, p. 72). Traditional administrative responsibilities such as planning, organizing, implementing, controlling, and evaluating are supplemented by cybernetically-oriented administrative practices aimed at providing foresight oriented leadership of the program stakeholders to collectively enhance excellence in a program structure, decision processes, operational outcomes, and the cultural milieu of the academic enterprise. Examples of attributes of a visionary type of (Cornesky, 1992; Hickman & Silva, 1984; Bensimon, Estella, Neumann, & Birnbaum, 1989) academic program director include the following:

- Promotes and develops a compelling, collective vision of the program by routinely completing such administrative practices as analyzing a montage of facts, trends, aspirations, traditions, opportunities, threats and information networks; articulating program mission and philosophy to permeate all program responsibilities; paying attention to program strengths; and keeping a focus on future development options to promote program quality.

- Searches for ideas, concepts, and ways of thinking to translate the program's vision into reality by (1) concentrating on key program components and strengths related to promoting overall effectiveness, (2) systematically networking the constituencies served by the program, (3) weighing different perspectives on a given situation, problem, or opportunity, (4) promoting creative problem solving and strategic planning by analyzing information gathered from multiple viewpoints, and (5) fostering participatory-oriented decision thinking and communication.

- Recognizes that administrative influence, leadership, and decision making consists of the incremental effects of many small actions aimed at enhancing the effectiveness of program structure, processes, attitudes, and norms that make some outcomes more likely than others.

- Enhances program quality by selecting, motivating, rewarding, retaining, developing, and unifying competent personnel.

- Maintains sensitivity to program personnel who want the employing organization to help fulfill their needs (e.g. sense of belonging, security, recognition), expectations (e.g. to be valued, respected, supported), and a sense of professional purpose by providing challenging, affirming, and rewarding work opportunities in an academic enterprise that functions as a concerned, supportive community.

- Models personal and professional commitment to the program and encourages initiatives that promote the commitment of all stakeholders to the vision, mission, philosophy, and purposes of the program.

- Functions in a warm, supportive, respectful manner in promoting the effectiveness of information, collegial, and operational networks.

- Demonstrates an understanding of administrative situations through the flexible application of the contrasting decision processes present in higher educational institutions and the ability to act accordingly in relation to programmatic needs and goals.

- Encourages innovation by fostering the creative insights of program stakeholders to discover opportunities, develop distinctive program strengths, create improved operational strategies, and support the testing of novel approaches that strategically promote program advancement.

A major leadership challenge for a contemporary program director is the broadening of vision — their own, their colleagues, and that held by program stakeholders — about the metamorphosis underway in the academy and the evolving opportunities to promote the relevance of the social work academic enterprise in the institution and within the broader communities that it serves.

## Summary

Chapter 8 has examined systems thinking as applied to academic program administration and the distinguishing characteristics of colleges and universities that form the administrative context for academic program leadership for a baccalaureate social work program. We hope to have led the reader to conclude that operating within these complex and dynamic elements requires more visionary-oriented leadership and administration, and to have helped provide or identify ways directors can mold that leadership style and development.

# References

Anderson, G. L. (1962). Professional education: Present status and continuing problems. In Education for the professions, Nelson B. Henry, editor. Chicago: University of Chicago Press.

Anderson R.E., & Carter, I.E. (1974). Human behavior in the social environment: A social systems approach. Chicago: Aldine

Baldridge, J. V. & Deal, T.E. (1977). Governing academic organizations. Princeton, New Jersey's Carnegie Foundation for the Advancement of Teaching. McCutchan Publishing Corporation, Berkeley, CA

Baldridge, J. V. (1971). Power and conflict in the university: Research in the sociology of complex organizations. New York: John Wiley and Sons, Inc.

Bass, B. M. (1985). Leadership and performance beyond expectation. New York: Free Press.

Belenky, M. F., Clinchy, B.M., Goldberger, N.R., & Tarule, J. M. (1997). Women's ways of knowing: The development of self, voice, and mind. New York, NY: Basic Books, Inc.

Bennett, J. B. (1983). Managing the academic department. New York: American Council on Education, Macmillan Publishing Co.

Bensimon, E., Estela, M., Neumann, A., & Birnbaum, R. (1989). Making sense of administrative leadership: The 'L' word in higher education. ASHE-ERIC Higher Education Report No. 1. Washington, DC: School of Education and Human Development, the George Washington University.

Berger, R. L., & Federico, R. C. (1982). Human behavior: A social work perspective. New York: Longman.

Bergquist, W. H. (1992). The four culture of the academy: Insights and strategies for improving leadership in collegiate organizations. San Francisco, CA: Jossey-Bass Publishers.

Bertalanffy, L. V. (1968). General system theory: Foundations, development, applications. New York: George Braziller.

Black, P. H., Jeffreys, D., & Hartley, E. K. (1993). Personal history of psychosocial trauma in the early life of social work and business students. Journal of Social Work Education, 29(2), 171-179.

Blau, P. (1994). The organization of academic work. (2nd Edition). New Brunswick, New Jersey, Transaction Publishers.

Blau, P. (1973). The organization of academic work. New York: Wiley and Sons.

Blau, P., & Scott, W. R. (1982). Formal organizations. San Francisco: Chandler Publishing Company.

Blostein, S. (1999). Social work education and university restructuring: A case study. ARETE, 23(1), 23.

Bolman, L. G., & Deal, T. E. (1984). Modern approaches to understanding and managing organizations. San Francisco: Jossey-Bass.

Brown, W. R. (1982). Academic politics. University, Alabama: The University of Alabama Press.

Capra, F. (1982). The turning point. New York: Ballantine Books.

Carlisle, H. (1973). Situational management: A contingency approach to leadership. New York: AMACOM.

Chess, W. A., & Norlin, J. M. (1991). Human behavior and the social environment: A social systems model (2nd ed.). Boston: Allyn & Bacon.

Cobb, N. H., & Jordan, C. (1989). Students with questionable values or threatening behavior: Precedent and policy from discipline to dismissal. Journal of Social Work Education, 25(2), 87-97.

Cohen, M. D., & March, J. G. (1974). Leadership and ambiguity: The American college president. New York: McGraw-Hill.

Cole, B. S., & Lewis, R. G. (1993). Gatekeeping through termination of unsuitable social work students: Legal issues and guidelines. Journal of Social Work Education, 29(2), 150-159.

Cornesky, R. A. (1992). Using Deming to improve quality in colleges and universities. Madison, WI: Magna Publications, Inc.

Council on Social Work Education. (1994). Handbook of accreditation standards and procedures. (4th ed.), Alexandria, VA.

DeGreene, K. (1990). Nonlinear management in technologically-induced fields. Systems Research, 7, 159-168.

Dressel, P., Johnson, C., & Marcus, P. (1969). Departmental operations: The confidence game. Educational Records, 50(3), 274-278.

Fiedler, F. E. (1967). A theory of leadership effectiveness. New York: McGraw-Hill.

Fiedler, F. E. (1971). Validation and extension of the contingency model of leadership effectiveness: A review of the empirical findings. Psychological Bulletin, 76(2), 128-48.

Fiedler, F. E., & Garcia, J. E. (1987). New approaches to effective leadership. New York: John Wiley & Sons.

Flax, N., & Swaine, R. L. (1996). Influence of administrative structure on BSW program objectives. The Journal of Baccalaureate Social Work, Vol. 1(2), p. 49-50.

Germain, C. B. (1979). Social work practice: People and environments. New York: Columbia University Press.

Germain, C. B. (1991). Human behavior in the social environment: An ecological view. New York: Columbia University Press.

Germain, C. B., & Gitterman, A. (1980). The life model of social work practice. New York: Columbia University Press.

Gibbs, P. (1994). Screening mechanisms in BSW programs. Journal of Social Work Education, 30(1), 63-74.

Gibelman, M. (1999). The search for identity: Defining social work - past, present, future. Journal of the National Association of Social Workers, 44(4), pp. 293-409.

Gmelch, W.H., & Miskin, V.D. (1993). Leadership skills for department chairs. Boston, MA: Anker Publishing Company, Inc.

Hafner, K. A., & Oblinger, D. G. (1998). The future compatible campus: Planning, designing, and implementing information technology in the academy. Bolton, MA: Anker Publishing Company, Inc.

Halter, A., & Gullerud. E. (1995). Academic mergers in social work programs: Autonomy or disharmony? Journal of Social Work Education, 31(2), 269-280.

Harper, K. V., Ramey, J. H., & Zook, L. J. (1991, Spring/Summer). BSW program administration: directors' perception of their power to manage. Journal of Social Work Education, 27(2), 176-186.

Havassy, H. M. (1990, March). Effective second-story bureaucrats: Mastering the paradox of diversity. Journal of the National Association of Social Workers, 35(2), 103-111.

Hersey, P., & Blanchard, K. H. (1977). Management of organizational behavior. 3rd Edition. Englewood Cliffs, NJ: Prentice-Hall.

Hickman, C. R., & Silva, M. A. (1984). Creating excellence. New York, NY: New American Library.

Hill, W., & French, W. (1967). Perceptions of power of department chairmen by professions. Administrative Science Quarterly, XI, 548-574.

Hobbs, W. & Anderson, L. (1971, December). The operation of academic departments. Management Science, 18(4), B-135.

Icard, L. D., Spearmon, M., & Curry-Jackson, A. (1996). BSW programs in black colleges: Building on the strengths of tradition. Journal of Social Work Education, 32(2), p. 227-235.

Johnson, H. W. (1990). Baccalaureate social work education consortia: Problems and possibilities. Journal of Social Work Education, 26(3), 254.

Johnson, H. W., & Hull, G. H. (1990). The rest of the story: Baccalaureate social work programs no longer accredited. Journal of Social Work Education, 26(3), 244-253.

Koerin, B., & Miller, J. (1995). Gatekeeping policies: Terminating students for nonacademic reasons. Journal of Social Work Education, 31(2), 247-260.

Longres, J. F. (1990). Human behavior in the social environment. Itasca, IL: F.E. Peacock.

Macy, H. J. (1990). Role analysis study of chairpersons in academic departments offering accredited baccalaureate social work degree programs. Unpublished doctoral dissertation, Ball State University, Muncie, Indiana.

Macy, H. J., Flax, N., Sommer, V. L. & Swaine, R. L. (1995). Directing the baccalaureate social work program: An ecological perspective. Jefferson City, Missouri, Association of Baccalaureate Social Work Program Directors (BPD).

McCorkle, C. O. & Archibald, S. O. (1982). Management and leadership in higher education. San Francisco: Jossey-Bass.

Merton, R. K. (1957). The role set. British Journal of Sociology, VIII, 106-120.

Mintzberg, H. (1973). The nature of managerial work. New York: Harper and Row.

Mobley, T. (1981). Selecting the department chairman. Educational Record, 52, 322.

Murdrick, N., Steiner, J., & Pollard, W. (1992). Strategic planning for schools of social work. Journal of Social Work Education, 28(3), 278-290.

Reinardy, J., & Halter, A. (1994). Social work in academia: A case study of survival. Journal of Social Work Education, 30(3), 300.

Roach, J. (1976). The academic chairperson: Functions and responsibilities. Educational Record, 57, 13.

Sayles, L. R. (1979). Leadership: What effective managers really do…and how they do it. New York: McGraw-Hill.

Schein, E. (1995). Organizational culture and leadership: A dynamic view. San Francisco: Jossey-Bass Publishers.

Shank, B., Piliavin, I., & Mailick Seltzer, M. (1994). Must schools of social work be freestanding? Journal of Social Work Education, 30(3), 286.

Sommer, V. (1995). The Ecological Perspective. In Macy, H. J., Flax, N., Sommer, V. L. & Swaine, R. L. (1995). Directing the baccalaureate social work program: An ecological perspective. Jefferson City, Missouri, Association of Baccalaureate Social Work Program Directors (BPD).

Sommer, V. L., & Macy, H. J. (1995). Environmental Scanning. In Directing the baccalaureate social work program: An ecological perspective. Jefferson City, Missouri, Association of Baccalaureate Social Work Program Directors (BPD).

Suppes, M. A., Drumm, R., & Kersting, R. (1999, Spring). What directors of small programs believe about program strengths and challenges. BPD Update - Association of Baccalaureate Program Directors, 21(1), 7.

Swain, R. L., & Flax, N. (1992). BSW program directors: Characteristics and role experiences. ARETE, 17(2), 16-28.

Sweet, V. K. (1998). Advancing the ecosystems perspective. Sixteenth Annual Baccalaureate Program Director's Conference, Albuquerque, New Mexico, 1998.

Tucker, A. (1984). Chairing the academic department: Leadership among peers (2nd ed.). New York: Macmillan Publishing Company.

Waltzer, H. (1975). The job of academic department chairman. Washington, D.C.: American Council on Education.

Warren, K., Franklin, C., & Streeter, C. L. (1998, July). New directions in systems theory: Chaos and complexity. Social Work, 43(4), 357-372.

Weiner, M. E. (1982). Human services management: Analysis and applications. Homewood, IL: The Dorsey Press.

Wheeler, B. R. & Gibbons, W. E. (1992). Social work in academia: Learning from the past and acting on the present. Journal of Social Work Education, 28(3), 300-311.

Wheatley, M. J. (1992). Leadership and the new science: Learning about organization from an orderly universe. San Francisco: Berrett-Koehler Publications.

Yukl, G. A. (1971). Toward a behavioral theory of leadership. Organizational Behavior and Human performance, 6, 414-40.

Yukl, G. A. (1981). Leadership in organizations. Englewood Cliffs, NJ: Prentice-Hall.

# Epilogue

The traditional instructional model used to prepare social work practitioners is based on the dynamic integration of academic and field-based learning. This evolving partnership, between social work education and practice, continues today within contemporary accredited baccalaureate social work programs that share the common purpose of providing fundamental knowledge, values and skills required for students to enter professional practice.

Responsibilities for the overall administrative leadership and day-to-day management of complex social work education program operations are lodged in the position of the program director. This position, which is formally embedded within the administrative hierarchy of the host institution, requires the flexible use of specialized technical, conceptual, interpersonal and leadership abilities in order to address the competing needs, interests and expectations held by program stakeholders and to promote program quality as a specialized academic discipline.

Very few directors of social work education programs have received formal training for completing the complex administrative tasks inherent in the position. An advanced degree in educational administration would approach most closely the body of content we have attempted to pull together in this volume, but even then such prior experiences as faculty leadership, instructional governance, project supervision and professional service assignments within the social work contextual factors would be needed. The program director role is very demanding, as these pages attest. The need for continual learning and renewal is everywhere apparent. This volume will hopefully be one, on-going source of information, ideas, and encouragement that improvement on the job is both possible and doable.

This volume should be considered as a working resource for program directors and for faculty and staff of social work programs - because this is a shared enterprise, only some of which must be accomplished by the director. Leadership and initiative must be looked for from all stakeholders: there is that much work in these programs if quality and excellence are sought, and there is that much at stake.

This volume hopes to have captured much of the flavor of directing a social work education program, identified professional challenges and rewards that can flow from the position and examined anticipated needs of directors and faculty for action orientations. We hope you will dialogue with this volume, dipping into chapters as your work presses on you, checking the administrative tasks in the Appendices to allow our ideas and yours to interact.

In the preface, we proposed a number of themes that we think are intrinsic to social work education. Some of these related to the nature of the program itself, some reflected directly on the work of the program director, and some stressed the contexts within which the social work program functions. We then tried to carry these themes through the chapters detailing the work of program directing. And now we again call your attention to these core messages; try not to lose them in the welter of detail that inevitably accompanies administrative responsibilities as broad and pressing as a director's are. These themes can help keep you focused, and can help you remember the larger arenas and purposes that the day-to-day grind often obscures. Balancing the manifold demands on a program director should be the realization of your ability to have a real and lasting impact on the program, on students, on colleagues, on your institution and on the quality of social work practice.

The degree of success of program directing may be directly proportional to the director's ability to facilitate the efforts of others irrespective of program size, sanction and structure. Helping others set goals within the context of the program and then working to enable their attainment is a basic means for promoting professional growth of individuals while leveraging program work across as many faculty and staff as possible. Again, this volume presents far more than a job description for a program director; rather, it attempts to map a common program perspective and then the vision and work to be accomplished to carry out that perspective by program stakeholders.

The obverse of the preceding point also bears remarking here. The individual whose needs a director is most likely to ignore is himself/herself. The line between the director and the program can become all too fuzzy, and what has the potential to get lost is the personal and professional development of the director. Hold back some time and energy to maintain a scholarly agenda, to build in professional replenishment at conferences and meetings, to retain a foothold in the social work practice community, and to work on professional growth targets. This may be a small part of the director's personal landscape given the work we have discussed in this volume, but its importance cannot be overstated if the director is to stay centered in the job and not overwhelmed by it.

We wish you a challenging and rewarding career as a program director.

# Appendix A • Academic Affairs

## Self-Evaluation Inventory

The purpose of this form is to help a program director identify and assess administrative responsibilities in the academic affairs domain. The two-step assessment process asks a director to consider each task in terms of its
- Level of importance of the administered task to the effectiveness or success of the program.
- Level of involvement in completing each specific administrative task.

This assessment can also be used as a starting point for setting administrative priorities by identifying: (1) relationships among domain-based tasks to increase one's efficiency; (2) domain-based tasks that can be delegated to other program personnel or other institutional officials; and (3) additional domain-based tasks that are related to such program features as sanction, structure or mission.

Read the list of tasks below and circle the level of assessment that matches your view of each task for your program. Additional spaces are provided to identify other tasks which you believe to be significant program responsibilities.

| Academic Affairs Domain Task Descriptions | Level of Importance | | | | | Level of Task Involvement | | | | | |
|---|---|---|---|---|---|---|---|---|---|---|---|
| | Not Important | Some Importance | Complete When Have Time | Very Important | Essential | Not A Formal Position | Responsibility | Assign to Ad Hoc Committee | Assign to Formal Committee | Assign to Faculty Colleague/ Admin. Assistant | Personally Complete |
| Promote the instructional effectiveness of the social work faculty and the performance quality of staff and technical personnel. | 1 | 2 | 3 | 4 | 5 | 1 | | 2 | 3 | 4 | 5 |
| Promote in-service training, development and technical competencies of social work faculty, staff and field practicum instructors. | 1 | 2 | 3 | 4 | 5 | 1 | | 2 | 3 | 4 | 5 |
| Schedule program-based academic offerings and complete instructional, orderly and service assignments for all academic personnel. | 1 | 2 | 3 | 4 | 5 | 1 | | 2 | 3 | 4 | 5 |

| Academic Affairs Domain<br>Task Descriptions | Level of<br>Importance | | | | | Level of<br>Task Involvement | | | | | | |
| --- | --- | --- | --- | --- | --- | --- | --- | --- | --- | --- | --- | --- |
| | Not Important | Some Importance | Complete When Have Time | Very Important | Essential | Not A Formal Position | Responsibility | Assign to Ad Hoc Committee | Assign to Formal Committee | Assign to Faculty Colleague/ Admin. Assistant | | Personally Complete |
| Provide administrative oversight of the program's curriculum decision structures to enhance academic quality, monitor faculty use of approved course syllabi and promote instructional effectiveness. | 1 | 2 | 3 | 4 | 5 | 1 | | 2 | 3 | 4 | | 5 |
| Promote the effectiveness of program-sponsored extra-curricular and experiential learning opportunities for students. | 1 | 2 | 3 | 4 | 5 | 1 | | 2 | 3 | 4 | | 5 |
| Monitor evaluative data that reports student progress toward program outcomes. | 1 | 2 | 3 | 4 | 5 | 1 | | 2 | 3 | 4 | | 5 |
| Support faculty applications for academic research proposals, grants, and special projects designed to enhance the instructional and academic quality of the program. | 1 | 2 | 3 | 4 | 5 | 1 | | 2 | 3 | 4 | | 5 |
| Assist faculty in adapting information technology (virtual textbooks, computer-based simulations, video-conferencing, electronic networks, etc.) as a means to enhance the program's effectiveness. | 1 | 2 | 3 | 4 | 5 | 1 | | 2 | 3 | 4 | | 5 |
| Notify institutional officers of curriculum changes and degree requirements; authorize publication of such changes; adapt and administrator procedures and standards caused by curriculum changes. | 1 | 2 | 3 | 4 | 5 | 1 | | 2 | 3 | 4 | | 5 |
| Schedule and supervise program examinations; monitor grading procedures and standards; resolve academic-based evaluation conflicts. | 1 | 2 | 3 | 4 | 5 | 1 | | 2 | 3 | 4 | | 5 |
| Teach courses required for the degree program, and/or instruct field practicum, special academic student projects (e.g. honors thesis, independent study, senior projects). | 1 | 2 | 3 | 4 | 5 | 1 | | 2 | 3 | 4 | | 5 |
| Other (please specify) | 1 | 2 | 3 | 4 | 5 | 1 | | 2 | 3 | 4 | | 5 |
| Other (please specify) | 1 | 2 | 3 | 4 | 5 | 1 | | 2 | 3 | 4 | | 5 |

# Appendix B • <u>Financial and Physical Resource Affairs</u>

## Self-Evaluation Inventory

The purpose of this form is to help a program director identify and assess administrative responsibilities in the fiscal and physical affairs domain. The two-step assessment process asks a director to consider each task in terms of its

- Level of importance of the administered task to the effectiveness or success of the program.
- Level of involvement in completing each specific administrative task.

This assessment can also be used as a starting point for setting administrative priorities by identifying: (1) relationships among domain-based tasks to increase one's efficiency; (2) domain-based tasks that can be delegated to other program personnel or other institutional officials; and (3) additional domain-based tasks that are related to such program features as sanction, structure or mission.

Read the list of tasks below and circle the level of assessment that matches your view of each task for your program. Additional spaces are provided to identify other tasks which you believe to be significant position responsibilities.

| Fiscal and Physical Affairs Domain Task Descriptions | Level of Importance | | | | | Level of Task Involvement | | | | | |
|---|---|---|---|---|---|---|---|---|---|---|---|
| | Not Important | Some Importance | Complete When Have Time | Very Important | Essential | Not A Formal Position Responsibility | Assign to Ad Hoc Committee | Assign to Formal Committee | Assign to Faculty Colleague/ Admin. Assistant | | Personally Complete |
| Formulate the annual operating budget; request documented personnel and physical resources on the basis of an evaluation of current and anticipated program needs. | 1 | 2 | 3 | 4 | 5 | 1 | 2 | 3 | | 4 | 5 |
| Administer the use of allocated fiscal and physical resources. | 1 | 2 | 3 | 4 | 5 | 1 | 2 | 3 | | 4 | 5 |
| In accordance with institutional policies and procedures, authorize the processing of receipts and disbursements by the institutional accounting office(s). | 1 | 2 | 3 | 4 | 5 | 1 | 2 | 3 | | 4 | 5 |
| Monitor routine expenditures (e.g. telephone charges, travel costs, etc.) to prevent excessive or unauthorized expenditures; complete timely budget transfers; document unanticipated expenses. | 1 | 2 | 3 | 4 | 5 | 1 | 2 | 3 | | 4 | 5 |

| Fiscal and Physical Affairs Domain Task Descriptions | Level of Importance | | | | | Level of Task Involvement | | | | | |
|---|---|---|---|---|---|---|---|---|---|---|---|
| | Not Important | Some Importance | Complete When Have Time | Very Important | Essential | Not A Formal Position | Responsibility | Assign to Ad Hoc Committee | Assign to Formal Committee | Assign to Faculty Colleague/ Admin. Assistant | Personally Complete |
| Submit authorized time/attendance reports to ensure accurate and timely payment of wages and salaries to program employees. | 1 | 2 | 3 | 4 | 5 | 1 | | 2 | 3 | 4 | 5 |
| Monitor purchases to ensure that accounts payable procedures are followed, purchases are inspected, and timely payments are made. | 1 | 2 | 3 | 4 | 5 | 1 | | 2 | 3 | 4 | 5 |
| Formulate policies and procedures for the efficient and appropriate use of supplies, materials, space, resources, and equipment by program personnel. | 1 | 2 | 3 | 4 | 5 | 1 | | 2 | 3 | 4 | 5 |
| Monitor and evaluate program-based student financial assistance; ensure compliance with institutional, legal, and vendor requirements for financial aid awards. | 1 | 2 | 3 | 4 | 5 | 1 | | 2 | 3 | 4 | 5 |
| Develop sources of in-kind support from the institution, professional and product/services communities to obtain supplementary program resources (e.g. office equipment, audio-visual equipment, furniture, student financial assistance, paid internships, etc.). | 1 | 2 | 3 | 4 | 5 | 1 | | 2 | 3 | 4 | 5 |
| Supervise grants/contract-funded projects to verify that all expenditures, commitments, activities, and reports are completed in compliance with the policies and procedures of the host institution and the sponsoring agency. | 1 | 2 | 3 | 4 | 5 | 1 | | 2 | 3 | 4 | 5 |
| Monitor income bearing accounts; approve expenditures from designated funds in accordance with program and institutional policies and procedures. | 1 | 2 | 3 | 4 | 5 | 1 | | 2 | 3 | 4 | 5 |
| Identify budget saving and reallocation opportunities, complete timely requisitions; strive to improve purchasing procedures. | 1 | 2 | 3 | 4 | 5 | 1 | | 2 | 3 | 4 | 5 |
| Document and personally acknowledge receipt of all gift and other forms of resource contributions; inform the providers of how their contributions help the program. | 1 | 2 | 3 | 4 | 5 | 1 | | 2 | 3 | 4 | 5 |
| Develop (in collaboration with institutional advancement offices) periodic restricted and unrestricted fund raising and resource development initiatives. | 1 | 2 | 3 | 4 | 5 | 1 | | 2 | 3 | 4 | 5 |

| Fiscal and Physical Affairs Domain<br>Task Descriptions | Level of<br>Importance | | | | | Level of<br>Task Involvement | | | | | |
|---|---|---|---|---|---|---|---|---|---|---|---|
| | Not Important | Some Importance | Complete When Have Time | Very Important | Essential | Not A Formal Position | Responsibility | Assign to Ad Hoc Committee | Assign to Formal Committee | Assign to Faculty Colleague/ Admin. Assistant | Personally Complete |
| Engage in proposal writing and other forms of resource development to increase program resources from grants, gifts, contracts, and other sponsored programs. | 1 | 2 | 3 | 4 | 5 | 1 | | 2 | 3 | 4 | 5 |
| Maintain relationships with institutional advancement offices (e.g. Grants and Sponsored programs, alumnae/alumni, Public information, Academic Assessment) to enhance program visibility and advocate program development and resource needs. | 1 | 2 | 3 | 4 | 5 | 1 | | 2 | 3 | 4 | 5 |
| Monitor the availability of improved supplies (e.g. software), equipment (e.g. computers), and educational resources (e.g. publications) to purchase the most reliable, cost effective resources. | 1 | 2 | 3 | 4 | 5 | 1 | | 2 | 3 | 4 | 5 |
| Oversee the collection, use, and distribution of program-based information (e.g. employment trends, alumnae/alumni data, program assessment results) for use in resource development institutional capitol campaigning initiatives. | 1 | 2 | 3 | 4 | 5 | 1 | | 2 | 3 | 4 | 5 |
| Submit annual long-range planning reports that identify needs, opportunities, and constraints in the development of resources needed for facilities, equipment, personnel, and student financial aid. | 1 | 2 | 3 | 4 | 5 | 1 | | 2 | 3 | 4 | 5 |
| Promote mutually beneficial professional, educational and research development initiatives (conferences, lobbying, media presentations, fundraising) between the program and social work practice constituencies and stakeholders | 1 | 2 | 3 | 4 | 5 | 1 | | 2 | 3 | 4 | 5 |
| Maintain an inventory system for all movable equipment and expendable supplies. | 1 | 2 | 3 | 4 | 5 | 1 | | 2 | 3 | 4 | 5 |
| Oversee policies for the creation, maintenance, movement, retrieval, safekeeping, storage, and destruction of program records needed for day-to-day and long-range operations | 1 | 2 | 3 | 4 | 5 | 1 | | 2 | 3 | 4 | 5 |
| Other (please identify) | 1 | 2 | 3 | 4 | 5 | 1 | | 2 | 3 | 4 | 5 |

# Appendix C • <u>Governance</u>

## Self-Evaluation Inventory

The purpose of this form is to help a program director identify and assess administrative responsibilities in the governance affairs domain. The two-step assessment process asks a director to consider each task in terms of its
- Level of importance of the administered task to the effectiveness or success of the program.
- Level of involvement in completing each specific administrative task.

This assessment can also be used as a starting point for setting administrative priorities by identifying: (1) relationships among domain-based tasks to increase one's efficiency; (2) domain-based tasks that can be delegated to other program personnel or other institutional officials; and (3) additional domain-based tasks that are related to such program features as sanction, structure or mission.

Read the list of tasks below and circle the level of assessment that matches your view of each task for your program. Additional spaces are provided to identify other tasks which you believe to be significant position responsibilities.

| Governance Affairs Domain Task Descriptions | Level of Importance | | | | | Level of Task Involvement | | | | | |
| --- | --- | --- | --- | --- | --- | --- | --- | --- | --- | --- | --- |
| | Not Important | Some Importance | Complete When Have Time | Very Important | Essential | Not A Formal Position Responsibility | Assign to Ad Hoc Committee | Assign to Formal Committee | Assign to Faculty Colleague/ | Admin. Assistant | Personally Complete |
| Promote and implement governance practices that adhere to institutional, legal, ethical, and professional standards. | 1 | 2 | 3 | 4 | 5 | 1 | 2 | 3 | 4 | | 5 |
| Promote the effectiveness of governance structures and formal decisions by representatives of key program constituencies and stakeholders (e.g. students, faculty, field instructors, etc.). | 1 | 2 | 3 | 4 | 5 | 1 | 2 | 3 | 4 | | 5 |
| Promote faculty involvement and leadership in the institutional-based governance structures and processes to represent and advance the program's interests within the institutional and professional environments. | 1 | 2 | 3 | 4 | 5 | 1 | 2 | 3 | 4 | | 5 |
| Resolve conflicts among competing constituencies; seek to promote effective governance processes. | 1 | 2 | 3 | 4 | 5 | 1 | 2 | 3 | 4 | | 5 |

| Governance Affairs Domain Task Descriptions | Level of Importance | | | | | Level of Task Involvement | | | | | | |
|---|---|---|---|---|---|---|---|---|---|---|---|---|
| | Not Important | Some Importance | Complete When Have Time | Very Important | Essential | Not A Formal Position | Responsibility | Assign to Ad Hoc Committee | Assign to Formal Committee | Assign to Faculty Colleague/ Admin. Assistant | | Personally Complete |
| Maintain records of meetings and correspondence to provide factual information for timely decision making. | 1 | 2 | 3 | 4 | 5 | 1 | | 2 | 3 | | 4 | 5 |
| Monitor trends and issues (e.g. economic, legal, demographic, educational, accreditation, professional) that influence program governance. | 1 | 2 | 3 | 4 | 5 | 1 | | 2 | 3 | | 4 | 5 |
| Other (please specify) | 1 | 2 | 3 | 4 | 5 | 1 | | 2 | 3 | | 4 | 5 |
| Other (please specify) | 1 | 2 | 3 | 4 | 5 | 1 | | 2 | 3 | | 4 | 5 |

# Appendix D • Student Affairs

## Self-Evaluation Inventory

The purpose of this form is to help a program director identify and assess administrative responsibilities in the student affairs domain. The two-step assessment process asks a director to consider each task in terms of its

- Level of importance of the administered task to the effectiveness or success of the program.
- Level of involvement in completing each specific administrative task.

This assessment can also be used as a starting point for setting administrative priorities by identifying: (1) relationships among domain-based tasks to increase one's efficiency; (2) domain-based tasks that can be delegated to other program personnel or other institutional officials; and (3) additional domain-based tasks that are related to such program features as sanction, structure or mission.

Read the list of tasks below and circle the level of assessment that matches your view of each task for your program. Additional spaces are provided to identify other tasks which you believe to be significant position responsibilities.

| Student Affairs Domain<br>Task Descriptions | Level of<br>Importance | | | | | Level of<br>Task Involvement | | | | | |
|---|---|---|---|---|---|---|---|---|---|---|---|
| | Not Important | Some Importance | Complete When Have Time | Very Important | Essential | Not A Formal Position | Responsibility | Assign to Ad Hoc Committee | Assign to Formal Committee | Assign to Faculty Colleague/<br>Admin. Assistant | Personally Complete |
| Maintain a student information system that provides academic, professional, program admission, personal, and employment reference data. | 1 | 2 | 3 | 4 | 5 | 1 | | 2 | 3 | 4 | 5 |
| Maintain academic, professional, and career advising services for students to: (1) review academic performance, (2) monitor professional development, (3) address competency needs, (4) revise academic program and schedules, (5) authorize students' academic schedule requests, and (6) audit students' applications for graduation. | 1 | 2 | 3 | 4 | 5 | 1 | | 2 | 3 | 4 | 5 |
| Promote a student registration process that permits qualified program matriculates to efficiently register for required sequential courses and provide assistance to resolve academic, financial and performance issues. | 1 | 2 | 3 | 4 | 5 | 1 | | 2 | 3 | 4 | 5 |

| Student Affairs Domain Task Descriptions | Level of Importance | | | | | Level of Task Involvement | | | | | | |
|---|---|---|---|---|---|---|---|---|---|---|---|---|
| | Not Important | Some Importance | Complete When Have Time | Very Important | Essential | Not A Formal Position | Responsibility | Assign to Ad Hoc Committee | Assign to Formal Committee | Assign to Faculty Colleague/ Admin. Assistant | Personally Complete | |
| Evaluate student enrollment, attrition, registration, and advising procedures; recommend policies, practices and procedures to improve current procedures. | 1 | 2 | 3 | 4 | 5 | 1 | | 2 | 3 | | 4 | 5 |
| Oversee the administrative structures, policies, and procedures designed to systematically evaluate students' academic and professional development; utilize institutional and community resources to address deficiencies. | 1 | 2 | 3 | 4 | 5 | 1 | | 2 | 3 | | 4 | 5 |
| Ensure that academic and professional behavior infractions by students are addressed in a timely and equitable manner and in compliance with all academic, legal, professional and institutional requirements. | 1 | 2 | 3 | 4 | 5 | 1 | | 2 | 3 | | 4 | 5 |
| Support faculty advisors to assist students with a range of matters including academic, psychological, personal, medical, and legal issues; develop service-provision agreements with institutional and community-based specialized service systems. | 1 | 2 | 3 | 4 | 5 | 1 | | 2 | 3 | | 4 | 5 |
| Evaluate career services provision and continuing education information to assure that timely, accurate information is available for students seeking employment. | 1 | 2 | 3 | 4 | 5 | 1 | | 2 | 3 | | 4 | 5 |
| Facilitate extra-curricular activities that enhance the educational process; oversee the enforcement of administrative, fiscal, institutional and legal policies and procedures covering such activities. | 1 | 2 | 3 | 4 | 5 | 1 | | 2 | 3 | | 4 | 5 |
| Oversee procedures to notify students of encumbrances (e.g., unpaid parking violations) that jeopardize academic standing; direct students to appropriate institutional resources and personnel to resolve such matters. | 1 | 2 | 3 | 4 | 5 | 1 | | 2 | 3 | | 4 | 5 |
| Assure the availability of catalogues, handbooks, and other materials that accurately state the program's and host institution's academic/ professional standards, policies, and procedures. | 1 | 2 | 3 | 4 | 5 | 1 | | 2 | 3 | | 4 | 5 |
| Other (please specify) | 1 | 2 | 3 | 4 | 5 | 1 | | 2 | 3 | | 4 | 5 |
| Other (please specify) | 1 | 2 | 3 | 4 | 5 | 1 | | 2 | 3 | | 4 | 5 |

# Appendix E • Human Resources

## Self-Evaluation Inventory

The purpose of this form is to help a program director identify and assess administrative responsibilities in the human resources affairs domain. The two-step assessment process asks a director to consider each task in terms of its
- Level of importance of the administered task to the effectiveness or success of the program.
- Level of involvement in completing each specific administrative task.

This assessment can also be used as a starting point for setting administrative priorities by identifying: (1) relationships among domain-based tasks to increase one's efficiency; (2) domain-based tasks that can be delegated to other program personnel or other institutional officials; and (3) additional domain-based tasks that are related to such program features as sanction, structure or mission.

Read the list of tasks below and circle the level of assessment that matches your view of each task for your program. Additional spaces are provided to identify other tasks which you believe to be significant position responsibilities.

| Human Resources Affairs Domain Task Descriptions | Level of Importance | | | | | Level of Task Involvement | | | | |
|---|---|---|---|---|---|---|---|---|---|---|
| | Not Important | Some Importance | Complete When Have Time | Very Important | Essential | Not A Formal Position Responsibility | Assign to Ad Hoc Committee | Assign to Formal Committee | Assign to Faculty Colleague/ Admin. Assistant | Personally Complete |
| Administer faculty promotion/tenure, sabbaticals, leaves of absence, and retention/non-retention policies and decisions; ensure compliance with all legal, standard, institutional, and professional regulations. | 1 | 2 | 3 | 4 | 5 | 1 | 2 | 3 | 4 | 5 |
| Support faculty scholarship, service, and teaching to enhance the program, the institution, and the profession; promote recognition of exemplary performance. | 1 | 2 | 3 | 4 | 5 | 1 | 2 | 3 | 4 | 5 |

| Fiscal and Physical Affairs Domain<br>Task Descriptions | Level of<br>Importance | | | | | Level of<br>Task Involvement | | | | | |
|---|---|---|---|---|---|---|---|---|---|---|---|
| | Not Important | Some Importance | Complete When Have Time | Very Important | Essential | Not A Formal Position | Responsibility | Assign to Ad Hoc Committee | Assign to Formal Committee | Assign to Faculty Colleague/<br>Admin. Assistant | Personally Complete |
| Delegate specific administrative functions to program personnel; conduct administrative and/or supervisor oversight, provide collaboration and consultation upon request and systematically evaluate the outcomes of delegated responsibilities. | 1 | 2 | 3 | 4 | 5 | 1 | | 2 | 3 | 4 | 5 |
| Approve documented personnel compensation reports (e.g. for sick leave, vacation, overtime, emergency leave, etc.) to obtain timely payroll and benefits disbursement. | 1 | 2 | 3 | 4 | 5 | 1 | | 2 | 3 | 4 | 5 |
| Resolve personnel conflicts, complaints, grievances, and appeals in a timely and effective manner. | 1 | 2 | 3 | 4 | 5 | 1 | | 2 | 3 | 4 | 5 |
| Evaluate the program's human resource system operations (e.g. search and selection, training and development opportunities, work performance documentation); use this evaluative data to improve operations. | 1 | 2 | 3 | 4 | 5 | 1 | | 2 | 3 | 4 | 5 |
| Maintain a personnel file that documents administrative decisions and complies with the institution's affirmative action equal opportunity procedures. | 1 | 2 | 3 | 4 | 5 | 1 | | 2 | 3 | 4 | 5 |
| Maintain position descriptions for each academic and non-academic position, including position title, responsibilities, education and skill requirements, compensation ranges and evaluation procedures. | 1 | 2 | 3 | 4 | 5 | 1 | | 2 | 3 | 4 | 5 |
| Compose program improvement proposals based on evaluative data (e.g. personnel performance, student achievements, and curriculum outcomes) and findings reported in educational, practice, and administrative publications. | 1 | 2 | 3 | 4 | 5 | 1 | | 2 | 3 | 4 | 5 |
| Other (please specify) | 1 | 2 | 3 | 4 | 5 | 1 | | 2 | 3 | 4 | 5 |
| Other (please specify) | 1 | 2 | 3 | 4 | 5 | 1 | | 2 | 3 | 4 | 5 |

# Appendix F • <u>Influencing Program Environmental Entities</u>

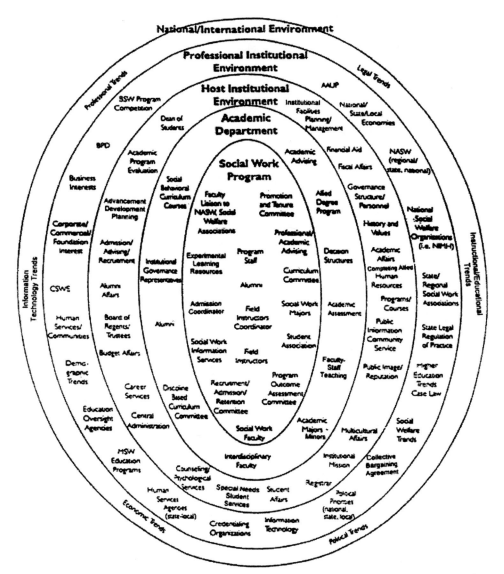

Adapted from Donald M. Loppnow, Utilizing Strategic Planning in a Department of Social Work, presented at the Annual Program Meeting of the Council on Social Work Education, Miami, Florida, March 9-12, 1986.

# Appendix G

## -SAMPLE-
## ACADEMIC AFFAIRS ANNUAL
## PLANNING CALENDAR
## 2000-2001

### AUGUST 2000

| | |
|---|---|
| 02-03 | Fifth Fall Orientation for Freshman |
| 03 | Summer Semester II Final Examinations |
| 04 | Commencement 7:30 p.m. Residence halls close after Commencement |
| 09 | Academic Council meeting 10:15 am. |
| 23 | Academic Council meeting 10:15 a.m. |
| 25 | New Faculty Orientation 8:00 a.m., 11th floor Library |
| 28 | President's Staff and Faculty Meeting 8:00 a.m. (7:30 coffee) |
| 29 | Registration and Orientation (freshman/transfer) |

### SEPTEMBER 2000

| | |
|---|---|
| 01 | Call for promotion and tenure applications by Vice President for Academic and Student Affairs. |
| 01 | Classes commence 7:30 a.m. Late registration |
| 01 | Graduate student applications for Fall graduation due to Graduate Office |
| 08 | Last day for registration and addition of courses to schedule |
| 13 | Academic Council meeting 10:15 a.m. |
| 15 | Last day to withdraw and receive 80% tuition refund |
| 18 | Fall 2000 applications for degree due to Admissions and Records |

### OCTOBER 2000

| | |
|---|---|
| 02 | Faculty professional development grant applications due to Professional Development Committee, Chair |
| 11 | Academic Council meeting 10:15 a.m. |
| 12 | Department Heads Council Meeting |
| 12-13 | Faculty Academic Advisement In-Service |
| 16 | Faculty portfolios submitted to department heads. |
| 16-27 | Departmental or college review of portfolios: promotion portfolios available for review by all faculty equivalent to, or higher rank than that being sought; tenure portfolios available for review by all tenured faculty. Portfolios must be complete with letters of recommendation by October 14, 2000 (no further documentation may be added by the candidate). |
| 16 | Visitation Day |

| | |
|---|---|
| 19 | Advisor DARS reports run |
| 20 | Mid-term grades due |
| 25 | Academic Council meeting 10:15 a.m. |
| 23 - | Nov. 5 Department heads review portfolios, complete evaluations, propose recommendations, and submit portfolios to the college promotion and tenure committee, where applicable, or dean. |
| 26 | Student DARS reports run |
| 26 | Last day to drop courses or withdraw without academic penalty |

## NOVEMBER 2000

| | |
|---|---|
| 01 | Academic Advisement begins for Spring 2001 |
| 08 | Academic Council meeting 10:15 a.m. |
| 13 | Spring 2001 pre-registration commences |
| 15 | Thesis for Fall graduation due in Graduate Office |
| 15 | May, Summer 2001 schedules must be loaded into the computer system |
| 22 | Academic Council meeting 10:15 a.m. |
| 29 | Last day to withdraw or drop passing from a course. |

## DECEMBER 2000

| | |
|---|---|
| 01 | Fall 2001 schedules must be loaded into the computer system |
| 01 | Faculty in their second year of employment notified of re-employment |
| 01 | Academic Council meeting 10:15 a.m. |
| 05 | Academic Preparation Day (NO ACTIVITIES ALLOWED) |
| 06-12 | Fall Semester Final Examinations |
| 13 | Filing of semester grades for graduating students by 1:15 in the Office of Admissions and Records. |
| 13 | Academic Council meeting 10:15 a.m. |
| 14 | Five Year Plan and Budget request due to deans & directors |
| 14 | Filing of all semester grades by 10:00 a.m. in Office of Admissions and Records |
| 15 | Commencement 6:30 p.m. Residence halls close after Commencement |
| 18 | Vice President for Academic and Student Affairs begins review of portfolios for promotion and tenure. |

# Appendix H

## Activities Toward BSW Program Completion

1. Student is admitted to University and receives University Catalogue and Student Handbook.

2. Academic advisor is assigned to student.

3. Student takes SW 330 (Intro to Social Work) and is given the BSW Program Handbook (grade of "C" or better is required for acceptance into BSW Program).

4. Student submits application for admission to the BSW Program upon successful completion of SW 330.

5. Student's application is reviewed by the Admissions Committee for a decision on admission (students must have completed at least 30 hours, have at least a GPA of 2.25, and have earned a "C" or better in SW 330, Intro to Social Work).

6. Decision is mailed to student concerning program acceptance.

7. Student meets with advisor each semester to review progress toward completing degree requirements and obtains approval for their next semester's course schedule.

8. Student passes English Competency Exam (MUST PASS PRIOR TO APPLYING FOR DEGREE AND PRIOR TO APPLYING FOR FIELD PLACEMENT).

9. Student submits application for Field Placement during the semester prior to the semester of Field Placement (all other social work courses required for the BSW must be completed with a minimum GPA of 2.25 in social work to be eligible for Field Placement).

10. Student is notified of a mandatory initial organizational meeting about Field Placement that is held during the semester before the Field Placement experience. Students are given an Application for Degree and information regarding the following: Major Area Achievement Exam, Exit Interview Survey, College Base Exam, and graduation.

11. Student completes and returns to the University Field Coordinator all required forms for Field Placement and degree. Student arranges to complete required C-Base exam and should at this point schedule an appointment with the Certification Secretary, College of Arts and Sciences.

12. Student is required to attend second Field Placement meeting (usually one month after the first meeting) and is given notification of any degree or Field Placement requirement deficiencies. However, the final determination for graduation is made by the Certification Secretary, College of Arts and Sciences. Formal planning for Field Placement proceeds with students having no identified deficiencies.

13. College of Arts and Sciences Certification Secretary reviews application for degree and notified the BSW Program Director and the student of any deficiencies in student's transcript.

14. Student completes degree requirements.

15. Dean's office certifies student for graduation.

# Appendix I

# Application for Admission To The
# Bachelor of Social Work (BSW) Degree Program

Name:_____ Date:_____ SSN:_____

Mailing
Address:_____

_____

Phone No._____Emergency Contact Person:_____

Phone:_____

> Overall GPA:_____    Grade in SW 330:_____
> Minimum requirements are 2.25 overall and a grade of
> "C" or higher in SW 330 (Introduction to Social Work)

List and briefly describe employment history


List and briefly describe volunteer work


Describe what influenced your decision to pursue a Major in Social Work


Do you have any physical or emotional illnesses or limitations which might limit
your ability to practice social work?                     Yes:____        No:____
Explain how you plan to address those limitations?


Have you ever been convicted of a felony?              Yes:____        No:____
Please explain:


I affirm that the information provided on this form is accurate and I understand that it
is to be reviewed by the Admissions Committee of the Social Work Program.


_____        _____

Signature                                                        Date

# Appendix J

# Application for Field Instruction

## I.    IDENTIFYING INFORMATION

Name_____    _____Semester

(to begin field placement)

Student I.D. #_____    Address_____

E-Mail Address: _____    _____

Telephone: _____(home)    _____(work)

Agency or Field of Interest _____

## II.    ELIGIBILITY REQUIREMENTS FOR FIELD INSTRUCTION (SW 449, SW 450)

1.    Students must apply for Field Instruction during the semester before the anticipated placement by submitting an application for Field Instruction to the University Field Coordinator. This application must be approved by the Administration Committee (Social Work faculty) before a student can participate in Field Instruction

2.    Students must have completed all required social work courses with the exception of SW448 which is taken concurrently with field instruction and be formally accepted to the Social Work Program before beginning Field Instruction or have permission of the University Field Coordinator. Exceptions may be granted on a case by case basis due to extenuating circumstances. (Complete attached progress report requirement for social work major)

3.    Applications will be considered on the basis of personal characteristics and behavioral traits regarded as necessary for professional Social Work practice Relationship/communication skills which indicate some self-awareness and ability to empathize with others are important factors. Also important are the ability to deal with abstract concepts and a value system congruent with the National Association of Social Worker's Code of Ethics.

4.    Students approved for field instruction by the Admissions Committee will meet with the University Field Coordinator to discuss various placement opportunities. After reviewing potential placements, students will be referred to agencies to be interviewed regarding the placement. Following the pre-placement interview, the student, agency representative and University Field Coordinator will make a determination as to the appropriateness of the placement.

## III. CURRICULUM INFORMATION (Complete)

### Required Courses:

| | | Grades |
|---|---|---|
| Intro to Social Work | SW 330 | _____ |
| Social Policy | SW 332 | _____ |
| Social Work Research | SW 350 | _____ |
| HBSE I | SW 380 | _____ |
| HBSE II | SW 381 | _____ |
| Practice I | SW 390 | _____ |
| Practice II | SW 391 | _____ |
| Ethnic Minority Relations | SY 360 | _____ |
| Social Work Practice III | SW 448 | _____ |
| Field Placement | SW 449 | _____ |
| Field Instruction Seminar | SW 450 | _____ |

### Social Work Electives:

| | | |
|---|---|---|
| Family & Child Welfare | SW 333 | _____ |
| Volunteerism | SW 334 | _____ |
| Social Work in Health Care | SW 335 | _____ |
| Crisis Intervention | SW 336 | _____ |
| Family Preservation Practice | SW 337 | _____ |
| Mental Health/Sub Abuse | SW 338 | _____ |
| Comm. in SW Practice | SW 339 | _____ |
| Rational Emotive Ed | SW 392 | _____ |
| Independent Study | SW 441 | _____ |
| | SW 442 | _____ |
| | SW 443 | _____ |

**Appeals Process**

*Any student dissatisfied with the decision made by the Admissions Committee has the right to appeal to the Student Academic Grievance Committee (SAGC) The student has further rights to appeal to the Social Work Program Coordinator, to the Dean of College of Letters and Sciences and further to the Vice-President for Academic Affairs*

*I, _____, understand the requirements for admission to field instruction and wish to apply.*

\*\*\*\*\*\*\*\*\*\*\*\*\*\*\*\*\*\*\*\*\*\*\*\*\*\*\*\*\*\*\*\*\*\*\*\*\*\*\*\*\*\*\*\*\*\*\*\*\*\*\*\*\*\*\*\*\*\*\*\*\*\*\*\*\*\*\*\*\*\*\*\*\*\*\*\*\*\*\*\*\*\*\*\*\*\*\*\*\*\*\*\*\*\*\*\*

_____     _____

*University Field Coordinator*                        *Date*

_____     _____

*Recommendation of Admissions Committee*          *Date*

# Appendix K

# Environmental Scanning Inventory

## Relevant Aspects of Systems in Environmental Scanning

Assessment of goodness-of-fit includes the identification of:

- tension points within and between systems
- obstacles located at any point
- opportunities located at any point
- energy and resource capacities of systems
- energy and resource exchanges across boundaries
- social role set expectations within each system
- effects of inertia and synergy
- capacity for self-renewal and self-organization

**And** consideration of these variables:

### *Program Director*
Knowledge
Values
Skills
Personality
Leadership style
Voice and vision

### *Social Work*
**Program**
History
Size
Faculty
Students
Staff
Advisory Committee
Field instructors
Alumnae/alumni
resources

### *Instructional System*
Public/private
Union/nonunion
Mission and history
Size and location
Values/culture
Academic programs
Administration
Faculty governance

Board of Trustees/Governors
Alumnae/alumni
Planning/development
Facilities
Admissions/recruiting/
advising
Economic condition

**Community System**
Size
Demography/diversity
Economic condition
Perception of institution
Perception of program
Social work professionals
Human services network
**State/Regional System**
Demography/diversity
Economic condition
Employment base/conditions
Educational resources
Educational competition
NASW chapter
Practice licensing/regulation
Human services needs, priority,
and funding

### *National System*
Demography/diversity
Economic condition
Political direction

Employment base/
conditions
Educational resources
Educational competition
Human services needs,
priority, and funding
CSWE
BPD
NASW
Research funding
priorities
Practice theory and trends

## Environmental Scanning Checklist

Assessment of goodness of fit will require consideration of both environmental and personal variables at any one point in time. The variables listed are not exhaustive, but offer a model to begin assessment of influencing forces, conditions, tensions, and needs. Consider the following in terms of whether the influence of each environmental and personal condition is:

1. A source of tension

2. An obstacle

3. An opportunity

4. A facilitating force of influence

5. A restraining force of influence

### Macro-Environment Variables

CSWE accreditation requirements _____

State system of universities, including:

> *Resources allocated to your institution_____*

> *Resources allocated to your program vs. other state programs of social work education _____*

State regulation of social work profession through registration or licensing (consider how this may influence your program) _____

Connection to the Council of Social Work Education, Baccalaureate Program Directors, and National Association of Social Workers (consider level of knowledge about what these organizations are doing and their impact on your program) _____

National trends in social work education and professional practice _____

### Mezzo-Environmental Variables

*Institutional Variables*

Type of institution:

> *Public _____ Private _____*

Faculty affiliation:

> *Union _____ Nonunion _____*

Are there religious affiliation expectations?

*No* _____ *Yes* _____
*If so, what are they?* _____
*Do they expect certain content in curriculum?* _____

Emphasis of institution:
*Research* _____ *Teaching* _____

Source of students:
*Urban* _____ *Non-urban* _____

Source of department budget (predominant):
*grants* _____ *college/university budget* _____

College/university institutional emphasis:
*professional programs* _____ *liberal arts* _____

Institutional valuing of program director work, highest value:
*publication* _____ *administration* _____
*teaching* _____ *grant-writing* _____

### *Program variables*

Program setting within institution:
*Combined with graduate* _____ *Undergraduate only* _____
*Combined with other disciplines* _____ *Free-standing* _____

Emphasis of program in terms of services:
*Urban* _____ *Non-urban* _____

Degree of program connectedness to community:
*Strong* _____ *Moderate* _____ *Weak* _____

Degree of high-level administrative support (division, college, dean):
*Strong* _____ *Moderate* _____ *Weak* _____

History of the program/department at the institution:

_____

Adequacy of program funding:
*Adequate* _____ *Inadequate* _____

Adequacy of number of faculty for program operation:
*Adequate* _____ *Inadequate* _____

Program evaluation from institutional perspective (what is success as far as institution is concerned): _____

Adequacy of systems/processes established for program operation (faculty evaluation, curriculum evaluation, student recruitment, student selection and retention, faculty development) _____

Adequacy of program/department's database that provides information needed to make change decisions _____

Program/department's vision of the future; clarity and degree that it is shared by members _____

Opportunities for members of the program to have consistent input into the development of the future vision _____

Opportunities for faculty to demonstrate ownership and commitment to this vision

_____

Effectiveness of communication networks allowing flow of information both "coming down" and "going up" _____

Amount of tension between academic freedom and accreditation standards regarding course content _____

Amount of tension between "generalist" and "specialist" knowledge, resources, and curriculum content _____

Overall strengths of the program _____

Overall weaknesses of the program _____

### Micro-environmental and personal variables

#### One to one faculty

Personal relationships with members of faculty within the program _____

Program faculty perceptions that there is an open, supportive atmosphere or climate _____

Frequency that director assists faculty in setting realistic goals and priorities

_____

Program faculty's perception of director as an advocate for them to higher levels of administration _____

Mentoring skills of director _____

Scholarly performance of program faculty _____

Teaching performance of program faculty _____

Degree of enthusiasm and vitality of program faculty _____

Director's awareness of strengths and weaknesses of program faculty _____

### One to one administration

Personal knowledge needed to direct the undergraduate social work program

_____

Skills needed for program/department administration _____

Personal relationships with department chairs closely related to social work program _____

Personal relationships with administrators _____

Demands on the director:
*too much expected* _____   *about right* _____   *too little expected* _____

Director's "visibility" within the organization _____

Director's ability to give feedback to faculty and administrators so that it is likely to be considered _____

Availability of relationships with one or more people in the organization who can serve as personal sources to the director (advising, listening, testing out)

_____

Skills needed to initiate change in the program when changes are required

_____

Skills to develop and manage resources for the program _____

Skills needed to monitor progress of the program and faculty toward accomplishing goals _____

Awareness of gender differences in communication and administrative styles

_____

Degree of "differentness" of director (sex, race) from program/ institutional norms_____

Knowledge of own strengths and weaknesses regarding administration, communication, planning, etc. _____

Degree of "fit" between role as an undergraduate program director and personal career goals _____

# Subject Index